The WTO

Crisis and the governance of global trade

This book explores the factors behind the collapse of World Trade Organisation (WTO) ministerials – as in Seattle in 1999 and Cancun in 2003
– and asks why such events have not significantly disrupted the development of the multilateral trading system. It argues that the political conflicts
played out during these meetings, their occasional collapse and the reasons
why such events have so far not proven detrimental to the development
of the multilateral trading system can be explained by examining the way
in which the institution was created and has developed through time.

In developing its argument the book:

* explores the development of the multilateral trading system from the
  creation of the General Agreement on Tariffs and Trade (GATT) in 1947
  to the WTO's Hong Kong ministerial in December 2005;
* examines the way in which the interaction of member states has been
  structured by the institution's development;
* assesses the impact of institutional practices and procedures on the
  heightening of political tensions; and
* explains why WTO ministerials exhibit a propensity to collapse but why
  the breakdown of a meeting has so far not prevented the institution from
  moving forward.

This book will be of interest to scholars and students of international politics,
economics and law.

Rorden Wilkinson is Professor of International Political Economy at the
University of Manchester. He is author of *Multilateralism and the World
Trade Organisation* (Routledge, 2000), editor of *The Global Governance
Reader* (Routledge, 2005), and co-editor of *Global Governance: Critical
Perspectives* (Routledge, 2002). He also co-edits the *RIPE Series in Global
Political Economy* and the *Global Institutions* series.

The WTO

Crisis and the governance of
global trade

Rorden Wilkinson

 Routledge
Taylor & Francis Group

LONDON AND NEW YORK

First published 2006
by Routledge
2 Park Square, Milton Park, Abingdon, Oxon OX14 4RN

Simultaneously published in the USA and Canada
by Routledge
270 Madison Avenue, New York, NY 10016

Routledge is an imprint of the Taylor & Francis Group, an informa business

© 2006 Rorden Wilkinson

Typeset in Times New Roman by
Florence Production Ltd, Stoodleigh, Devon

Printed and bound in Great Britain by
MPG Books Ltd, Bodmin

British Library Cataloguing in Publication Data
A catalogue record for this book is available from the British Library

Library of Congress Cataloging in Publication Data
A catalog record for this book has been requested

ISBN10: 0–415–40553–X (hbk)
ISBN10: 0–415–40554–8 (pbk)

ISBN13: 978–0–415–40553–9 (hbk)
ISBN13: 978–0–415–40554–6 (pbk)

For Lizzie, Lucy, Isabella
and Paolo

Contents

Tables

Preface and acknowledgements

The argument that follows develops aspects of, but is quite different from, an idea which first appeared in the *Journal of World Trade* (Wilkinson, 2001). In that article I argued that the collapse of the Seattle ministerial meeting had thrown the WTO into a crisis the causes of which had been incompletely and insufficiently diagnosed. Commentary on the collapse of the Seattle meeting had divided on how best to understand that crisis. For many scholarly (and, it has to be said, a large number of practitioner) commentators, Seattle revealed a weakness in the ability of the WTO to act as a forum for multilateral trade liberalisation. While the most optimistic and problem-solving minded of this group saw the crisis as only temporary (or at least one that could be made temporary), others worried that the collapse of the Seattle meeting might be the trigger for, or an indication of, a more worrying phenomenon: a resurgence of protectionism and, at the extreme, a fragmentation of the global economy. Others sought to understand Seattle in another way. More radically minded scholars and civil society commentators saw Seattle as the precursor to a sea-change in global politics. In this analysis, Seattle was perceived to be broadly positive: it pointed to the growing maturity of a global civil society upon which rested hopes of a more democratic, accountable and transparent world order; a shift in the balance of power between countries of the North and those of the South; and/or the beginning of the end of the WTO and the neoliberal project for which it stood.

None of these pictures was, to my mind, satisfactory. Certainly something appeared to be 'wrong' with the WTO but it looked to be much more than a collective action problem (that is, the ability of the WTO as an institution to mediate the behaviour of political actors in such a way that a successful outcome would be produced); and little of substance seemed to support the thesis that the meeting's collapse would bring about a resurgence of protectionism. With regard to the civil society/global South perspective, while Seattle witnessed clashes between political-economic élites and those purporting to speak on behalf of the many, and industrial states and their developing counterparts, these contests seemed to be ignited more by happenings in the WTO, rather than by instances of wider systemic contestations.

I was also worried that the commentary on Seattle was surprisingly ahistorical. The collapse of ministerial meetings and attendant proclamations that the end of the multilateral trading system was nigh were not new. In fact, GATT/WTO ministerials have collapsed five times since 1982 alone; and the fear of a slide towards a new era of protectionism akin to the 1930s has been a perennial feature of post-war trade politics. What surprised me most was that little effort had been made to understand Seattle within the context of the development of multilateral trade regulation: that is, from its beginnings as an Allied project to revitalise international trade in the post-war era to the present day. Commentators occasionally paid lip-service to 'history' or made mention of a prior collapse; but none sought to understand these happenings historically and within the context of the institution's development. The result was to leave too many questions unanswered and, more importantly, to misunderstand (and in many cases exaggerate) the collapse of the Seattle meeting. For me, Seattle was merely a moment (albeit significant) in the development of multilateral trade regulation. As such, it had to be understood in that context.

In that original article I suggested that the collapse of the meeting had generated an inertia within the Organisation – not the Secretariat, though (as many of those recently and currently employed in the Organisation testify) that too was affected, but among the membership and within the process of trade liberalisation. But I was too quick to term the post-Seattle stasis 'inertia'; it clearly was not, though the root causes of the meeting's collapse – as the following pages illustrate – were nevertheless to be found in the way in which trade regulation had evolved in the post-war era and were not specific to the meeting's time and place. What I had previously characterised as inertia in fact belay the onset of a post-crisis politics wherein a process of institutional and political readjustment was at play that eventually resulted in the launch of the Doha Development Agenda (DDA). This process was an inevitable response to the crisis of Seattle – in this way it is intrinsically connected to the prior development of multilateral trade regulation – but it resulted in the emergence of a new political compromise that secured the further development of that system of trade regulation.

Of course the post-Seattle settlement proved deficient to the extent that it failed to prevent the collapse of the Cancún ministerial meeting four years later. The collapse of that second meeting nevertheless resulted in the readjustment of the original Seattle settlement (in the form of what is known as the July 2004 package) thereby leaving the way open for the ongoing development of multilateral trade regulation. In both instances, the collapse of a ministerial meeting generated a post-crisis politics that eventually bore fruit and, in so doing, took the trade agenda forward. But, importantly and somewhat paradoxically, it was not a progression that has addressed the distinct asymmetry of economic opportunity to which WTO rules give rise – an asymmetry that lies at the heart of the political contestation underpinning the collapse of GATT/WTO ministerials. Rather, in both cases the onset of a post-crisis politics has facilitated the possibility of a perpetuation of inequalities of opportunity in the Organisation's legal framework and, as a consequence, ensured that ministerial meetings continue to exude a propensity to collapse. In this way, crisis has played a more *dynamic* role in the development of multilateral trade regulation than I, and much of the literature, had previously given credit – a dynamism that has served to preserve the privileges of trade regulation accorded to its principal architects and chief industrial players. This book illustrates how.

What follows, then, is both an argument about the causes, consequences and role played by the collapse of ministerial meetings in the evolution of multilateral trade regulation and a corrective to, and development of, my earlier argument. The argument advanced hereafter is as much a product of time spent poring over primary materials, secondary literature, popular commentary and interview data as it is the outcome of discussions, debates and conversations with many people. While I claim the argument as my own, it inevitably reflects aspects of that dialogue. I am grateful to Hardeep Basra, Christophe Bellmann, Simon Bulmer, Carolyn Deere, Andrew Gamble, Catia Gregoratti, Anje Halle, Sophie Harman, Bernard Kuiten, Bernice Lee, Suguthan Mashesh, Linda Miller, Simon O'Meally, Katsuhiko Mori, Craig Murphy, Amrita Narlikar, Tony Payne, Nicola Phillips, Malena Sell, Seamus Simpson, Alexandra Strickner, Diana Tussie and Gil Winham for their comments on and help with aspects of this work. Maggie Levenstein, Liz Mandeville, Inderjeet Parmar, James Scott and Tom Weiss kindly put time and effort into reading the manuscript and commenting thereon. Their efforts are much appreciated. I am particularly grateful, and much indebted, to Claire Annesley and Donna Lee for their enthusiasm, encouragement and support. They each read several drafts of the manuscript and pressed me to think harder about my assertions. I am grateful also to those individuals who indulged me with their time during the many interviews conducted for this project but who, for reasons of confidentiality, remain anonymous; and I would like to thank the many member state delegates, international organisation officials, NGO representatives, and other interested parties who have chewed the proverbial fat with me over the course of the research.

The final phase of research for this book could not have been completed without the financial support of the British Academy (Award SG-36194) or the institutional assistance of the Academic Council on the United Nations System (ACUNS) which I represented at the WTO's Cancún and Hong Kong ministerial meetings. I am indebted to both. The argument would also not have evolved in quite the way it has without the administrative and institutional support of the Watson Institute at Brown University where I was a Visiting Associate Professor for the academic year 2003/4 or without the intellectual, personal and institutional support of the students and faculty of the Department of Political Science at Wellesley College during my time as Visiting Faculty there (2002–4). My home institution has also been the source of much intellectual and personal encouragement. My colleagues and students in what was the Department of Government at the University of Manchester (and is now Politics at the relaunched University of Manchester) have been a constant source of support, guidance and mentoring. My families Wilkinson, Singler and Cars have also supported me throughout; Frances Spriggs helped me beyond that which ought to be expected of friends in the final stages of writing – assistance for which I am enormously grateful; and Craig Fowlie and the team at Routledge shepherded this book through in seamless fashion. These debts notwithstanding, I remain responsible for the argument developed herein and any mistakes that I have made.

Rorden Wilkinson
Manchester, UK
3 January 2006

Abbreviations

ACP	African, Caribbean and Pacific states
ACP/LDC/AU	African, Caribbean and Pacific/Least Developed Country/African Union Group (also known as the G90)
ACUNS	Academic Council on the United Nations Systems
AD	Anti-dumping
ADD	Anti-dumping duty
AGOA	African Growth and Opportunity Act (US)
APEC	Asia Pacific Economic Co-operation
ASEAN	Association of South East Asian Nations
ASPS	American Selling Price System (Kennedy round side agreement on the)
ATN	Africa Trade Network
AU	African Union
Benelux	Belgium, the Netherlands and Luxembourg
C4	Group of 4 West and Central African Cotton Producing States
CAFTA	Central American Free Trade Agreement
CAP	Common Agricultural Policy
CG18	Consultative Group of 18
CHOGM	Commonwealth Heads of Government Meeting
CTD	Committee on Trade and Development
CTE	Committee on Trade and Environment
CTG	Council for Trade in Goods
CTRIPs	Council for Trade Related Aspects of Intellectual Property Rights
CTS	Council for Trade in Services
CVD	Countervailing duty
DDA	Doha Development Agenda
DDG	Deputy Director-General
DDsG	Deputy Directors-General
DG	Director-General
DSB	Dispute settlement body
DSM	Dispute settlement mechanism

DSU	Dispute settlement understanding
EC	European Community
ECLA	Economic Commission for Latin America (UN)
ECLAC	Economic Commission for Latin American and the Caribbean (UN)
ECOSOC	Economic and Social Council of the United Nations
EEC	European Economic Community
EU	European Union
FAO	Food and Agriculture Organisation
FIP	Five Interested Parties
FOGS	Functioning of the GATT system
FRG	Federal Republic of Germany
FTAA	Free Trade Agreement of the Americas
G7	Group of 7 leading industrial states
G8	Group of 7 leading industrial states plus Russia
G9	Group of 9 industrial countries (Uruguay round)
G9/10	Group of 9/10 industrial net food-importing countries
G10	Group of 10 developing counties (Uruguay round)
G21	Group of 21 (post-Dillon round)
G20/21/22	Group of 20/21/22 developing countries
G20 Finance	Group of 20 industrial and developing country finance ministers
G33	Group of 33 developing countries (also known as the SPSSM alliance)
G77	Group of 77 developing countries
G90	Group of 90 developing countries (also known as ACP/LDC/AU group)
G110	Group of 110 developing countries
GATS	General Agreement on Trade in Services
GATT	General Agreement on Tariffs and Trade
GC	General Council
GNG	Group of Negotiations on Goods
GNS	Group of Negotiations on Services
GSP	Generalised System of Preferences
HDR	Human Development Report
IBRD	International Bank for Reconstruction and Development (World Bank)
ICCICA	Interim Co-ordinating Committee for International Commodity Arrangements
ICFTU	International Confederation of Free Trade Unions
ICITO	Interim Committee for the International Trade Organisation
IGDC	Informal group of developing countries
IGTN	International Gender and Trade Network
ILO	International Labour Organisation

IMF	International Monetary Fund
IOS	International Organisation of Standards
ISI	Import substitution industrialisation
ITC	Interim Trade Committee (of the GATT)
ITO	International Trade Organisation
ITU	International Telecommunications Union
LDC	Least developed country
LMG	Like Minded Group
LTA	Long-Term Agreement (on Cotton Textiles)
MAI	Multilateral Agreement on Investment
MEAs	Multilateral Environmental Agreements
MFA	Multi-Fibre Agreement
MFN	Most favoured nation
MTN	Multilateral Trade Negotiation
MTO	Multilateral Trade Organisation
NAFTA	North American Free Trade Agreement
NAM	Non-Aligned Movement
NAMA	Non-agricultural market access
NATO	North Atlantic Treaty Organisation
NGO	Non-governmental organisation
NIEO	New International Economic Order
NICs	Newly industrialising countries
OECD	Organisation for Economic Co-operation and Development
OEEC	Organisation for European Economic Co-operation
OPEC	Organisation of Petroleum Exporting Countries
OTC	Organisation for Trade Co-operation
PGA	People's Global Action
Prepcom	Preparatory Committee
QRs	Quantitative restrictions
SAARC	South Asian Association for Regional Co-operation
SPSSM	Strategic Products and Special Safeguard Mechanism alliance (also known as the G33)
STA	Short-Term Agreement (on Cotton Textiles)
SG	Secretary-General
TBM	Textile monitoring body
TBT	Technical barriers to trade
TNC	Trade Negotiations Committee
TPRB	Trade policy review body
TPRM	Trade policy review mechanism
TRIMs	Trade Related Investment Measures (Agreement on)
TRIPs	Trade Related Aspects of Intellectual Property Rights (Agreement on)
UN	United Nations
UNCICT	United Nations Commission on International Commodity Trade

UNCTAD	United Nations Conference on Trade and Development
UNDP	United Nations Development Programme
UNEP	United Nations Environment Programme
UNO	United Nations Organisation
USTR	United States Trade Representative
VERs	Voluntary export restraints
WIPO	World Intellectual Property Organisation
WTO	World Trade Organisation

1   The WTO, crisis and the governance of global trade

Since the collapse of the Seattle meeting a cottage industry has grown up around WTO ministerials. This industry has at its core a biennial contest among journalists, academics, practitioners, policymakers and the NGO community to predict the outcome of a meeting and bask in the glory of vindication should events go their way. The cycle of this industry is now well established. In the six months prior to a WTO ministerial, journalistic pieces – either op-eds by notable academics, (increasingly) NGO officials and past participants, or slightly longer pieces in weekly, fortnightly and monthly periodicals – begin to appear, arguing either that progress so far has been slow but there is room to be optimistic, or that the meeting is destined to collapse threatening the Organisation's very survival and raising the spectre yet again of another Orwellian (but invariably unrealised) fragmentation of the world economy.

Four weeks before a meeting the commentary intensifies and the range of individuals and institutions professing to have a stake in the outcome multiplies exponentially. Each commentary marks out the issues perceived to be crucial citing the need to reconcile outstanding differences as key to the success of the meeting. In the days immediately prior to the meeting, leading newspapers in the developed world run opinion pieces by notable commentators while the print media in the global South either recycle excerpts from their northern counterparts, or else attempt to put a southern spin on the meeting's unfolding. All nevertheless tend to recycle familiar 'room to be optimistic/outcome uncertain/tensions remain/destined to collapse' arguments peppered with pointers to the latest hot issue or source of tension; or else they remark on the contribution of a successfully concluded meeting to economic development in the global South, the predictability of public demonstrations, the relationship between trade and the environment, or the plight of vulnerable workers in the world's periphery. In an effort to persuade readers of their various perspectives these pieces are complemented by the posting of innumerable 'guides to' WTO ministerials/free trade/the anti-globalisation movement/agriculture/development/trade and environment, and US foreign policy on newspaper, periodical, NGO, think-tank and government websites.

As the meeting begins, a competition commences to be the first to break the story and become *the* source of reference. Myriad NGOs produce daily and sometimes half-daily 'updates' reporting the minutiae of the meeting, pointing out anything that might later be deemed to have been the authoritative first comment on the impending collapse of the meeting, or the deal-clinching bargain. In this information rush, the 'official' account of events (not, it has to be said, the WTO's version, but more often than not an overview produced by the host nations' organising committee) fights a losing battle, reporting yesterday's and the day before's events as if novel (though inevitably superseded) coupled with the odd picture of pensive delegates, NGO street theatre or agricultural production in a nameless land. As the meeting progresses the intensity of commentary increases, changing focus from accounts of substantive issues to who-said-what-to-whom and the various tactics deployed to generate a consensus. Rumours of arm-twisting, through-the-night meetings, phone calls to capitals and frenzied work abound as the meeting nears an end.

With the close of play comes a barrage of commentary, most of which tries to turn what-was-originally-said-but-wasn't-quite-right into how-it-could-be-read-as-if-it-were, and identifies the meeting's principal victors and villains as well as the heroes and vanquished. This is followed by a second round of op-eds – increasingly including commentaries from national trade negotiators – offering their opinion of the meeting's outcome. In the immediate aftermath, national parliaments and other governmental and trans-governmental agencies solicit reports designed to examine the reasons for the collapse of the meeting or the impact of an agreement reached. NGOs pronounce various degrees of victory or impending doom. As the media spotlight begins to turn elsewhere the frenzy slowly fades into a background noise comprising a steady flow of academic articles trying to catch up on the commentary and add their particular slant to the debate, interviews in weekly periodicals with key protagonists in the trade and NGO community, a trickle of pieces offering various proposals for reforming the WTO and the steady reporting of all things trade in specialist newsletters.

For all the useful information generated by its activities, this cottage industry has come to shape understandings of the collapse of WTO ministerial meetings in a way that obscures both the causes and consequences of these events. While the collapse of two of the WTO's first six ministerial meetings inevitably made them newsworthy and diverted much-needed attention towards the politics of international trade, the Seattle and Cancún meetings are understood more in terms of the images they produced and the events that unfolded in compressed moments in time, than for their location within and significance for multilateral trade regulation.[1] Conceptions of the collapse of the Seattle meeting tend to focus on the demonstrations that disrupted the meeting and, to a lesser extent, the fracture that emerged between developing countries and their industrial counterparts over the extension of the trade agenda, rather than on the ministerial's contribution to shaping the further development of multilateral trade regulation. Similarly, the breakdown of the Cancún meeting is widely perceived to be a moment wherein developing country coalitions were able to resist First World agendas, rather than a point within a wider process of adjustment necessary to take the trade agenda forward.

In shaping the way in which we have so far conceived of the collapse of WTO ministerials, a number of important issues have been left unresolved. For instance, the collapse of two of the WTO's first six ministerial meetings has not significantly disrupted or derailed the liberalisation project as many scholarly and practitioner commentators had feared; nor has it resulted in a redistribution of power from industrial to developing states, or from political-economic élites to self-appointed representatives of the global many, as more radically minded scholars and members of the NGO community had suggested. If anything, multilateral trade regulation is stronger and more robust than it has been at any time since the negotiation of the GATT in 1947; and the way in which it structures the relations of its member states remains firmly intact. Seattle did not prevent the launch of a new trade round; it merely delayed the launch until the next ministerial meeting (in Doha in 2001). Moreover, the political settlement reached to enable a new negotiating round to commence did not promise to correct the sharp inequities and asymmetries in the WTO's legal framework or the way in which that framework is deployed as a means of liberalising trade; nor did it result in a fundamental overhaul of the WTO's operating procedures or the way in which negotiations are conducted, rendering them either more open to developing world participation or to third party scrutiny. Likewise, the collapse of the Cancún meeting did not result in a fundamental revision of the content of the Doha Development Agenda (DDA) but merely some minor fettling. The much-touted resurgence in Third World power resulting from the actions of the Group of 20 (G20), Group of 33 (G33) and Group of 90 (G90) has not significantly altered the balance of power among WTO members. And little progress has been made on the intractable problem of agriculture; yet the round will inevitably be concluded, further deepening and widening multilateral trade regulation.

The failure of the outcomes projected by many analyses of the Seattle and Cancún meetings to materialise suggests that a more nuanced understanding of the causes and consequences of the collapse of ministerial meetings is necessary. Moreover, given that the breakdown of the Seattle and Cancún meetings has not significantly disrupted the development of multilateral trade regulation (indeed, it may actually have helped drive it forward, as the following analysis shows), a better understanding of the role that these moments of crisis play in multilateral trade regulation needs to be advanced. These are the aims of this book.

The argument

The book's underlying premise is that much of the commentary on the breakdown of WTO ministerials has failed to see beyond the events that unfolded in those compressed moments in time to the root causes of heightened political contestation and a meeting's collapse. The book seeks to move beyond the politics of the moment to explain not only why WTO ministerials collapse (and continue to exude a propensity to do so), but also why such instances have not disrupted the development of multilateral trade regulation, and why significant changes have not been made to redress those asymmetries in the institution's legal framework, the manner of its deployment, and the practices and procedures employed in its operation that have underpinned the onset of heightened political contestation.

By drawing from a body of literature concerned with how and why institutions emerge and change, the book shows that the political contestation underpinning the collapse of WTO ministerials results from the way in which multilateral trade regulation was created and has developed through time. It argues that multilateral trade regulation has come to shape the interaction of participating states in such a way that contestation over the shape and direction of the trade agenda is an inevitable feature of contemporary trade politics. This contestation is the result not just of the use of political bargains as the means by which liberalisation is pursued, but also because of an acutely asymmetrical institutional evolution that has privileged the liberalisation of those sectors of greatest advantage to the economic interests of the institution's founding members and principal states while at the same time protecting those of economic and political sensitivity to that leading number (precisely those that are of economic interest to the institution's less significant largely developing country and least developed participants). The book also argues that meaningful alterations to the asymmetries in the WTO's legal framework have not been forthcoming precisely because they require the giving of concessions for those received. This has the effect of trading a modicum of corrective action for the creation of further economic opportunities. As the balance of exchange has always resided with the institution's most dominant members, this has, in turn, contributed at least to the perpetuation of asymmetry, and at most to its amplification. It is this asymmetry in economic opportunity and the persistence of practices and procedures that concentrate decision-making power in the hands of the dominant trading powers which has given rise to heightened political contestation and which has imbued ministerial meetings with a propensity to collapse.

However, the book also argues that, rather than significantly disrupting the development of multilateral trade regulation or resulting in its substantive alteration, those moments wherein political contestation has reached a peak and a ministerial meeting has collapsed have all, without exception, been followed by a period of reflection that has enabled the trade agenda to be taken forward. These periods have facilitated the institution's further development because of a shared belief in, and commitment to, the centrality of trade to economic growth and development among the participating states; the absence of a competing institution in which trade objectives might also be realised; a widespread acknowledgement that multilateral liberalisation promises far greater gains and is much less costly than regional or bilateral mechanisms; the persistence of a global configuration of power which is not fundamentally different from that which existed at the institution's creation, and a fear of a resurgence of protectionism and a return to the insularity of the inter-war years should the process of trade liberalisation be allowed to stall. That said, while the argument shows that collapse is not a fatal feature of multilateral trade regulation and that it has a progressive function in that it is often the precursor to further agreement, the breakdown of a ministerial meeting is nevertheless a spectacular reminder of the system's historical structural flaws and the manner in which it continues to disproportionately serve the interests of the dominant powers rather than those of the poorest and weakest members. In this way, collapse has an important symbolic, as well as procedural, function.

The remainder of this chapter sets the foundations for the development of the argument. It begins by exploring the existing scholarly literature on the collapse of WTO ministerials. In so doing, it reveals that while the literature comprises much that is of value, in large measure it misdiagnoses – and, as a result, fails to fully explain – the causes of the breakdown of these meetings and the consequences of their collapse. Thereafter the chapter sets out a series of conceptual markers that help make sense of the analysis which follows. These markers map out an understanding of institutions and institutional development that helps better understand patterns of trade politics. This section does not, however, engage in an involved discussion of institutional theory in all its variants. This is not the place (see, among others, Keohane, 1989, 2002; North, 1990; Steinmo *et al.*, 1992; Ruggie, 1993b; Thelen, 1999; Murphy, 2005). It is merely intended to be an aid to understanding. Once this is complete the chapter sets out how the book unfolds in the development of its argument.

Existing wisdom

Much of the existing scholarly and practitioner literature on the collapse of WTO ministerials identifies tensions between developed and developing countries, the significance of the issues at stake, disagreements among the leading industrial states (Annan, 2001: 19; Sampson, 2001: 9; Sutherland *et al.*, 2001: 87) and the inadequacy of existing procedures for conducting negotiations as important factors in the breakdown of the Seattle and Cancún meetings. Few beyond the politics of the moment (and even then beyond Seattle) emphasise the role of public demonstrations. As Chakravarthi Raghavan put it in the wake of Seattle:

> The week-long street protests and demonstrations . . . and the way the
> conference ended in shambles, led to a perception among the unwary
> that the protests and demonstrations had derailed the process and that
> the [NGOs] were a broad, organized movement, and posed the greatest
> threat to the 'rules-based' trading system protecting the weaker coun-
> tries. Nothing . . . could be further from reality. The Seattle meeting
> failed because of substantive differences among the major trading
> nations, and between them and the developing nations, and the refusal
> of the large majority of the membership to be pushed around.
>
> (Raghavan, 2000: 495–496; also Moore, 2003: 111)

Jeffrey Schott's analysis (2000) of the causes of the collapse of the Seattle
meeting is indicative of much of the scholarly literature. He suggests that
substantive disagreements among member states over the proposed content
of a new trade round (what was to be the 'millennium' round) were the principal causes of the Seattle collapse. Much of this disagreement brought
developed and developing countries into conflict over how to address trade
in industrial goods, agriculture and services as well as the expansion in the
WTO's agenda. Of particular note were the tensions that unfolded over the
labour standards issue, though trade and the environment was also a significant source of conflict. Schott also notes that differences of opinion among
the quad (the US, EU, Japan and Canada) on the level of reduction in
agricultural subsidies, peak tariffs and anti-dumping, the incorporation of
investment and competition policy in a new round, and exemptions for
'cultural industries' were also significant factors in the collapse of the
meeting; and he suggests a portion of blame lies with the Clinton administration's mishandling of the politics and organisation of the meeting as well
as its failure to nurture a consensus ahead of the meeting (Schott, 2000: 7;
also Arai, 2000: 62). Schott further suggests (with co-author Jayashree Watal)
that policy differences among the WTO membership could have been bridged
had the 'WTO's decision making process [understood as the 'process by
which member governments resolve issues concerning the conduct of trade
negotiations'] not broken down' (Schott and Watal, 2000: 283). He cites the
difficulty of building a consensus among a significantly expanded membership under the constraints placed on negotiations by the principle of a single
undertaking (where all parties agree to be bound by all aspects of an agreement) as the primary problem; and he also identifies the persistence of the
GATT practice of attempting to forge consensus through small numbers of
self-selected members meeting to decide on divisive issues (the so-called
'green room' process)[2] as a contributing factor (Schott and Watal, 2000:
283–286).

Two problems present themselves in accounts such as these. First, the
events that unfolded in the run-up to and during the Seattle meeting tend to
be divorced from the wider development of multilateral trade regulation.

While they offer a useful sense of the degree of political contestation during the meeting, they are nevertheless taken out of context. The result is that the events themselves are viewed to be more significant than they actually are, while the root causes of the collapse remain obscured. A second problem is that accounts such as these tend to underplay the role of the institution and its attendant procedures, practices and ways of operating in a meeting's collapse. While mention is made of institutional anomalies such as the quality of preparation and the manner of the meeting's organisation, these accounts do not fully appreciate the way in which the interaction of WTO members has been and is shaped by the institution.

Jagdish Bhagwati offers a slightly different account. Like many others, Bhagwati attributes the collapse of the Seattle meeting to a combination of factors of which the holding of a ministerial in the US in the run-up to a presidential election, the paralysis caused by and hostility generated towards the demonstrations that accompanied the meeting, the failure to build a consensus among the membership on the proposed content of a new trade round prior to the meeting, and President Clinton's ill-advised attempts to make domestic political capital out of the conference figure prominently (Bhagwati, 1999; 2001). However, he also suggests that the level of political contestation was heightened by what he sees as an anomaly in the WTO's legal framework that enabled a debate to emerge on the merits of extending the Organisation's remit to include certain trade-related issues (of which labour standards were seen as the most inflammatory). He argues that the conclusion of the Agreement on Trade Related Intellectual Property Rights (TRIPs) during the preceding Uruguay Round introduced a precedent wherein a reasonable case could be made for the future introduction of any other 'trade and' (or, to use his words, 'trade unrelated') agreement (Bhagwati, 2001: 25; also Wolf, 2001: 201–203).

What is significant about Bhagwati's account is his willingness to see the collapse of a ministerial meeting not just as the consequence of the politics of the meeting's time and place, but also to locate an element of the reason for the heightened political contestation in the manner in which the WTO's legal framework has been fashioned. Yet Bhagwati's account of the impact of the institution and its role in structuring the political interaction of its member states stops at the inclusion of a 'trade and' agreement. While he points to other problems in the WTO's legal framework (such as the imbalances in the single undertaking), he does not subject these to the same kind of sustained analysis that he does the TRIPs. Moreover, Bhagwati does not set the collapse of either the Seattle or Cancún meetings (see Bhagwati, 2004c), or the politicking therein in an historical context that allows the full extent of such imbalances to be appreciated. Similarly, though his role as one of the WTO's (now defunct) panel of experts[3] gives him an important insight into the politics of ministerials, he is nevertheless silent on the impact of ministerial practices and procedures in the collapse of such meetings (such as the selection of 'friends of the chair',[4] the green room process, and mini-ministerials) – practices and procedures about which developing and developed country delegates alike complain.

John Odell's work takes us a little further into the causes and consequences of the collapse of WTO meetings and enables us to get a better sense of the role played by institutional factors therein. Rather than attributing the collapse of the Seattle ministerial simply to the unbridgeable gulf in the negotiating positions of key players or the impact of the demonstrations outside the conference, Odell argues that a combination of factors caused the meeting to break down. Crucially, he suggests that the principal causes of the collapse relate to the *process* of the negotiations married to the pursuit of negotiating strategies that were not conducive to consensus building. Moreover, he argues that the collapse of the meeting was not inevitable; had a more appropriate process been followed, the substantive differences among member states could have been bridged and a new round launched. Odell identifies two aspects of the negotiating process as particularly troublesome (see also Ricupero, 2001): (i) the management of the pre-ministerial preparatory process in Geneva; and (ii) the management of the Seattle conference itself (see Odell, 2002; also Odell, 2001).

Odell develops his argument by comparing and contrasting the events in the run-up to and during the Seattle meeting with those that immediately preceded and occurred during the launch of the Uruguay Round (1986–1994). He suggests that the political and economic climate leading up to the Seattle ministerial was perhaps more conducive to the launch of a new round of negotiations than the comparable Uruguay phase. However, he argues, the tensions generated among the membership by the election of a successor to Renato Ruggiero as WTO Director-General (DG), the knock-on effect this had on shortening the time available for the preparatory process (down from 18 weeks during the run-up to the 1986 Punta Del Este ministerial to eight weeks prior to Seattle), the unusually weak positions of the Chair of the General Council (Ali Said Mchumo) and newly appointed DG Moore (coupled with Moore's relative newness to the job – appointed just eight weeks before the Seattle meeting was due to take place), the lack of appointed Deputy Directors-General (DDsG) until November 1999, the impossibility of drafting a negotiating text that reflected the various interests of the member states (and the manner in which the text was constructed), and the inability of the green room process to generate a consensus combined to undermine the chances of successfully launching a new round (Odell, 2002: 419–424; see also Moore, 2003: 111). Moreover, the ministerial itself was mismanaged in such a way that the meeting was destined to fail. Odell cites unfavourable local arrangements (malfunctioning telephone and sound systems, shortages of places to eat, limited time available for the negotiations), the ill-advised comments made by President Clinton in an interview with the *Seattle Post-Intelligencer* on the labour standards issue, and the lack of impartiality and overly robust manner of Charlene Barshefsky as conference Chair as the principal problems (for an alternative view see Sutherland *et al.*, 2001: 87–88) – though he notes that in spite of these problems, areas of agreement were nevertheless emerging (Odell, 2002: 422–424).

Odell's argument is persuasive, and his account of the problems in the process of the negotiations meticulous. Moreover, his assertion that '[d]eadlocks in multilateral WTO negotiations are more likely and more difficult to resolve today than prior to 1994' is certainly correct (Odell, 2005: 445). Four questions nevertheless present themselves. First, his comparative analysis of the pre-Uruguay and pre-Seattle phases rightly sharpens the problems of process in the latter. Yet Odell says little about the development of that process between the two meetings (Punta Del Este and Seattle). As Ricardo Melendez-Ortiz points out, the Uruguay Round was conducted under GATT auspices, and while many of the GATT's mannerisms have been carried over into the new institution, there are some differences that need to be taken into account (Melendez-Ortiz, 2004). Odell does mention some of these differences in the opening sections of his argument. He does not, however, fully explore the impact of these developments on the interaction of the member states in the run-up to the Seattle meeting. Second, Odell's historical view is in a number of ways not historical enough. When viewed in the context of the Uruguay negotiations, the pre-Seattle process and the mishandling of the meeting appear to be the principal causes of the collapse of the meeting. However, these processes themselves have an historical root and are more consequences of the way in which the WTO's institutional culture was fashioned and has developed than causes in themselves. Third, and relatedly, Odell's comparative analysis treats Seattle and the run-up to the Uruguay Round as directly comparable. This is also true of other commentators who acknowledge that the collapse of ministerial meetings is not unique to the WTO era (see, for example, Ricupero, 2001: 38; Sampson, 2001: 5). Although Odell acknowledges that differences in context exist, he underplays the fundamentally different setting in which the Seattle ministerial took place. Finally, though Odell's analysis rightly points to the role played by institutional factors in the meeting's collapse, it omits to show the extent to which they are entrenched features of the GATT/WTO's operating culture and, in so doing, implies that they can be corrected more easily than would likely be the case otherwise. Moreover, although Odell's account is pathbreaking in its focus on institutional factors, he nevertheless underestimates their role in the collapse of the Seattle meeting.

Amrita Narlikar's work picks up from and develops aspects of Odell's argument (Narlikar, 2004a). Like others, Narlikar points to the inability of the Geneva preparatory process to reconcile differences between principal players ahead of the Seattle meeting, and she points to a lack of adequate preparation preceding the Cancún ministerial. But, she suggests, in large measure the collapse of both meetings was the result of the ministerial process itself. Central to Narlikar's argument is an understanding that the practices and procedures that have developed and become part of ministerial meetings can structure the conduct of negotiations in such a way that their propensity to collapse increases; or else (as she argues was the case at the Doha meeting) the consensus reached at meetings 'reflects . . . an unstable equilibrium' that will inevitably unravel shortly thereafter (Narlikar, 2004a: 414, 420). She singles out seven practices that together combine to heighten political contestation at ministerial meetings and increase the chances of a collapse (see also Jawara and Kwa, 2003; Narlikar and Wilkinson, 2004). These may be summarised as: (i) the frequency of ministerials and the time set aside for negotiations; (ii) the disjuncture between the Geneva preparatory process and the ministerial meeting itself; (iii) the role of the Chair of the conference; (iv) the selection of facilitators (so-called friends of the Chair); (v) the choice and timing of venue; (vi) the persistence of green room diplomacy; and (vii) the reliance on 'flexibility' as the guiding operational principle.

Like Odell's, Narlikar's argument is persuasive. She usefully identifies the institutionalisation of particular practices and the development of a culture of ministerials as important factors in explaining their collapse. As she aptly puts it:

> [f]ailures of substance are often driven by failures in process . . . the proximate causes of the collapse at Cancún lay in the irreconcilable positions of members . . . [b]ut the reasons why countries adopted the entrenched positions that they did, and why standard negotiating tactics were unable to break the deadlock . . . had much to do with the flaws that underlie the institutional design of the WTO.
>
> (Narlikar, 2004b)

There are, however, some missing elements in Narlikar's argument. Like Odell, she does not probe sufficiently deeply into the factors that led to the development of these practices, nor does she explore other factors embedded in the WTO's institutional fabric that may also contribute to the breakdown of each meeting, like the way in which the Organisation's legal framework has developed and its impact in structuring negotiations. Part of the problem results from the relatively narrow focus of Narlikar's analysis. In focusing on the process of ministerials she is seeking to advance a more sophisticated explanation of their collapse; but in so doing, she extracts the ministerial process from the wider institution of the WTO. For instance, Narlikar says very little about the structural inequalities embedded in the WTO's legal framework, or the issues at stake in the negotiations. Narlikar is also reluctant to place the development of a culture of ministerials in an historical context. She notes that three ministerial meetings held under GATT auspices also collapsed, yet she does not strive to explore these and draw any findings therefrom into her analysis.

Fatoumata Jawara and Aileen Kwa (2003) develop some of the themes highlighted by Narlikar in their account of the naked use of power in the conduct of trade negotiations. Like Narlikar, their focus is primarily on the post-Seattle era, and their task is to reveal the myriad ways in which developing countries are disadvantaged in WTO negotiations. They do not, however, set out explicitly to explain why WTO meetings collapse, though they do so in a tangential fashion.

Jawara and Kwa are more critical of the WTO than Narlikar. Whereas Narlikar is persuaded that a redesign of WTO procedures can mitigate the power asymmetries which certain of its practices and procedures amplify and she holds stock in the broad idea of trade liberalisation, Jawara and Kwa see the Organisation and its system of rules as part of a wider global machinery that seeks the subordination of developing countries (Jawara and Kwa, 2003: 269, 304). As they put it:

> What happens in the WTO is part of a broader pattern of neocolonialism in the global economy. This has two strands. The first is the self-interest of the major powers; their close ties with multinational companies . . . and their willingness to use their political and economic strength to achieve their ends, what ever the effects on other countries. . . . The second strand is a combination of ideology, paternalism and missionary zeal. The true believers in globalization and liberalization feel sure that they know best – that markets work and globalization benefits all – but that the poor benighted heathens of the South have yet to realize this.
> (Jawara and Kwa, 2003: 269–270)

Like Narlikar, Jawara and Kwa point to the emergence of a particular culture of ministerials as a root problem with the conduct of trade negotiations. However, they do so within a wider critique of the WTO which draws upon an analysis of the Organisation's legal aspects and the structural disadvantages that many developing countries face in the global economy (such as lack of technical capacity, adverse terms of trade, underdeveloped legal and physical infrastructures and so on). Jawara and Kwa add to Narlikar's list the following as cause for concern: (i) the partisan nature of the secretariat; (ii) the lack of development sensitivity in WTO obligations; (iii) the financial constraints on developing countries in using the dispute settlement process; (iv) the practice of holding mini-ministerials, comprising only a limited number of members, ahead of ministerials in an effort to forge consensus among the principal trading powers; (v) the tension between the large number of meetings during negotiations and the limited number of developing country delegates available to attend; (vi) imbalances in the WTO's legal framework that favour the economic interests of northern states over their southern counterparts; (vii) the politics of issuing draft texts as the basis upon which negotiations are conducted; (viii) the lack of adequate and speedy facilities for translating draft documents into official WTO languages other than English; (ix) the lack of widespread consultation in deciding issues such as the extension of a ministerial meeting; (x) the power of secretariat lawyers in drafting texts; and (xi) the residue of a GATT mindset (Jawara and Kwa, 2003).

Like those of Odell and Narlikar, Jawara and Kwa's analysis is rich and insightful. It does not, however, fully uncover the sources of the imbalances they point to in either the WTO's legal framework or the practice of conducting trade negotiations. This is largely the result of a limited time-frame in which their analysis is set. By focusing on the post-Uruguay Round era generally, and post-Seattle more specifically, they do not fully appreciate the entrenchment of these practices (albeit that their work is peppered with pointers to historical happenings that do have an impact on contemporary trade politics). Moreover, they focus too much on the politics (rather than the political economy) of trade negotiations to offer a complete and wholly compelling account of the asymmetries confronting developing countries.

Elsewhere in the literature, pointers to a more historically sensitive analysis may be found. Robert Wolfe's analysis of Seattle, Doha and Cancún, for instance, attempts to stand back from the politics of the moment and take a longer (what he calls 'conjunctural') view of trade politics. His analysis begins with the observation that since the 1982 Geneva ministerial most GATT/WTO meetings 'have apparently been near catastrophes, yet the trading system is stronger, deeper and wider now than it was a generation ago' (Wolfe, 2004: 575); and, as he rightly puts it, the outcome of one ministerial meeting is a 'poor sign of the health of the institutions of the global trading system'. As such, the failure of Seattle and Cancún and the success of Doha point to 'neither imminent collapse nor new grand design but a continuation of a long process of evolution' (Wolfe, 2004: 575). Wolfe's idea is that the long run development of multilateral trade regula-tion is 'that the WTO always proceeds in a step-by-step fashion, solving problems as they appear in the daily life of the trading system without itself [i.e. the WTO] being able to lead the process of change' (Wolfe, 2004: 577). Yet, while he importantly emphasises changes and developments through time, his focus on haphazard institutional development wherein problems encountered are fixed, and where these fixes are glued to others in time lacks an appreciation of a developmental process shaped by institutional design and relations of power embedded therein as well as the outcome of politi-cal bargaining designed to ensure continued development but which follow from the institution's core purposes. Put differently, the development of multilateral trade regulation is less haphazard and solution-orientated than Wolfe suggests, and rather more the result of institutional dynamics, design and path-dependent evolution seldom acknowledged.

Others too offer important insights. Ricardo Melendez-Ortiz suggests that the WTO's current problems are the inevitable consequences of (i) a process of transition from the trade liberalising function of the GATT to what he terms the 'economic integration arrangements of the WTO' (Melendez-Ortiz, 2004: 1), and (ii) the result of the youthfulness and novelty of the current system. In this account, the difficulties of concluding trade negotiations are amplified by the move from 'shallow integration' to a harmonisation of domestic regulations (the latter of which is considerably more time consuming and complicated to undertake than the former). Jean-Christophe Graz offers a slightly different account. He argues that it is not so much the move from shallow to deep integration that underpins the WTO's current difficulties; rather it is the content of that deep integration and its guiding principles that are the subject of contestation and which accounts for the tensions that pervade the Organisation (Graz, 2004: 598). As Graz puts it:

> [the WTO is] facing a fundamental crisis because of its failure to strike an acceptable balance between market and non-market provisions. . . . Although the mandate of [the DDA] includes provisions giving a more balanced interpretation of the embeddedness of international trade in non-trade concerns, it remains unclear whether this slight revision . . . [is] anything more than a pragmatic response to the tensions between developed and developing countries, and growing domestic concerns regarding the goals of the multilateral trading system.
>
> (Graz, 2004: 611)

Somewhat differently, Katsuhiko Mori suggests that the collapse of the Cancún meeting was the result of an unpicking of the compromise between protectionist and liberalising forces in previous incarnations of the GATT/WTO; changing relations of power among the WTO membership; and the constraints placed on the major players by the 'two-level' game – that is, the problems of satisfying two constituencies at once: the first domestic, the second fellow participants (Mori, 2004: 394–414).

What exists then is a rich literature on the collapse of WTO meetings; yet it is a literature that explains the breakdown of ministerials in large measure as a consequence of the negotiating strategies and political actions of key players, the political and economic significance of the negotiations themselves, the inadequacy of existing procedures for forging consensus, blended with the politics of the moment. Underpinning these accounts is an assumption that the WTO currently fashioned is unable to co-ordinate negotiations among its member states so that each member's pursuit of self-interest is satisfied and a stable equilibrium produced. The corollary is that the problem can be solved and an equilibrium produced through the implementation of measures designed to make the WTO deal more effectively with the sources of trouble: that is, through institutional modification and rationalisation. In this sense, the root causes of the collapse of WTO ministerials are generally deemed to hold constant and represent problems to be solved.

This received wisdom, however, leaves too many questions unanswered. It fails to explain why the collapse of ministerial meetings emerged as a feature of multilateral trade regulation *prior to* the establishment of the WTO;

it ignores the dynamic quality that the collapse of ministerial meetings has had on driving the trade agenda forward; it does not explain the consequences of the emergence and entrenchment of a politics of crisis (as well as post-crisis) as an institutional culture and the impact of this on relations among member states; and it mistakenly attributes the collapse of ministerial meetings to causes that are in reality consequences of the way in which multilateral trade regulation was established and has developed through time. Most certainly these accounts offer useful explanations of a measure of the political contestation that pervades WTO ministerials; but they do not reveal the degree to which this contestation is a consequence of the way in which multilateral trade regulation was created and has evolved. Moreover, they do not locate the collapse of WTO ministerials in a wider historical setting that takes account of the way in which multilateral trade regulation has evolved through time and explore the role of institutional developments in giving rise to crises. Also absent from those works is a detailed account of the consequences of their collapse. Mention is made of the need to place development more firmly at the core of WTO negotiations and the consequences of not doing so as 'fixes' to the WTO's problems so conceived, but little is said of the longer term consequences of these collapses on the WTO's institutional evolution or the economic opportunities arising therefrom. In short, these works do not sufficiently explain the way in which the interaction of the membership and the issues negotiated is structured by the institutional context in which it takes place.

The conceptual framework

In contrast, this book takes the causes, consequences and role of crisis in the WTO to be a function of the way in which multilateral trade regulation was created and has evolved through time. It does not perceive the collapse of ministerial meetings merely as problems that need solving, that is, as moments of disequilibrium which require the causes of that upset to be identified and remedial action undertaken. Nor does it take the development of multilateral trade regulation to be the result of functional answers to problems posed. The argument advanced here draws from a body of literature that takes as a starting point a different understanding of institutions and institutional development. This literature is principally concerned with how and why institutions emerge and change through time; and it seeks to better understand the consequences of their emergence and evolution (see, among others, Murphy, 1994, 2005; Cox, 1996; Lowndes, 1996; March and Olsen, 1996; Hall and Taylor, 1998; Hay and Wincott, 1998).

The approach begins from the assumption that institutions matter. Institutions are not neutral, autonomous entities; nor do they influence actor expectations and political outcomes only at the margins. Instead, they reflect particular relations of power and shape actor expectations and political outcomes accordingly (though they do not, as Susan Sell rightly points out, *dictate* outcomes – Sell, 2002: 482). At their broadest, institutions may be thought of as systems of rules, norms, practices and procedures that structure relations and affect outcomes in a manner that reflects the particular power configurations of which they are a product. In this way, they structure power relations among actors in a manner that privileges some while putting others at a disadvantage (Thelen and Steinmo, 1992: 2). As Simon Bulmer and Martin Burch put it, institutions reflect 'a particular bias, allowing access to some interests while denying it to others and encouraging and highlighting some points of view at the cost of others'. They continue, 'institutions can be evaluated in terms of the opportunity structures they create and of which actors, and interests they represent, are most benefited' as well as 'the extent to which and the ways in which these opportunity structures have changed over time' (Bulmer and Burch, 1998: 604).

The argument presented here assumes that institutions are not merely structures 'holding together' (Thelen, 1999: 384) particular patterns of behaviour that are replicated and perpetuated through time, though such patterns may appear to persist for identifiable periods. Instead, the argument understands that institutions, once created, develop and change. This development and change is the product not only of an institution's interaction with the environment in which it is located, the result of refinements implemented to ensure its smooth functioning, or a direct result of the role for which it was originally created. An institution's development and change is also the result of a degree of institutional autonomy developed through its very functioning. To put it another way, once created institutions develop a life of their own. This is not, however, an existence divorced from the circumstances of an institution's establishment; rather it is an existence organically connected to the institution's core purposes and any internal and external changes that may arise.

The approach also assumes that much institutional development is incremental: that is, through modifications at the margins and in keeping with existing formats and ways of operating as opposed to adjustments to core purposes and constitutive principles. These modifications may be a response to a technical problem, such as the need to establish a means of overseeing the administration of a set of rules, or the result of pressure from actors subject to the institution's rules and whose participation is essential to its purposes, but who are not dominant therein. They nevertheless imbue institutional development with a path-dependent quality – by which I mean a bounded evolutionary trajectory.

A corresponding assumption is that at particular moments in time fundamental change in the nature and direction of an institution's evolution has the capacity to occur. These moments can result from a single or a combination of multiple exogenous and endogenous factors, such as changes in prevailing configurations of power, through alterations in existing rules, to changes in personnel within a particular office or division; or they can result from pressure brought to bear as a critical mass develops from a long process of incremental adjustment. Nevertheless, these moments contain within them the potential to produce a fundamental, qualitatively distinct shift in trajectory. This potential for change, however, only becomes part of an institution's evolution if it is used. In this sense, we can differentiate between a 'critical moment' wherein change has the capacity to take place, and a 'critical juncture' whereupon change emerges signalling a clear departure from existing patterns of practice (Bulmer and Burch, 1998: 605).

The approach also acknowledges that the creation of an institution imbues its architects with certain advantages. The advantages arise from the construction of rules that serve the needs of dominant actors, but which also put in place significant barriers to new entrants such that challenges to the prevailing configuration of power are attenuated. As Robert Hunter Wade puts it, institutional innovators are able to 'kick away the ladder' thereby enabling them to perpetuate the advantages accrued by them from the institution's creation (Wade, 2003: 632; also 621–630). This does not mean, however, that institutions are free from conflict or tension. Rather, it is precisely because institutional structures reflect prevailing configurations of power that they are also sites of potential contestation. In this way, institutions have a transformative potential; but their development is also a reflection of the outcomes and accommodations resulting from contestations between dominant and non-dominant actors. It is by observing these moments of contestation and understanding their causes, consequences and significance that a more accurate understanding of an institution and its development may be advanced. As Robert Cox puts it:

> [i]nstitutionalization is a means of stabilizing and perpetuating a particular order. Institutions reflect the power relations prevailing at their point of origin and tend, at least initially, to encourage collective images consistent with these power relations. Eventually, institutions take on their own life; they become battlegrounds of opposing tendencies, or rival institutions may reflect different tendencies.
>
> (Cox, 1996: 99)

Applying the conceptual framework and the development of the argument

With these conceptual markers in mind, the book develops its argument through an exploration of the development of multilateral trade regulation in the post-war era focusing on the purposes for which it was constructed and the manner in which it has developed through time. This exploration is necessarily descriptive. As Richard Blackhurst puts it, such description is an essential part of 'understanding ... how the [GATT/WTO] functions' (Blackhurst, 1998: 31). However, where this book differs is in the way in which it describes the institution. For many, the WTO can simply be reduced to certain facts and features: its organisational structure, legal framework, dispute settlement machinery, potted history and so on. Yet certain of these facts and features are not set appropriately within their proper context, nor are they told in a value-neutral fashion (something I do not profess to do either). Mindful that the presentation of fact and argument always serves a particular purpose, the argument presented hereafter draws upon a particular reading of the WTO consistent with the conceptualisation of institutions set out above.

The historical narrative developed throughout focuses on the evolution of multilateral trade regulation from the moment of its inception up to, and including, the WTO's Hong Kong ministerial meeting (December 2005). In so doing, it draws attention to those moments wherein a significant aspect of the development of multilateral trade regulation emerges and becomes part of its evolutionary trajectory as well as those that have passed by the wayside. It does not offer a comprehensive and formulaic analysis of each round – the preparatory phase, the negotiations themselves and the aftermath. This is *not* the purpose of the book. Rather, it explores the GATT and WTO's institutional development identifying those factors important to a better understanding of why ministerial meetings collapse and why this is now an entrenched feature of trade politics. As such, it focuses on those aspects of trade rounds and other developments that are intrinsic to understanding the causes, consequences and role of crisis in the WTO. Moreover, this is a narrative that builds through time focusing on those instances of note to the overall development of the argument. As a result, the book unpacks in detail the foundations of multilateral trade regulation, the manner in which the GATT was deployed as a vehicle for liberalisation, and the development of practices and procedures for that purpose tracing its development from 1947 to the present day.

It is also important to note at the outset that this is not an argument against or in defence of free trade. It is an argument about institutional development, its consequences and the inequities arising therefrom. Despite a prevailing perception and attendant rhetoric to the contrary, the WTO is not about free trade; nor has it, or the GATT, ever been. It has always been, and remains, a political institution constructed and deployed to serve a particular purpose. It is about facilitating and entrenching in international law political bargains that enable the economic agents of participating governments to pursue opportunities in some markets while protecting others. While those bargains may ease the flow of goods and services in some sectors, this is entirely different from the blanket liberalisation of trade. As such, an understanding of the WTO cannot be conflated – as is all too often the case – with a normative preference for free trade.

In offering a more detailed account of the causes and consequences of the collapse of WTO ministerials and exploring the role that the crises generated by these events play in the development of multilateral trade regulation the book advances four claims. First, it argues that the collapse of WTO meetings is a consequence of the way in which the institution of multilateral trade regulation was created and has evolved through time; second, it posits that far from being a disruptive force, crisis has come to be an important feature of the way in which multilateral trade regulation as an institution evolves; third, it argues that the causes, consequences and role of crisis in the WTO can only be understood by viewing the evolution of multilateral trade regulation as an historical process; and fourth, it contends that until or unless a dramatic shift in the global balance of power occurs (in which a vastly different institutional architecture is put into place), an alternative ideological consensus develops, a viable competing institutional framework emerges, and/or a fundamental overhaul of the WTO takes place (involving an alteration of its core principles) the collapse of ministerial meetings and the onset of a post-crisis politics thereafter will continue to be features of multilateral trade regulation for some time to come.

Hereafter, the evolution of multilateral trade regulation is conceived as the product both of bargains struck among participating states during trade negotiations and the ongoing adjustment and development of practices and procedures designed to oversee the conduct of world trade as well as the institution's functioning. At its creation, multilateral trade regulation took the form of a limited agreement among 23 contracting parties (the GATT) designed for the specific purpose of liberalising trade in goods and kick-starting the reversal of the protectionism that characterised the inter-war world economy. Inevitably, the GATT reflected the interests of its architects. As the dominant party, its principal purpose was to assist the US in the realisation of post-war economic opportunities. However, reflecting the accommodations necessary to reach agreement on the creation of this system, it also offered the European allies a measure of assistance with reconstruction. Thereafter, the practices and procedures governing the conduct of world trade evolved steadily over time and the striking of bargains during trade rounds placed new layers of regulation on top of those previously negotiated. And while there has been some superseding of provisions and the modification of bargains struck, in large measure the development of multilateral trade regulation has preserved and enhanced rules, norms and ways of operating first developed under the GATT and extended them into new arenas. At the same time it has protected those areas of key political import-ance to the institution's principal architects and dominant players. Inevitably, given the GATT's original purpose, this system has regulated international trade in such a way that the balance of economic opportunity lies with the industrial states. The result has been that as each new layer of regulation is added, whether in terms of rules and disciplines in new areas or tariff reduc-tions and other concessions, the asymmetries in multilateral trade regulation have been perpetuated and, more often than not, amplified. This, in turn, has produced a deeply asymmetrical system of regulation in terms of the economic opportunity to which it gives rise; and it is in the development of this system of multilateral trade regulation that we find the causes of height-ened political contestation that has come to pervade WTO ministerials.

How it unfolds

The analysis begins in Chapter 2 with an exploration of the manner in which the modern system of trade regulation was forged. Here the chapter places emphasis on understanding the unique circumstances of the GATT's creation – as the predecessor institution to the WTO – and the way in which it was institutionalised as the principal machinery for multilateral trade regulation and liberalisation. Chapter 3 picks up on that story and explores how the GATT was deployed as a mechanism for liberalising trade in its formative quarter-century. In so doing, it examines how the application of the General Agreement came to structure the relations of its contracting parties by removing impediments to trade in some sectors while protecting others. The chapter also surveys the major developments in multilateral trade regulation during this period and explores the emergence of pressures that led, two decades later, to the creation of the WTO.

Set against this backdrop, Chapter 4 examines the developments that paved the way for, and ultimately shaped, the creation of the WTO. Here emphasis is placed on understanding the critical moment that had been reached in multilateral trade regulation following the conclusion of the Kennedy round (1964–1967), exploring the 'reform' of the GATT during the Tokyo round (1973–1979), and detailing the major developments in the run-up to the Uruguay round (1986–1994). The chapter also explores the impact of the breakdown of three ministerial meetings (Geneva 1982, Montreal 1988 and Brussels 1990) upon the development of multilateral trade regulation. It also discusses the way in which the creation of the WTO resulted in the amplification of an asymmetry in multilateral trade regulation that developed during its formative years, focusing on the consequences of the deal brokered at the conclusion of the Uruguay round and the significance of the 'single undertaking'.

Chapter 5 explores the development of multilateral trade regulation since the creation of the WTO and the negotiations currently being conducted under the DDA. The chapter begins with the emergence of political efforts to forge a new consensus for the launch of a 'millennium' round of trade negotiations in the run-up to and during the Geneva ministerial meeting (May 1998). It then considers the collapse of the Seattle ministerial; the readjustment process that occurred thereafter; the breakdown of the Cancún meeting; the July 2004 agreement reached in the wake of Cancún aimed at revitalising the DDA; and the continuation of a post-crisis politics in the run-up to and during the Hong Kong ministerial meeting (December 2005). Throughout, the chapter places these events in the overall context of the development of multilateral trade regulation.

Chapter 6 brings the argument full circle and offers a series of concluding comments. These not only deal with the significance of understanding the causes, consequences and role of crisis in the WTO as the inevitable result of the institution's historical development but they also examine the impact of these developments on the future shape of multilateral trade regulation. Ultimately the chapter argues that until or unless a dramatic shift in the global balance of power occurs (in which a vastly different institutional architecture is put into place), an alternative ideological consensus develops, a viable competing institutional framework emerges, and/or a fundamental overhaul of the WTO takes place, the asymmetry at the core of multilateral trade regulation, and the propensity of its meetings to collapse, will remain among its most characteristic features.

2 Forging multilateral trade regulation

The post-war settlement and the rise of the GATT

Crisis has always loomed large in the politics of international trade. Indeed, the system of multilateral trade regulation over which the WTO presides was itself borne out of crisis: twin crises to be exact. Its body of rules, associated institutional practices and procedures, and the manner in which trade negotiations are conducted evolved from the Allied response to the interwar depression and the slide into war, *and* from the collapse of a project designed to build a trade organisation as the most significant third of a post-war economic triumvirate. What emerged and was salvaged from these crises in large measure has shaped the modern system of multilateral trade regulation.

Yet it is not only the institutional features of modern multilateral trade regulation that are continuities of past endeavours. The *memory* of one of these crises has played and continues to play a crucial role in shaping WTO politics. Warnings of a return to the economic fragmentation of the 1930s serve as a frame for the political interactions of the WTO's member states. In the wake of the collapse of the Cancún ministerial meeting, for instance, US Trade Representative (USTR) Robert Zoellick's admonishment of the 'won't do' countries for their part in the breakdown of the meeting and his suggestion that the US would pursue its trade objectives outside of the WTO (see Zoellick, 2003) ignited a hyperbole at the centre of which sat this memory. Press commentary warned of the dire consequences of the collapse of the DDA and the US's imminent rush to conclude bilateral agreements and strengthen its regional interests through the Free Trade Agreement of the Americas (FTAA) forsaking the WTO. The hyperbole was such that then EU Trade Commissioner Pascal Lamy attempted to allay such concerns in the wake of a November 2003 meeting with Zoellick suggesting that bilateral trade agreements were a normal and entirely understandable part of a nation's commercial portfolio (Lamy, 2003b). The spectre of the 1930s nevertheless continued to lurk in the background.

Comparable warnings framed the first GATT negotiations in 1947 and have been a feature of every trade round since. The Uruguay round (1986–1994), to cite just one example, was conducted under the threat of a US withdrawal and worries of a global fragmentation resulting therefrom;

and fears of what might happen if the round was not concluded served as constant encouragement to keep the negotiations on track. As Alan Winters put it:

> [To] many commentators the era of liberal and multilateral international trade is in the melting pot, if not actually doomed. To them the Uruguay Round . . . represents the last chance to re-assert the virtues of multi-lateralism which, if unsuccessful, will herald a descent into restricted and bilateral or plurilateral trading arrangements.
>
> (Winters, 1990: 1288)

Remarkably, however, while the memory of the crisis of the inter-war years is and has been used repeatedly as a rhetorical device to frame nego-tiations and to keep the trade bicycle going, no such memory exists of the way in which a system of trade regulation was fashioned in response to that crisis or the impact that the manner of its development thereafter has had on contemporary trade politics. Yet, as this chapter and the rest of the book illustrate, the creation and subsequent evolution of multilateral trade regu-lation has played a crucial role in nurturing the collapse of WTO ministerial meetings by shaping member states' interaction and by constraining the expectations of what can be achieved during trade negotiations. It is here that this tale of institutional evolution, the interests that it has served, and the manner in which it has served those interests begins.

This chapter focuses on the way in which the modern system of multi-lateral trade regulation was forged. It locates the creation of that system within a political project which sought to create a new international econ-omic order in the wake of the Second World War. The chapter focuses not only on the structural context in which the WTO's antecedent institution was forged, but also on the political accommodations reached that were necessary to secure its creation. The chapter also explores the role trade liberalisation was to play within a wider post-war international economic policy and sets the creation of a trade institution within a much larger political and economic institutional complex; and it examines how these ideas, inter-ests and accommodations were reflected in the institutional framework that came to govern international trade.

The wartime foundry – structural context

It is important to reiterate that the WTO's evolution from and intrinsic connection to a post-Second World War institutional apparatus designed to implement a quite specific international economic policy *and* the collapse of that project shortly thereafter is seldom sufficiently acknowledged in the scholarly literature. The Organisation's general purpose, core principles, legal framework and operating procedures are all continuations, adaptations, variations or developments of aspects of a trade institution – what began as the International Trade Organisation (ITO) but which, as we see below, became the General Agreement on Tariffs and Trade (GATT) – fashioned for the purposes of reconstructing a war-ravaged world economy and resurrecting a system of international commerce around the broad notion (though, as it turns out, not a realisation) of non-discrimination in international commerce. Working in conjunction with two sibling institutions – what became the International Monetary Fund (IMF) and the International Bank for Reconstruction and Development (IBRD and later, albeit slightly differently, the World Bank) – and under the umbrella of a world organisational structure known as the United Nations Organisation (UNO), this institutional apparatus also served to lock into place the Allied victory and facilitate the realisation of the economic opportunities resulting from the changed circumstances of the post-war order.

However, though it is often portrayed as such, this was not strictly an 'Allied' project. While the final shape of the post-war economic architecture was the result of a process of negotiation among the Allies (and in particular the US and UK), it was US power, its special interests, its ideas and its material capabilities that provided the structural context in which this post-war institutional apparatus was forged (Knorr, 1948; Crick, 1951; Diebold, 1952; Stern, 1987b; Ikenberry, 1992; cf. Gardner, 1956: 369). The other Allies were merely Greeks at the Rome Court. It was inevitable that the post-war economic institutions would reflect US preponderance.

The active crafting of a post-war institutional architecture by the US signalled a significant departure from its pre-war policy. Prior to the outbreak of war the US had sought to remain apart from the Old World, engaging only with those areas – largely confined to Latin America and Asia Pacific – it had previously designated its sphere of influence. The US had chosen not to become involved in the League of Nations – an organisation whose existence is credited to the pronouncements, if not the ideas, of President Woodrow Wilson, but in whose design the US had little input, and for much of the post-civil war era US economic policy had been largely protectionist.

This new-found US internationalism was guided by a self-interest that had emerged from its changed political and economic circumstances. Politically, the end of the war posed new strategic challenges. While the Second World War had settled one ideological conflict, its conclusion brought another centre-stage. The emergence of the Soviet Union as an economic, military and, most importantly, an ideological competitor threatened American interests; but this posed different problems for the various facets of the post-war institutional architecture. While the UN struggled to bring about (with varying degrees of success) 'the maximum possible amount of co-operation between the United States and the Soviet Union' (Toynbee, 1947: 469), the economic institutions presented the US with an opportunity for economic aggrandisement and strategic consolidation. Although in principle open to Soviet membership, the post-war economic architecture proved to be of little interest to the USSR (see Feis, 1948, 41; Knorr, 1948: 35–36; Kock, 1969:

54–55). The result was to put the US in the unique position of not only wielding influence in the institutions' creation but also their subsequent development.

Economically, the two world wars had proven uniquely beneficial to the US. The First World War decimated the industrial base of the European powers assisting in the elevation of the US from 'a bold pirate of intellectual property' (Wade, 2003: 626) to a major producer and exporter of mass-produced goods. American industrial expansion was further enhanced by the demand for US products stimulated by Europe's post-First World War reconstruction process. The net result was to accelerate the rate at which the US overtook its principal rivals. The onset of the Second World War and its impact on European industry stimulated further demand for US produce, and the post-war reconstruction process promised additional returns. By the end of the war, the US accounted for approximately one-third of total world production and more than 50 per cent of its output of manufactured goods. As Clair Wilcox observed, the US was in a position to sell 'everything to everybody' and needed to buy 'little of anything from anybody' (Wilcox, 1949a: 10–11). It was thus in US interests to pursue a post-war international economic policy that would enable American industry to take full advantage of these opportunities.

There were, however, notable obstacles to the US's trade-led industrial expansion. First, the spread of depression in the inter-war years had caused many governments to implement trade restricting and trade diverting commercial policies in an effort to protect their national economies. Second, the persistence of trade barriers in many of the US's key industrial markets offered domestic producers a respite in which to meet the challenge of American competitivity. Third, much of the colonised world was effectively closed to the US's commercial reach. Those imperial preference systems still in operation guaranteed markets for products from the colonial powers and provided exclusive access to vital raw materials. The effect was to restrict American commercial presence in, and the extraction of raw materials from, these markets.

The US, however, faced a fourth and potentially more costly obstacle to economic aggrandisement. It needed not only to ensure that its goods entered foreign markets as competitively as possible, it also needed to ensure that there existed sufficient demand for its products. Some of this demand could be stimulated by prising open the preference systems that tied former and continuing colonial territories to the imperial powers, but this alone would be insufficient. While European colonies represented emerging markets, the core of demand for US products would come from the Old World itself. A series of problems confronted the planners here. Much of Europe lacked the means with which to purchase US goods. In the absence of a reconstruction package European demand for both capital and consumer goods would evaporate. Moreover, for US producers to take advantage of any European demand, the means by which goods were purchased had to be fully convertible into dollars. Given the poor health of the European economy, and the potential for bouts of hyper-inflation (which, as the planners were only too aware, were not without historical precedent), a managed system of currency convertibility had to be put into place. The solution then was to implement a set of policies that provided the wherewithal for economic reconstruction and to put into place a mechanism for ensuring currency convertibility. Only then would the US's trade possibilities be realised.

However, the route to trade-led growth and recovery was not to be fashioned in the way that previous commercial relations had been conducted: that is, through the negotiation of myriad bilateral agreements with various states with which such arrangements were deemed beneficial (see Ruggie, 1993a). This was not only cumbersome and time-consuming; they promised, as Herbert Feis noted, 'only gradual and limited results' (Feis, 1948: 40). As Klaus Knorr put it:

> Multilateral commerce is eminently suited to the American system of government and economic organization. Prewar trade practices were not, and their continuation would either harm American trade or compel further extensions of governmental controls over private business.
>
> (Knorr, 1948: 19)

The decimation of Europe's industrial base provided a unique but not ever-lasting moment of high demand for US products. The longer European industry was left to recover and satisfy domestic demand, the more restricted American commercial opportunities would become. Thus, to enable the US to take greatest advantage at the earliest possible opportunity of the possibilities presented by a revitalised commercial order, a multilateral approach to trade had to be adopted. In this way, the US could secure trade concessions across a number of countries in one set of negotiations. Furthermore, as Feis noted, the carry-over of wartime co-operation into the immediate post-war period provided an instance in which America's allies, with the exception of the Soviet Union and its satellite states, would be less inclined to 'the customary resistance to the idea of lowering import barriers' (Feis, 1948: 41). What existed, then, was a unique moment of opportunity to refashion the global commercial order in such a way that US interests could maximise any benefit (Gorter, 1954: 2).

To ensure the congruity of the new order to American economic needs, the US also sought to fashion this order in its image – that is, by internationalising American commercial methods, legal frameworks and economic ideas. As Feis so aptly put it, 'the American government was eager to preserve in as much of the world as possible the American type of trading system; one shaped mainly to private initiative and calculation, ruled mainly by competition, nominally open to all on equal terms, unclamped by rigid controls' (Feis, 1948: 41). The result was the construction of international

economic frameworks that drew from and entrenched practices and principles long used within the US as well as in relations with its primary trading
partners. In the field of trade, this was manifest in the use of the principles
of most favoured nation (MFN), national treatment and reciprocity as corner-
stones of post-war commercial regulation. As John Ruggie has noted, it was
to be not just a new commercial order, but a quintessentially *American* order
(Ruggie, 1993a: 31).

US plans for an integrated international economic policy designed to
enable American goods to flow more freely did, however, have a significant
caveat. Price deflation during the 1920s and the depression of the 1930s
had hit the US agricultural sector particularly hard. The economic and social
distress resulting therefrom had ushered in tariffs, production controls, price-
support schemes, import quotas and export subsidies (Evans, 1971: 61–63,
66–69). Moreover, the relative political strength of the agricultural lobby –
accentuated by Congressional districting and non-population-based Sena-
torial electing – made any attempt to pursue a blanket liberalisation policy
unlikely and at variance with US national interests (Gardner, 1956: 3, 20–21).
The result was that while the US was willing to liberalise trade in those
sectors in which it could accrue economic gain (and wherein, it should be
noted, the US faced little competition), it was not willing to do the same in
areas of political and economic sensitivity. This selective approach to liberalisation, particularly with regard to agriculture, was to become a cornerstone
of the GATT.

US efforts to create a post-war economic architecture were thus guided
by the desire to secure increasing market opportunities for its burgeoning
industrial sector while at the same time protecting domestic agricultural
production. Such a system could not, however, be achieved alone despite
the opportunities presented by Soviet exclusion; it required the agreement
of the remaining allied powers. Yet despite the obvious material benefits for
the European powers of the US plan – in terms of providing a machinery
for, and assistance with, reconstruction – and the potential to carry through
the wartime alliance, the American vision was far from a *fait accompli*.
The crisis of the interwar years had severely damaged the idea of a liberal
world economy: as Jacob Viner noted at the time, 'there are few free traders
in the present-day world, and no person in authority anywhere advocates
free trade' (Viner, 1947: 613). What emerged in its stead was a growing
preference among European policymakers and leading economists (of which
John Maynard Keynes was perhaps the most notable) for a measure of
economic planning and government intervention to correct market failure.
Europe, much more so than the US, also faced the very real spectre of mass
unemployment arising from the post-war demobilisation of military personnel and the possibility for social unrest that this might create. The pressing
concerns for Europe's political élites, then, were reconstruction *and* full
employment to forestall any shift in public opinion towards a socialist alternative. As Knorr noted, this situation made the revival of 'multilateral trade

a goal of something less than overriding concern to most nations or else render[ed] its implementation more difficult' (Knorr, 1948: 20).

The involvement of the UK proved particularly important in this regard. British involvement in the American post-war order had a number of benefits. Not only did it build upon a wartime alliance, and a common commercial *lingua franca*; British involvement was strategically and economic beneficial to the US. By binding Britain to a wide-ranging commercial agreement based on a commitment to non-discrimination in trade, the US could prise open the UK's system of imperial preferences as well as ensure British domestic demand for its goods. Moreover, not only did a collaborative relationship with the UK open the US up to new markets for its produce, it had a uniquely strategic dimension in the unfolding Cold War. Tying Britain into a comprehensive post-war economic programme would better enable the UK to manage the breakup of its empire, thus preventing the US from having to actively forestall any Soviet influence developing therein (Toynbee, 1947: 466).

Although they initially shared differing visions of the post-war order, British and American economic interests were also congruous in other regards. Britain's economic complexion – as a nation and imperial power built on trade, and as a state lacking the necessary resources for self-sufficiency – ensured that its post-war economic growth was also contingent on a revitalisation of trade. Like the US, this was a trade-centred vision that gave particular importance to industrial products. Moreover, like the US, the UK was reluctant to open up its agriculture sector to full liberalisation (Gardner, 1956: 33). While imported foodstuffs would inevitably be cheaper than those produced domestically, it would create a level of agricultural dependence incompatible with Britain's national security objectives. It was thus also in Britain's interest to press for a revitalisation of world trade targeted specifically at stimulating demand for industrial goods, while protecting its agricultural sector, married to a comprehensive reconstruction programme.

While these shared interests laid the foundations for an Anglo-American reconstruction of the global economy, the policy designs and the institutional architecture overseeing their implementation were less clear-cut. The US and UK visions of the post-war economic order were initially quite different. British policymakers favoured an order based on a continuation and development of its imperial ties; whereas their US counterparts preferred a more universalistic approach drawing in as many areas of the post-war world as possible. What ensued was a process of negotiation on the specifics of post-war economic policy and the shape of the institutions charged with its implementation (see Gardner, 1956; Ikenberry, 1992).

Anglo-American post-war planning was set in motion early into the war. A broad vision of the post-war economic order was set out during the Atlantic Conference of August 1941 and was furthered by the February 1942 Lend-Lease Agreement. The Atlantic Charter put forward the idea of an integrated set of economic institutions designed to implement a coherent international economic policy centred on non-discrimination in trade – albeit that the commitment to non-discrimination was commercially selective and contingent on reciprocal action (what became known as the American version of MFN – see Viner, 1951). However, in recognition of the economic exigencies of the European powers, this policy was also to 'bring about the fullest collaboration between all nations in the economic field with the object of securing, for all, improved labour standards, economic advancement and social security' (Atlantic Charter, 1941: paragraphs 4, 5). The commitments outlined in the Atlantic Charter, and in particular the centrality of a trade body to plans for the post-war world order, were furthered by the 1942 Lend-Lease Agreement (Article 7 of the Agreement provided the mandate for discussions to commence between the two powers on the issue of liberalising international trade).

Once agreement had been reached on the broad post-war agenda, internal discussions and negotiations between US and British officials separated out into two streams. The first centred on the financial issues thrown up by the designs for the post-war order culminating in the July 1944 Bretton Woods Conference and the subsequent establishment of the IMF and World Bank. The second stream dealt with making provisions for the establishment of a quasi-liberal international trading order. Yet, while the negotiations diverged, the key to the success of the overall project was the high level of coherence between the two streams. The mechanisms devised for stabilising balance-of-payments situations were to have no effect unless subsequent progress was made in restricting, and ultimately eroding, trade barriers; and increases in productive capacity as a prerequisite for accruing the benefits of trade liberalisation could only be achieved in some cases through capital provision for reconstruction.

Forging a trade institution – shaping politics

The designs for what would have eventually become the ITO emerged from a plan for a Commercial Union drafted by the Economic Section of the British War Cabinet and Members of the Board of Trade, and designs for a Multilateral Convention on Commercial Policy doing the rounds in the US. The designs were not, however, in themselves new. Rather they were what Robert Hudec has described as a résumé of ideas developed across myriad interwar international and bilateral conferences (Hudec, 1990: 10). Both the outline for the Commercial Union and that for the Multilateral Convention envisaged, to greater or lesser degrees, the establishment of a permanent body that would administer a series of rules designed to promote non-discrimination in international commerce; have the legal authority to interpret such rules; and provide a mechanism for settling any disputes arising among member states (Gardner, 1956: 103).

Although Anglo-American discussions on the shape of a trade institution did take place during the latter stages of the war – in particular during a meeting in Washington in September 1943 famously characterised by Gardner as a 'university seminar' (Gardner, 1956: 104; Penrose, 1953: 97–104) – it was not until early 1945 that the negotiations proceeded with any vigour. The success of the Bretton Woods Conference in establishing the IMF and World Bank increased the pressure for the completion of the trade project. In December 1945 the US took the lead by preparing and sending out for discussion a draft Charter of the ITO. This was followed, in February 1946, by the passing of a resolution by the Economic and Social Council (ECOSOC) of the newly created United Nations (UN) calling for an international conference on trade and employment to be convened (Fawcett, 1951: 269). The resolution, in turn, established a Preparatory Committee to discuss the creation of the ITO. Nineteen states were involved in the subsequent discussions that took place when the Preparatory Committee met to discuss a 'Suggested Charter' put forward by the US in London in Autumn 1946 (15 October to 26 November), though the bulk of the negotiations remained between Britain and the US (Viner, 1947: 612; Brown, 1950: 67–134; Gardner, 1956: 269–270).

The Suggested Charter comprised 26 articles covering most aspects of commercial policy central to US post-war aims. As Hudec puts it, 'the suggested Charter clearly reflected the interests of the author government. The firmest rules were those on which the United States had no practice to the contrary'. He continues:

> Thus, for example, the "National Treatment" rule – the requirement that internal taxes and other internal laws do not discriminate against foreign products once they enter local commerce – was absolute. Similarly, the exception authorizing the use of quantitative restrictions to deal with balance-of-payments problems was far more rigorous than IMF Article XIV. On the other hand, the Suggested Charter provisions dealing with U.S. trade practices – export subsidies, quantitative restrictions to protect agricultural price supports, and the "escape clause" – were considerably more relaxed . . . [and] [t]here was not much opposition over the exception for agricultural price supports . . . [Moreover, the] Suggested Charter prohibited all export subsidies which lowered export prices below domestic prices, but an exception permitted such subsidies in the case of products in chronic oversupply. Most exports being subsidized under the U.S. farm program were assumed to fall into the excepted category. The Suggested Charter left the subsidizing country free in the end to determine for itself whether market conditions fit the exception. It was, in short, a rule without any means of enforcement.
>
> (Hudec, 1990: 17–18)

Despite this level of authorship, the US was compelled to give ground. The need for exceptions to assist in times of balance-of-payments crisis – a situation that faced much of the developed world in the wake of the war but not, notably, the US – was pressed for by the UK with the support of much of Western Europe. The British case was reinforced by a poor balance-of-payments performance and little prospect of the restoration of currency convertibility. Yet an exception to the suggested Charter's balance-of-payments rules would effectively undermine the rest of the agreement by permitting widespread discrimination thereby nullifying any benefits accrued from the agreement by the US. In the end, the US gave ground, enabling states to act in anticipation of a balance-of-payments crisis, to do so without a concomitant policy of internal adjustment, and to water down the surveillance of exceptions. The concession, however, began to diminish the value of the Charter in the eyes of US negotiators. This was compounded by the debate that also raged over quantitative exceptions provisions in which the US was again forced to give ground by accepting a provision that permitted the continuation of restrictions already in existence (Hudec, 1990: 19–20). American frustrations were further fuelled by pressure from – to which they ultimately conceded – the British delegation to make full employment a central feature of the Charter.

As a result, and in spite of reports that agreement had been reached on 'approximately ninety per cent of the text of the charter' (ITO Report, 1947a: 361), American enthusiasm for the project had begun to wane. American frustrations were further fuelled by persistent tensions over the 10 per cent of the Charter that had yet to be agreed. Inevitably, the document produced by these negotiations – the so-called 'London Charter' – pleased no one. Nevertheless, it provided the prelude for what was to become the ITO Charter, developed first by a technical drafting committee in New York between January and February of 1947, then at the Preparatory Committee's second session in Geneva between 10 April and 30 October 1947 (during which the GATT was also negotiated), and finally at the 1948 Havana Conference on Trade and Employment itself. Although the planners were yet to realise it, the fate of the ITO had been all but decided.

Negotiating the GATT and the Draft Charter

The Preparatory Committee's second session in Geneva had two aims: first, to engage in a 'round' of negotiations (as it turned out, the first GATT round) designed to erode impediments to trade; and second, to move as far as possible towards the completion of the ITO negotiations. The first of these aims, pushed for strongly by a US delegation anxious to make the most of the President's authority to negotiate tariff reductions prior to its expiry (Finlayson and Zacher, 1981: 562), proved by far the easiest and resulted in an agreement among the 20 parties represented in the Preparatory

Committee to commence the liberalisation process. Yet, although it was the easier of the two aims, the round proved to be far from straightforward.[1] The round was momentarily threatened with collapse by a dispute between the US and UK over the latter's imperial preference system. Crisis was averted only when the US agreed to accept reduced concessions on British access to associated markets, 'while the dominions agreed to make greater reductions in the preferences they enjoyed in Britain' (Kock, 1969: 70). The crisis, nevertheless, proved crucial to the negotiation's conclusion. The possibility that the negotiations might break down ushering in a return to interwar insularity served to focus British and American energy on the conclusion of the negotiations. The emergence of crisis as a frame for trade negotiations had begun.

With regard to the second aim, disagreements among the leading players proved to be a significant brake on the completion of the ITO negotiations. However, despite a lack of progress, the members of the Preparatory Committee shared a view that it was important to agree among themselves the fundamental principles of the Charter in order to give contractual force to the tariff concessions already negotiated (Fawcett, 1951: 270) as well as to lock in progress towards the completion of the larger ITO project. The result was the negotiation and subsequent adoption of the GATT.

The format of the GATT was largely derived from Chapter IV (Commercial Policy) of what was to become the Havana Charter. Most significant among its articles were commitments to: (i) engage in periodic negotiations directed at the further liberalisation of trade; (ii) conduct trade negotiations in accordance with the principle of reciprocity – that is, the receipt of roughly equivalent value for concessions offered; and (iii) apply the results of negotiations, with some notable exceptions, in a non-discriminatory manner – that is, in accordance with the principle of most favoured nation. The GATT was to be administered by an Interim Trade Committee (ITC) comprised of one representative from each contracting party; and it would be subsumed into the ITO once the latter was up and running, whereupon the interim committee would be dissolved.

The successful conclusion of the GATT aside, disagreements between the main players continued to plague designs for the ITO. During the Geneva meeting's July 1947 deliberations, all-too-familiar tensions began to emerge. Principal among these were agriculture and, yet again, Britain's imperial preferences. Tensions over the latter remained a perennial feature of the negotiations, particularly as – much to the annoyance of the American delegation – the head of the British delegation had announced at a press conference prior to the Geneva discussions that imperial preferences were not up for negotiation. More important, for our purposes at least, were the fractures that began to emerge between industrialised and agricultural producing states. In an infamous incident a three-way conflict broke out between Britain, the US and Australia (a recipient of British preferences) over tariffs on wool. Part-way into the negotiations the US Congress passed a bill increasing tariffs on wool imports and putting into place a price support system for the American wool industry. In response to threats from both the British and Australian delegations that they would, as Gardner puts it, 'bolt the conference if the wool bill became law' President Truman vetoed the bill (Gardner, 1956: 356). The discussions were again stalled, as shortly thereafter the Australian and US delegations reached deadlock over the extension of an American duty reduction on wool and a corresponding Australian unwillingness to lower import duties (ITO Report, 1947b: 530).

Disagreements over agriculture were also evident during discussions on quota restrictions. This time, however, the protagonists were aligned slightly differently with Australia, Canada, Belgium, the Netherlands and the US all resisting pressure to allow quota restrictions under the terms of the ITO Charter, while India and pre-Castro Cuba defended such measures as necessary to protect infant industries. The US, in particular, sought to force the issue by warning that Congress would not ratify an agreement that allowed such restrictions. At the same time, the US delegation was also embroiled in a disagreement over agricultural export subsidies, finding itself on the losing end of an eight to one vote on the inclusion of language in the Charter sanctioning such subsidies (ITO Report, 1947b: 530–531).

In another prescient aspect of the discussions, disagreements broke out over the provisions governing the relationship between trade policy and economic development. Most controversial was the question of quantitative measures and their deployment to protect infant industries. What resulted was an agreement to allow such measures to encourage the development of particular industries (including agricultural sectors), but only after prior consultation, and approval and control by the ITO.

After hard-fought negotiations, the Geneva meeting was able to overcome these and other disagreements and resulted, first, in the 22 August 1947 agreement on a draft ITO Charter, and second, the 30 October 1947 signing of the GATT by 23 contracting parties (effective 1 January 1948). Given the degree of disagreement that had pervaded moments of the Preparatory Committee's second session the production of a Charter was significant, and the extent of the duties negotiated seemed, at least at first glance, impressive: some 45,000 items were discussed (compared with, for instance, 8,700 items during the later Torquay round (1950–1951) – ITO Report, 1951c: 609). Not all of the duties discussed were, however, subject to reductions. Many were bound against future increases until 1951, while a smaller proportion were actually cut. Moreover, the degree of liberalisation during this first round was facilitated by two factors: (i) the existence of a sellers' market making it easier to gain consent for tariff reductions; and (ii) the sheer height of existing tariffs which ensured that substantial cuts could be offered without significantly reducing their protective effect (Gardner, 1956: 11–12).

The Havana Conference and the ITO

However, the successes of the Preparatory Committee's discussions were quickly overshadowed by the reappearance of many of the Geneva disagreements during the Havana conference. This was most pronounced on the issue of economic development, particularly with regard to commitments relating to tariff reduction negotiations, the establishment of new preferential systems, the ability to impose import quotas, and the employment of other trade restrictions without prior notice (Wilcox, 1949a: 48–49). Particularly contentious was the requirement that countries seeking to implement protective measures secure 'prior approval'. This saw the participants divide along varying axes.

The Swiss delegation protested over the proposed deployment of restrictive measures by Britain and France to assist in rectifying the latter's balance-of-payments difficulties; India pressed for provisions enabling developing countries to freely deploy tariffs, quantitative restrictions and subsidies to assist with industrialisation; the US delegation clashed with their British, Canadian and French counterparts over a proposed relaxation of the export subsidy controls agreed in Geneva; Norway and Sweden disagreed with a South American proposal (minus Brazil) to establish a preferential trade agreement; Britain and the US again found themselves at odds over balance-of-payments safeguards; controversy reigned over the ITO's proposed system of weighted voting, causing the US to accept the principle of one-member-one-vote albeit with the caveat that it and the seven other countries of the greatest economic significance be granted permanent seats on the Organisation's executive board; and US pleas for delegates to resist overloading the Charter with exception and escape clauses drew criticism, since four of the eight exceptions incorporated into the Charter were included expressly at American insistence – (i) the suspension or withdrawal of tariff or other concessions if increases in the importance of a particular product causes or threatens to cause serious injury to domestic producers; (ii) the imposition of quotas on those agricultural products subject to domestic control; (iii) the right to subsidise exports of agricultural produce; and (iv) in instances pertaining to national security (ITO Report, 1948a: 135; ITO Report, 1948b: 366–367; Wilcox, 1949b: 493). Indeed, the fractious nature of the negotiations led economic adviser to the US State Department Herbert Feis to comment that '[a]lmost every one ... [was] trying to re-write important sections of the [Charter], in the service of its special necessities, ideas, wishes or prejudices. The number of suggested amendments runs into hundreds' (Feis, 1948: 51; see also Knorr, 1948, 20). Clair Wilcox put the number of amendments at 800 and suggested that 'among them as many as two hundred ... would have destroyed the very foundations of the enterprise' (Wilcox, 1949a: 47–49).

Five aspects of the Havana discussions require our attention, as they established patterns of practice that by degree affect the way in which trade negotiations are conducted today. The Havana deliberations resulted in: first, and already mentioned, the practice of one-member-one-vote decision-making (a procedure that persists but which is nevertheless overridden by the pursuit of consensus, as we shall see later); second, the election of the head of the host nation's delegation as Chair of the Conference – head of the Cuban delegation, Sergio Clark, was elected as Chair of the Havana Conference (a protocol that is more a rule-of-thumb than a hard-and-fast requirement, as its application has been patchy); third, drawing upon a practice used during the preceding Geneva Preparation session, the practice of attempting to settle disagreements between participants through specially convened subcommittees (ITO Report, 1948a: 135–136); fourth, a culture, and expectation, of extending the proposed end date of the conference in order to reach agreement (the Havana Conference had been scheduled to run from 21 November 1947 to 15 January 1948, but was finally concluded over two months later on 24 March); and fifth, the *de facto* exclusion of developing countries from the core of decision-making and the emergence of a perception of a North/South fracture.

The latter point is perhaps among the most apposite for contemporary trade politics. While there were undoubtedly differences of interest between developed and developing countries during the negotiations, spiced with the political assertiveness inevitable in the wake of collapsing empires, poorly handled decolonisation processes and colonial legacies, the disagreements were often more complex than an industrial/developing country split (as the discussion above illustrates), though they were often portrayed in such broad-brush terms. Feis's account of the negotiations offers such an image. In Havana he observed that it was 'the smaller countries which have little industry and small variety of natural resources . . . [that seem] most assertive of all; they seem carried away by the hope of rapid development' (Feis, 1948: 51). He continues:

> At Havana many countries, carried away by a vision of nurturing new and diversified branches of manufactures, heedless of cost or the size of markets, seem determined to cling to the right freely to use quantitative restrictions for this purpose. The nations of Latin America, the Middle East and Asia seem to think that they really cannot be nations unless they make within their own border many of the things which the older industrial nations have in the past supplied.
>
> (Feis, 1948: 47)

Hemispheric tensions were similarly noted in a report carried by the then relatively new journal *International Organization*. The report commented that 'although every chapter became the subject for prolonged debate and disagreement, many of the disputed issues could be grouped together as a manifestation of the divided opinions which existed between industrially developed counties and the underdeveloped countries' (ITO Report, 1948b:

365). The perception of a North/South dynamic, fanned by inequalities in substance and practice, as we see below, became (and remains) a primary dynamic of post-war trade politics. In reality, the fault lines have never been quite as clear cut even if, for clarity of mind, it is useful to portray them as such.

Disagreements notwithstanding, the Havana Conference was eventually concluded and 53 states signed the Final Act of the United Nations Conference on Trade and Employment (which comprised the Charter for the ITO).[2] Their industry resulted in a weighty and often contradictory document that dealt in minute detail with tariffs levels, preferences, discriminatory taxation régimes and regulations, customs procedures, quota systems, state subsidies and trading, cartels, commodity agreements, economic development, investment, and the relationship between domestic stability and international commerce. Reflecting the sheer size of the task undertaken by its architects, the Charter comprised nine chapters: (i) purposes and objectives; (ii) employment and economic activity; (iii) economic development and reconstruction; (iv) commercial policy; (v) restrictive business practices; (vi) intergovernmental commodity agreements; (vii) the composition and structure of the Organisation; (viii) the settlement of differences; and (ix) general provisions.

The Charter envisaged an organisational structure composed of an Executive Board, a Conference and a series of Commissions to be established at the discretion of the Executive Board. The Executive Board was intended to be a council of leadership comprising 18 members elected by the Conference on the basis of a two-thirds majority – albeit that the negotiations had already demonstrated that the major economic powers formed what Hudec terms a 'ruling Directorate' (Hudec, 1990: 27). Membership of the Board was to include eight states of 'chief economic importance' and ten others reflecting varying levels of economic development as well as geographic distribution – though of course the requirement that the Board include eight states of chief economic importance ensured that both the US and Britain would continue to have a large degree of influence in the Organisation's workings. The Board was to be responsible for the execution of the policies of the ITO, to supervise the activities of the Conference, and to make recommendations to the Conference as well as to other intergovernmental organisations. The Conference – the Organisation's principal decision-making body – comprised all of the ITO's members. It was to have the authority to determine trade policy, or empower an individual member to forego a particular obligation (dependent on a two-thirds majority), as well as approve the budget and other related matters. And the functioning of the Organisation was to be administered by a permanent staff, headed by a Director-General appointed upon the recommendation of the Executive Board.

The conclusion of the Conference was, however, the high point for the ITO. Of the 53 signatory states, only two sought its ratification: Australia and Liberia (ITO Report, 1950a: 325).[3] This reflected the fact that, with the exception of Lebanon, all of the Charter's signatories made their ratification contingent on the US doing the same (Gardner, 1956: 369; Kock, 1969: 57). Once this had occurred a general process of ratification would take place among the other participants. However, despite the repeated efforts of President Truman, Congressional ratification of the Charter proved impossible (Kock, 1969: 58). In December 1950 Truman announced the decision to postpone indefinitely plans for US participation in the ITO, stating that the Havana Charter would not be resubmitted to Congress for approval (*New York Herald Tribune*, 7 December 1950). This was followed in February 1951 by similar announcements from the UK and the Netherlands (ITO Report, 1951b: 384–385). It was, in the end, an Organisation that did not serve the interests of its principal architects, nor did it suit the political climate into which it was born. The GATT, however, did.

Institutionalising the GATT

The GATT's elevation in place of the ITO had and continues to have a marked impact on the manner in which international trade was and is regulated. As John Jackson put it, the 'odd circumstances of [the] birth of the GATT as an institution . . . left it with certain defects that . . . plague[d] its efficient performance' (Jackson, 1987: 379) but, it should be added, which has also left an indelible mark on the development of multilateral trade regulation. Although the three core ITO principles remained at the centre of the GATT's regulatory framework – most favoured nation (MFN – and its corollary national treatment), reciprocity, and a commitment (albeit rather weak) to dispute settlement (see Wilkinson, 2000: 43–51) – as did the exception clauses enabling contracting parties to withhold preferential trading terms *vis-à-vis* other contracting parties in particular circumstances (of which the balance-of-payments provisions were the most noticeable and troublesome – see Patterson, 1966: 22–66) the General Agreement was without its ill-fated sibling's more elaborate and much more extensive provisions on the relationship between trade liberalisation and the maintenance of fair standards of labour, restrictive business practices, commodity agreements, state trading, and development and reconstruction (see Wilkinson, 2002a). Moreover, the GATT was intended merely to be a mechanism for the liberalisation of trade in goods; and even then only *some* goods. This meant a focus on trade in manufactured, semi-manufactured, industrial and capital goods. It was not the intention that the GATT be used as a tool for prising open agricultural markets or assisting with increases in the volume and value of textile production from the developing world – as Chapter 3 clearly demonstrates.

For many, the narrow focus of the GATT and the absence of an extensive set of highly prescriptive rules lent the General Agreement a streamlined, informal and malleable quality (see Gorter, 1954: 7–8). The GATT was perceived to be neither a tightly binding set of rules nor a constraint on the sovereign autonomy of the contracting parties (a feature that was particularly important to the US – see Pigman, 1998). While this fluid character came to serve the political and economic interests of the GATT's most economically significant contracting parties, it was far from beneficial to its smaller, more vulnerable, developing, primary and agricultural producing counterparts. For this latter group, the GATT's fluidity – and lack of procedural clarity and selective deployment that resulted therefrom – was the source of much consternation. Yet, though it came to serve a particular purpose, the GATT's distinctive character and its place as the principal mechanism for regulating trade was more by accident than design – at least initially.

Between 1948 and 1950 it was fully expected that the ITO project would be successful. As a result, little attention was paid to the way things were done under the GATT. As Hudec (1990: 54) remarks:

> [the] GATT's personality simply grew, more or less spontaneously out of the complex situation in which it was launched. Later when the likely course of events became clearer, governments began to look more closely at what they had wrought, and found, to their surprise, that GATT had acquired a distinctive character much to their liking.
>
> (Hudec, 1990: 54)

These were not, however, appropriate foundations upon which to construct an equitable and mutually beneficial trade régime, as the GATT's evolution from these early years has proven. But then the original intention of the post-war institutional architecture was to serve US economic interests while at the same time offering reasonable prospects for trade-led economic growth for the other contracting parties, most notably in Western Europe. This remained; and the GATT's institutional character evolved throughout the following years in a manner that consolidated rather than attenuated its birth defects. It also did so in a fashion that cloaked the emergence of an asymmetry of opportunity arising from the way in which the GATT was deployed (see Chapter 3); but not before the uncertainty over its status was resolved.

The story of the GATT's rise is one of a slow and incremental institutionalisation coupled with a growing reliance upon its function nurtured by the collapse of more ambitious projects. It is also one of relative obscurity, cloaked as it was by much grander projects. As it became increasingly apparent that the ITO was moribund, the contracting parties set about securing a future for and developing a machinery to administer the GATT. Initially, this was done by simply extending the GATT's period of operation. However, as the collapse of the ITO looked increasingly likely, particularly with the US's announcement that it would not seek Congressional ratification of the Havana Charter in December 1950, the need to preserve and take forward the liberalisation that had so far been achieved became more acute. The GATT was the inevitable beneficiary.

In fact, the GATT had already begun to develop a life of its own. The convening of trade negotiations under its auspices had given rise to the need for an administrative and institutional apparatus which, in turn, consolidated its emerging institutionalisation. But rather than formalise its rules and procedures with increasing degrees of bureaucratisation and stipulation, the creeping institutionalisation reinforced and entrenched its slippery character. From the outset, a strong resistance to mission-creep, over-bureaucratisation and formal institutionalisation existed to the extent that, as Hudec puts it, every 'hint of organizational existence was ruthlessly hunted down and exterminated' (Hudec, 1990: 51). This stretched as far as distancing the General Agreement from any association with the ITO for fear of it being a Trojan horse for the Organisation's resurrection. In so doing, it served to consolidate the General Agreement's character of informality and to have real consequences for its implementation. Three aspects of this institutionalisation of informality are worth pointing out. First, the GATT was to be accepted by contracting parties as a provisional agreement. Second, contracting parties were bound by its dictates only 'to the fullest extent not inconsistent with existing legislation' (*Protocol of Provisional Application of the General Agreement on Tariffs and Trade*, 1947: paragraph 1(b)). And third, the GATT's status as a mere trade agreement devoid of organisational trappings enabled it to avoid US Congressional ratification. The contracting parties nevertheless needed a means of administering the General Agreement. This was solved by employing the contracting parties (referred to as the 'Contracting Parties') as a committee-of-the-whole to indicate their role in this capacity (to which we return below).

Yet, it was not just in the crafting of the GATT that the strong resistance to mission-creep, over-bureaucratisation and organisation-ness was evident; this was also a feature of the discussions (and resulting decisions) that took place over the General Agreement's ongoing administration. The discussions that took place over the development of a machinery to deal with the administration of the GATT between sessions – annual meetings of representatives of the contracting parties – illustrate well this resistance, though it should be noted that concerns were expressed about almost every facet of the administration of the General Agreement and stretched to worries that aspects of the work of the GATT secretariat (such as it was) might duplicate work undertaken in areas of the UN system (GATT, 1952b: 209). The December 1950 report on the 'Continuing Administration of the General Agreement' recommended to the contracting parties the establishment of a standing committee. The committee's purpose was to undertake pressing intersessional action and serve to expedite the business of sessions by putting together agendas and corresponding documentation. Such a committee would comprise 15 members and would include, on a permanent basis, representations from those contracting parties of chief economic importance, as well as adequate geographic and level of development representation. The report was at pains to point out – though ultimately in vain – that the committee would not have executive authority; any work undertaken would be of a preparative character; its functions would not include 'the taking of decisions, which would be reserved exclusively to the contracting parties' (GATT, 1952b: 197); the establishment of such a committee would merely formalise existing aspects of GATT practice; and it would be consistent with established practice in UN institutions (such as in the Economic and Social Council).

The working party's second report noted, however, that 'there was not a sufficient measure of agreement on the establishment of a standing committee to justify proceeding with the suggestion at the present time' (GATT, 1952b: 206). The report nevertheless proposed that provision should be made to deal with pressing matters between sessions; and that the work of the regular sessions could be dealt with more expeditiously if there was greater preparation prior to their convening. By way of a solution, the report recommended that between the sixth and seventh sessions (September–October 1951 and October–November 1952, respectively) an 'experimental arrangement' should operate wherein the contracting parties agree to the establishment of an *ad hoc* Committee for Agenda and Inter-sessional Business. Again the report emphasised that the committee would act only at the behest of the contracting parties; its remit was limited to urgent matters and agenda setting only; it was to have no executive authority; and its existence did not set a precedent for a proliferation of inter-sessional bodies.

The idea of an *ad hoc* committee was revisited at the eighth session of the contracting parties (September–October 1953) and the proposal developed further. Crucially, aside from the inclusion of various semantic caveats designed to be seen not to circumscribe the role of the contracting parties, the final proposal (adopted at the ninth session – October 1954 to March 1955) resembled the original plan for a standing committee in nearly all but name. Even the stipulation that composition of the committee's membership comprise the contracting parties of chief economic importance remained (GATT, 1954: 8–13; GATT, 1955b: 9–15, 244–247). Importantly, the committee appeared to be a practical solution to an administrative problem of a provisional agreement rather than the trapping of a formal organisation; it nevertheless contributed to the institutionalisation of *ad hoc*-ery that came to characterise the GATT.

The appearance of *ad hoc*-ery belay a formality to the committee and, more importantly, the opportunity for the work of each session to be constructed in such a way that it served the interests of the GATT's principal contracting parties. The eleventh session of the contracting parties

(October–November 1956) clarified the *ad hoc* committee's (now the Intersessional Committee) procedures. The session confirmed that the committee's membership would be elected at each session in accordance with the membership criteria set out above. It required the committee to meet three weeks before (amended to 'when necessary' at the thirteenth session – October–November 1958 – GATT, 1959: 8) the opening of an ordinary session to consider matters likely to arise at that session, assess the adequacy of any required documentation, and recommend a provisional agenda in light of any documentation submitted; and that the committee examine all items on the provisional agenda with a 'view to clarifying and defining the issues involved' (GATT, 1957: 17–18). Instructively, in its deliberations the committee could recommend that an item be ejected from the agenda should the documentation available be deemed insufficient. Moreover, the committee was empowered to undertake any preparatory work that might expedite a session's business; it could establish and convene, in advance of a session, working parties to explore matters of a 'complex technical character' and a technical working party to 'begin work on questions relating to trade and customs regulations and schedules', and a working party on budgetary questions; the committee could make recommendations to the contracting parties on matters relating to balance-of-payments restrictions, the administration of quantitative restrictions, exceptions to the rule of non-discrimination, and exchange arrangements including consulting with the IMF; and it was authorised to examine applications made by contracting parties regarding government assistance for economic development that required prompt attention, modifications to tariff schedules, and any other urgent business (GATT, 1957: 18–19). The significance of these procedures is that, despite its supposed informality (and until its dissolution at the sixteenth session – May–June 1960), in the GATT's formative years the Intersessional Committee had very real opportunities to influence the business of sessions as well as to preside over the actions of contracting parties as they related to the General Agreement. And although the composition of the committee was to be decided at each session, the stipulation that its membership of 17 comprise, among others, contracting parties of chief economic importance ensured that the interests of the industrial states would hold sway.

Efforts to maintain the GATT's informality also stretched to the General Agreement's application. The review of the General Agreement at the ninth session saw the contracting parties debate the GATT's status. The working party report on this issue noted that in the seven years it had been in operation the GATT had so far operated on a provisional basis. As such, there seemed to be reasonable grounds for the contracting parties to seek the GATT's definitive application. This suggestion, however, raised a number of concerns. Its provisional status ensured, for many contracting parties, that the GATT did not require national ratification. This was particularly important in ensuring the continued participation of the US. Attitudes towards the GATT within the national legislature were at best contrary. Although the GATT served US post-war purposes, it and any attempt to formalise a trade organisation was treated with suspicion by Congress. The General Agreement's provisional status, presidential authority and a combination of already-existing US statutes had sheltered the GATT from the need for Congressional approval (Jackson, 2000: 210–219); and any attempt at further formalisation would remove this shelter and jeopardise US involvement. The Danish, Norwegian and Swedish delegations also raised concerns that the movement towards definitive acceptance of the GATT would have significant domestic consequences, as the ratification of an international treaty 'had the automatic effect of modifying domestic legislation' (GATT, 1955b: 48, 248).

The debate over the GATT's provisional status also brought confirmation that a large proportion of the General Agreement's obligations (principally Part II – dealing with the core principles and corresponding practices governing international trade) were effective only to 'the extent [that they were] not inconsistent with existing legislation' (GATT, 1955b: 247–250). The notion of 'the extent not inconsistent with existing legislation' was itself vague and was the source of some discussion during the ninth session. In discussing this point, John Jackson notes that 'existing' related to the date specified (30 October 1947) in paragraph 1 of Article XXIV (Acceptance, Entry into Force and Registration), and was clarified in a 1949 ruling by the Executive Secretary of the contracting parties; 'existing legislation' referred to all national legislation with some ambiguity relating to the legislation of administrative subdivisions in federal systems; and 'not inconsistent with existing legislation' related to all legislation that could not be modified by executive action (that is, legislation which did not give an executive the authority to undertake particular action in a given set of circumstances) (Jackson, 2000: 24–27). This provision (the so-called 'grandfather clause') enabled the contracting parties to implement the General Agreement without having to repeal any existing legislation that might be GATT-inconsistent and was used consistently by various states up to the late 1980s (most notable was US recourse to grandfather rights *vis-à-vis* its lack of an injury text on countervailing duties – see Jackson, 2000: 268–269).

The Organisation for Trade Co-operation

The resistance to formal institutionalisation was also much in evidence during the wider review of the General Agreement during the ninth session. Despite widespread agreement among the contracting parties over the desirability of establishing a permanent organisation to oversee the implementation of the GATT – the Organisation for Trade Co-operation (OTC) – during that session, the GATT's provisionality continued to hold sway. The purposes of the OTC were: (i) to administer the GATT; (ii) to facilitate intergovernmental consultation on questions related to trade; (iii) to sponsor trade negotiations; (iv) to provide research and to make recommendations on matters to do with international trade and commercial policy; (v) to collect, analyse and publish data on international trade and commercial policy; and (vi) to provide a more effective means of settling disputes (Articles 3 and 14 of the Agreement on the OTC – GATT, 1955c: 75–76, 80). The OTC was also to resurrect the governance structure of the ITO comprising an executive board and an assembly of representatives of the contracting parties, together with associate representatives for those non-members seeking to participate in its discussions. The assembly would consist of all of the members of the Organisation. The executive committee would comprise 17 members elected periodically by the assembly. Each member was eligible for election (and re-election). However, the election of the committee was to be 'guided' by three criteria: (i) that it include the five members of chief economic importance (determined in large measure by their share of world trade); (ii) that it be representative of the broad geographic complexion of the membership; and (iii) that it represent members of different 'degrees of economic development, different types of economies and different economic interests' (GATT, 1955c: 77). The Organisation would be headquartered in Geneva; and the day-to-day functioning of the OTC would be overseen by a small staff under a Director-General.

Similar to the passage of events during the ITO's negotiation, the US delegation signed the necessary protocols amending the GATT's provisional status and the agreement establishing a permanent organisation but warned that American entry into the proposed organisation required Congressional ratification (scheduled for 1956). As it had done in the wake of the Havana Conference, Australia announced that it accepted the revisions to the GATT and the establishment of a new organisation, but that it would only be bound by its decision once the US and UK had successfully ratified the agreement (ITO Report, 1955c: 599). However, unlike the ITO, the OTC was put forward for Congressional consideration. Yet, in spite of warnings by Dana Wilgress (Chair of the ninth session) that the failure to give the GATT more permanency risked encouraging the emergence of alternative and potentially divisive commercial machineries (principally bilateral and regional solutions) (GATT Report, 1957: 205), and repeated extensions to the time period in which contracting parties could ratify the agreement (GATT, 1957: 22–25; GATT, 1958b: 12–13; GATT, 1959: 22), Congress failed to agree to US membership of a formal trade organisation (Jackson, 2000: 211). It was not, however, Congressional hostility to the OTC that finally sank the organisation. It was rather the consequence of the way in which the initiative was presented. As Karin Kock (1969: 80) notes:

> The general protectionist trend in and outside Congress made the spokesmen of the Administration minimise the importance of the OTC, by characterising its functions as routine business, quite different from the functions which had once been assigned to the ITO. This defence

in negative terms weakened the position of the Administration and gave the impression that the creation of the OTC was not an urgent measure. [The result was that the] House found itself too preoccupied by other matters to take action on the proposal. A new attempt was made in 1957, but it came to nothing, and, in Geneva, the member countries had to find other means [of administering the GATT].

The GATT triumphant

The stillbirth of a second trade institution further contributed to the growing institutionalisation of the GATT as the principal machinery for the liberalisation of trade. Moreover, it proved not to be the trigger for a collapse of the trade régime or a fall-back into protectionist and discriminatory commercial policies – as Wilgress, among others, had warned (though proclamations to the contrary nevertheless assisted in keeping the GATT bicycle moving). Yet the collapse of the OTC was in many ways much less significant than that of the ITO. Whereas the ITO had been organically connected to the institutional architecture built upon the Allied victory, the OTC had no such connection. Moreover, the case for the creation of a formal trade organisation had been circumscribed by the creeping manner in which the GATT had become institutionalised, initially through the establishment, and subsequent modification, of rules of procedure governing contracting party sessions (see GATT, 1952a: 95–100; GATT, 1957: 11–16) as well as intersessional activities. In the end, the degree to which the GATT had become an institution (or, as Kenneth Dam boldly suggested, an organisation – see Dam, 1970) ensured that the demise of the OTC proved little more than a minor and soon-forgotten moment in the evolution of multilateral trade regulation.

The collapse of the OTC also served to consolidate an expectation that initiatives undertaken by the contracting parties do not necessarily bear fruit and that, occasionally, they break down (and periodically quite spectacularly). But, and importantly, it quickly became accepted that these periodic setbacks were merely part of the drama and rhythm of trade politics and not fundamental ruptures in the development of multilateral trade regulation. Moreover, in each case, these setbacks produced settlements and solutions that resulted in the *further* development of the GATT – as the remainder of this book shows.

The General Agreement's body of rules in the end proved sufficient to give multilateral trade regulation a more permanent operational framework. In order to overcome the lack of organisational formality, the contracting parties improvised by using Article XXV (Joint Action by the Contracting Parties) as the basis upon which to build a series of functions that approximated those of a formal organisation (Curzon and Curzon, 1974: 300). In the absence of a formal assembly, Article XXV enabled the contracting parties to act as if they were such a body. From this evolved a quasi-organisational structure, which added to its ranks a permanent secretariat, a council to oversee GATT activities between the meetings of the contracting parties (and which superseded the Inter-sessional Committee), and the development of a series of committees and working groups convened at the discretion of the council concerned with various aspects of international commerce (GATT, 1960: 23; GATT, 1961, 7–9). Tellingly, however, the contracting parties did not formalise or explicitly set out the processes and procedures by which decisions were made; instead, these were developed through practice at the behest of the dominant powers and in a fashion that kept the General Agreement congruous with its original objectives (and, it should be said, concentrated decision-making power in the hands of its principal trading states).

This improvisation did not, however, result in the significant bureaucratisation of the GATT. Rather, the contracting parties sought to check any movement in this direction (as well as any agency that might be emerging in areas wherein a bureaucracy had been formalised). Again, the workings of the Intersessional Committee are instructive here. In the wake of the collapse of the OTC project the working group on organisation and procedures sought to whittle away the power of the Intersessional Committee by removing two of its functions – the review of documentation prior to a session and the power to appoint working parties on questions of a technical nature – and to dilute a third (its role in facilitating the conduct of balance-of-payments consultations). These functions were, the working group argued, better carried out through other means. The group recommended that the review of documentation be devolved to an informal contact between the Executive Secretary and representatives of the contract parties. It also recommended that the establishment of working groups would remain the preserve of the contracting parties, and that to facilitate this, as well as deal with an increasing work-load, sessions should be biennial (which has become the practice for WTO ministerial meetings) rather than yearly as had been existing practice (GATT, 1959: 108–110). The result was that, while the improvisation of existing GATT articles enabled the General Agreement to survive the collapse of a second attempt at establishing a formal trade organisation, it also preserved its *ad hoc* character.

The argument so far

At first glance the story of the construction of a post-war trade machinery appears to be one of haphazard development and of the modification of political design and intention out of disappointment and collapse. A more considered view reveals, however, that the GATT emerged as precisely the kind of trade institution best suited to the satisfaction of industrial (largely US) interests and evolved thereafter in a tightly path-dependent fashion. While it remains the case that aspects of its legal framework were forged in response to demands from other states, the institution's principal features

were crafted to facilitate the realisation of US post-war economic opportunities. Its streamlined and *ad hoc* character proved useful in quelling
hesitancy in the US about any constraint on sovereign decision-making,
opening markets from which the US sought to gain and in protecting those
of a politically sensitive nature (in these early years, largely agriculture); its
informal character also enabled the US and its principal allies to continue
to exercise control over its development and deployment – as Chapter 3
clearly demonstrates. The GATT, then, was neither an insufficient nor a
haphazard tool; rather, it was a precise instrument facilitating the realisation
of US trade interests in a way that the ITO proved not to be. It was upon
this foundation that the post-war multilateral trade machinery evolved.
Robert Hudec (1990: 57) offers the following summary:

> As the leading countries saw it, the original GATT was not intended to
> be a comprehensive world organization. It was a temporary side affair
> meant to serve the particular interests of the major commercial powers
> who wanted a prompt reduction of tariffs among themselves. GATT was
> their property, and they did not have to accommodate the rest of the
> world. . . . When the ITO Charter began to fail, GATT stood ready as
> an alternative model for carrying out the same trade policies. It would
> provide a place where the leading countries could go off to do business
> by themselves, unencumbered by the complexities of the larger organ-
> ization. The smaller group of GATT countries might even come to say
> "good riddance" to the niceties of world politics, for it was comforting
> to have one place (one might almost say a club) where likeminded people
> could get together and do their work in peace.

Importantly, crisis played a key role in these developments. The fear of
a slide back to the 1930s focused minds in the early negotiations and enabled
agreement to be reached on a post-war trade institution despite disagreement
among the participating states. However, when that first institution failed,
the crisis it produced served yet again to drive multilateral trade regulation
forward – this time in the shape of the GATT; and when the OTC befell a
similar fate to that of the ITO, the GATT was again consolidated and multilateral trade regulation driven forward. This is, however, only part of the
story. To better understand how crisis has become an entrenched feature of
the development of multilateral trade regulation we next need to explore
how the General Agreement was deployed as an instrument of liberalisation
in its formative years.

3 Establishing asymmetry
Liberalising trade under the GATT

With the settling of the debate over the GATT's future came certainty about the final shape of the post-war economic architecture. The GATT would fill the role originally intended for the ITO and work alongside the IMF and World Bank (a place it would occupy until the creation of the WTO). What the debate did not settle, however, was the precise manner in which the GATT would operate as a machinery for liberalising trade. Like much else associated with the General Agreement's early development the manner of its operation emerged out of practices and procedures developed and put into place through time. These practices and procedures were seldom formally specified. Rather, they tended merely to be elaborations of the way in which the principal contracting parties had always done business. One consequence of this lack of formal elaboration was that during the GATT's formative years the manner in which impediments to trade were reduced and removed was subject to almost constant change and modification. Decision-making power nevertheless lay with the principal trading powers; the smaller, less significant contracting parties were largely signatories in name only. Indeed, it was not until the GATT's practices and procedures had become relatively settled that the contracting parties sought a measure of codification in international trade law. Even then, however, few of its practices and procedures were subject to explicit and precise specification (to which we return in Chapter 4).

This process of experimentation, and the codification of the practices and procedures resulting therefrom, has come to profoundly affect the way in which GATT contracting parties and later WTO members interact. Not only do we find in these early years the operationalisation of a process of liberalisation that formally excluded areas of commerce of key interest to developing countries (and acute political sensitivity to their industrial counterparts), we also see the emergence and entrenchment of particular practices and procedures that excluded all but the most significant trading nations. These two facets of the GATT's unique evolution have combined to produce the heightened political contestation that has come to be associated with contemporary trade politics and imbue ministerial meetings with a propensity to collapse; and together they form part of the wider foundation upon which the modern system of multilateral trade regulation is built. For these reasons, the book now turns to an examination of the way in which the GATT was deployed as a machinery for liberalising trade and the manner in which its practices and procedures developed through the institution's formative quarter-century.

The chapter begins with the first trade negotiations held under GATT auspices and ends with the financial and commercial crisis that developed in the wake of the Kennedy round (1964–1967). It focuses on the use of the GATT to facilitate post-war recovery and the growing problems of agricultural protectionism, non-tariff barriers, trade in primary commodities, and textiles and clothing. It also explores growing pressure to amend the General Agreement to take account of the specific needs of developing countries, the challenge to the GATT posed by the creation of an alternative trade institution in the form of the UN Conference on Trade and Development (UNCTAD), and the tensions that emerged during and after the conclusion of the Kennedy round. The chapter draws to a close with a summary of the argument developed thus far.

Deploying the GATT

The emergence and subsequent consolidation of a culture of informality (detailed in the previous chapter) was just one of the GATT's emerging defects. More troubling was the emerging asymmetry of opportunity arising from the way in which the General Agreement was deployed as an instrument of liberalisation. From the outset, the GATT evolved as an industrial nations club. Its original design as a mechanism for facilitating trade-led US growth and Allied reconstruction ensured that the GATT was better suited to enhancing the economic opportunities of its industrial contracting parties than the primary, agricultural and textile producing economies of their developing counterparts. As Tigani Ibrahim recalled, the GATT served 'to govern the conduct of the major trading countries in: (a) their trade with each other; (b) their competition with each other in third countries; and (c) the way in which third countries could behave towards their major trading powers in relation to that competition' (Ibrahim, 1978: 25). It was inevitable, then, that the liberalisation conducted under GATT auspices would target those areas best suited to these ends (see Wells, 1969: 64–65) as the following examination of its early history clearly shows.

The first three rounds of negotiations held under GATT auspices (see Table 3.1) were governed by the rules and procedures set out in the Havana Charter. In each case, the negotiations were organised around five basic rules with particular importance being given to the gradual elimination of preferences. The five rules were:

(i)   that negotiations be conducted on a selective product-by-product basis;
(ii)   that requests for tariff concessions could only be made by principal suppliers to the contracting parties from which greater market access was required;

Table 3.1 Trade negotiation rounds under the GATT and WTO

1947	Geneva, Switzerland
1949	Annecy, France
1950–1951	Torquay, United Kingdom
1956	Geneva
1960–1961	The Dillon round (Geneva)
1964–1967	The Kennedy round (Geneva)
1973–1979	The Tokyo round (Geneva)
1986–1994	The Uruguay round (Geneva)
2001 on	The Doha Development Agenda (Geneva)

(iii)   that each contracting party was free to grant concessions, refuse concessions, or bind a tariff at a specified (and potentially higher) level;

(iv)   that the binding of a tariff was to be treated as a concession of significant value and equal to a 'substantial reduction of high duties or the elimination of preferences';

(v)   that the negotiations should be conducted on a reciprocal basis

(Hoda, 2001: 27)

Karin Kock describes the general technique that was to be deployed during the negotiations – what she terms 'bilateral–multilateral' and what has become known as multilateralisation (see Hoekman and Kostecki, 1995: 70–71; Rhodes, 1995: 86; Wilkinson, 2000: 106–113) – as follows:

> Before the negotiations started, each member was to transmit to all other members a preliminary list of concessions which it proposed to request, and, on the opening of the negotiations, they were to present a corresponding list of the concessions they were prepared to grant. The negotiations would then take place between two countries as was the custom in traditional trade negotiations, or possibly between three or four countries. The result of the negotiations would be periodically reviewed by the Preparatory Committee as a whole, thereby enabling the negotiators to follow the general trend of the negotiations ... the results of the negotiations would take the form of a tariff schedule for each participating country; the schedule would contain the negotiated most-favoured-nation rates of duty for the members of the group as well as such preference rates or margins that had been subject to negotiations. ... The tariff schedules which resulted from the negotiations would [then] be incorporated into an agreement among the members of the Committee.

(Kock, 1969: 63–64)

Not one of the first three rounds, however, produced spectacular results (they were certainly not as forthcoming as much of the literature on the early years of the GATT suggests). The first round was significant because of its place in kick-starting post-war liberalisation and its role in beginning the reversal of the trends of the 1930s. Rounds two and three were, however, disappointing. During the second round, for instance, concessions were not exchanged between the UK, Australia and New Zealand, and the US. Indeed, negotiations between the US and UK actually broke down. Yet again, at issue was Britain's system of imperial preferences (upon which it refused to negotiate), but this was further complicated by the UK's dollar shortage. The British delegation argued that due to the shortage of dollars US concessions should be larger than those offered by the UK and its other European counterparts: a proposal flatly rejected by the American delegation. While they proved unable to reconcile their differences of opinion the lack of an exchange of concessions between the US, and Britain and the dominions had an effect on the overall value of the round. Each of the protagonists worried that any concessions they made would, under the MFN rule, be enjoyed by all parties (including those with which they were in dispute) but would not be appropriately reciprocated. This, in turn, led each to contribute less than their best endeavours. Reducing further the value of the round was the spread of this cautiousness to the other contracting parties, each of which withheld their best endeavours for fear that those received in return would not be of roughly equivalent value. The result was to rob the round of much of its potential (Kock, 1969: 71).

The Torquay round – the GATT's third – was also a qualified affair. One of the factors contributing to the relative underperformance of the Torquay negotiations was the inability of low tariff countries to prosper under the request-and-offer system.[1] The problem here was that in order for meaningful concessions to be extracted from their trading partners, concessions of roughly equivalent value had to be offered. However, with relatively low tariff levels to start with, these countries were unable to gain meaningfully because they had very little to offer in return. This advantaged those contracting parties with relatively high general tariff levels or those with considerable tariff peaks in key products (which included the US). As an Interim Commission for the International Trade Organisation (ICITO) report published in the wake of the Torquay round asked, '[h]aving bound many of their rates of duty in 1947 and 1949, what could these low-tariff countries offer . . . in order to obtain further concessions from the countries with higher levels of tariffs?' (ICITO report cited in Hoda, 2001: 28). The result was the adoption (on 13 October 1953) of a French plan to reduce tariffs by a fixed percentage (see GATT, 1954: 67–92).

The plan did not, however, solve the problem of how to conduct tariff negotiations. Although it was adopted by the contracting parties, the plan was not operationalised in the next round of negotiations – as we see below. Instead, the plan became one of a number of attempts to refashion the GATT's birth defects. In the end, the pursuit of tariff reductions by a fixed percentage did not, at that time, serve the interests of the dominant trading nations. The failure of the French plan did, however, mark the beginning of what was to become an established feature of trade politics. By not developing hard-and-fast rules governing the cutting of tariffs, the contracting parties ensured that this would be the subject of debate during future rounds – as has consistently proved to be the case. Moreover, as the number of contracting parties grew and the range of economic interests swelled this debate became ever more heated. The result was to lock into the GATT's evolutionary trajectory a measure of contestation over the method of cutting tariffs. This, in turn, would contribute to the general heightening of political contestation that would become a feature of trade politics in the GATT's later years and which would contribute to the collapse of ministerial meetings.

After the first three rounds, the GATT took a back seat to the reconstruction programme underway in Europe and in particular to the trade liberalisation programme of the Organisation for European Economic Cooperation (OEEC). The wider political context also took on a markedly different character. The euphoria of the end of the war quickly gave way to an escalation of Cold War tensions. The GATT played a key role in, and was affected by, this changed political climate. The place of borderline states in a Western alliance of market economies was secured by their accession to the General Agreement and other international organisations. Much to Czechoslovak consternation West Germany was given observer status to the GATT in February 1950, and formally acceded to the General Agreement 18 months later (*New York Times*, 24 February 1950; ITO Report, 1952a: 127–128); and Japan, after a protracted and politically fraught period, secured associate membership in the GATT in October 1953 and formally acceded in September 1955 (ITO Report, 1953: 586; Patterson, 1966: 285). The industrial character of the GATT was further consolidated by the withdrawal of China (effective 6 May 1950) following the establishment of the People's Republic in 1949 and the Kuomintang Government's relocation to Taiwan (ITO Report, 1951a: 213); Lebanon and Syria announced their intention to withdraw from the General Agreement upon the dissolution of their customs union (effective 1951); and Liberia, a founding contracting party and one of only two states to ratify the Havana Charter, also chose to withdraw (effective 13 June 1953).

Cold War tensions were also played out in the GATT. The US and Czechoslovakia clashed over the withholding of American exports of coal-mining drills and ball-bearings with the former justifying its actions on the grounds that these goods could be used in the extraction of uranium and the production of aircraft and other military applications respectively (*New York Times*, 9 April 1949). They clashed again over the inclusion of a text in the 1951 Trade Agreements Extension Act withholding MFN from 'countries dominated or controlled by communists' (Kock, 1969: 73) – indeed, the incident resulted in the suspension of obligations between the US and

Czechoslovakia, and the issuing of a declaration to that effect (GATT, 1952b: 36). In addition, the Korean war diverted attention away from the GATT during the opening years of the 1950s.

Agriculture

The Cold War politics played out in the GATT cloaked a series of developments that had a more fundamental hand in fashioning the contours of the institution's development and contracting party interaction therein. Almost from the outset the US and its industrial counterparts began to withdraw agriculture from the purview of the GATT – a move consistent with its post-war objectives. In 1950 the US implemented restrictions on Canadian potato imports (ITO Report, 1950b: 496); and in August 1952 the US administration announced an increase in its duty on imports of dried figs from Turkey to 4.5 cents per pound, thereby reneging on a commitment made during the Torquay round (GATT, 1953b: 28–29). More significant (and notorious) was the US's imposition of import restrictions on dairy products justified first under Section 104 of the United States Defense Production Act and, once the Act had been repealed, later under the 1933 Agricultural Adjustment Act (GATT, 1952b: 16–17; GATT, 1953b: 31–32; GATT, 1954: 28). Indeed, US discrimination against a range of dairy products lasted the life of the GATT and was carried over into the WTO (see Hudec, 1990: 181–200).

US actions did not, of course, go unnoticed. During the sixth session of the contracting parties (September–October 1951) the Netherlands and Denmark, supported by Italy, New Zealand, Norway, Australia, France, Canada and Finland, complained that the US restrictions on the import of dairy products were a 'serious violation of the agreement' (ITO Report, 1952a: 128). During the seventh session (October–November 1952) 12 delegations complained of the effects of US import restrictions on dairy products (ITO Report, 1952b: 648), resulting in the Netherlands being granted permission to restrict imports of US wheat flour to 60,000 metric tons in retaliation (GATT, 1953b: 32–33, 62–63) – the only instance of retaliation authorised under Article XXIII of GATT dispute procedures (indeed, consistent with its *ad hoc* and provisional character, dispute settlement under the GATT relied on 'organized normative pressure' – Hudec, 1990: 198, 201–202). Turkey sought retaliatory action for US tariff increases on dried figs and raisin imports (GATT, 1953b: 28–30), while Greece and Italy also voiced their displeasure. And complaints were heard regarding US import restrictions on dairy products and subsidies on exports of raisins, oranges and almonds during the eighth session (September–October 1953).

During the ninth session (October 1954 to March 1955) a Danish resolution supported by Australia, Canada, the Netherlands, Italy and Sweden censured the US for restricting trade in dairy products and permitted other contracting parties to take retaliatory measures until such restrictions were terminated was adopted. USTR Waugh responded by declaring that the US could not permit unrestricted entry of agricultural products into its domestic markets and that there existed little probability that restrictions would be removed in the near future (ITO Report, 1955a: 174–177). The reluctance of the US to modify its agricultural import quotas, and the reticence of those countries taking action under the Danish resolution, nevertheless contributed to the delay in the session's conclusion. The issue of import quotas was not the only source of tension in agriculture. The ninth session also saw the US submit a proposal for a waiver of its contractual obligations for dairy products. After much debate the waiver was eventually granted (GATT, 1954: 81; GATT, 1955b: 32–41). Importantly, unlike other waivers granted by the contracting parties, the US secured the permanent exclusion of its dairy sector from GATT rules – a move that was, unsurprisingly, the subject of continual debate thereafter.

The US was not, however, the only country seeking to protect its agricultural markets. Quantitative restrictions on agricultural imports were also imposed and maintained by most of the European powers (including the majority of those that complained of US actions), and many subsidised both the production and export of agricultural produce. Norway and the Federal Republic of Germany (FRG) quarrelled over changes to the latter's tariff schedules for sardines (GATT, 1953b: 30–31, 53–59). Belgium, the Netherlands and Luxembourg (Benelux) complained about the FRG's failure to bring German duties on cereal starch and potato flour down to Benelux levels (GATT, 1955b: 7). Belgium, and later Luxembourg, sought and were granted waivers to restrict imports of a range of dairy, meat, fruit and vegetable produce (GATT, 1956: 22–29), and Australia complained that French export subsidies on wheat and wheat flour were displacing its trade in these products in South and Southeast Asia (GATT, 1959: 46).

The disruption to agricultural trade caused by the growing incidence of tariffs and other barriers in industrial markets was not the only source of tension in this sector. Similarly problematic was the disposal of large quantities of over-production in foreign markets thereby disrupting normal patterns of trade and national production (so-called 'dumping'). The extent of the problem proved to be quite considerable and accounted for a significant share of exports for some contracting parties. As the 1955 GATT report noted, the dumping of surplus agricultural produce accounted for a 'large part of the increase in United States exports in 1955' (ITO Report, 1956a: 516). In an attempt to address the problem, on 4 March 1955 a resolution requested that contracting parties enter into a process of consultation designed to minimise the disruption to world markets of dumping and 'contribute to the orderly liquidation of such surpluses' (GATT, 1955b: 50). In characteristic GATT fashion, the resolution did not, however, seek to mitigate dumping through substantive regulation. This was in large part the result of the importance of dumping to industrial states to rid themselves of surplus produce. As a result, not only did deployment of the GATT in its early years remove agriculture from the General Agreement's purview; the lack of substantive action on dumping codified it as a normal commercial practice. Not only has this contributed to the continuation of massive subsidy régimes and farm programmes in the EU and US, it has ensured that consternation over the persistence of these programmes, the continuation of dumping as a commercial practice, and the removal of agriculture from the GATT's remit became entrenched features of the General Agreement's evolutionary trajectory and remain key points of contention in the DDA. It was inevitable, then, that as the number of contracting parties with an interest in agriculture expanded, so would tensions over these developments. They would also, in turn, come to be important elements in the heightening of political contestation underpinning the collapse of ministerial meetings.

Manufactures, primary commodities and development

The emergence of agriculture protection and dumping were not, however, the only noticeable anomalies that developed from the way in which trade was regulated under the GATT. Similarly troublesome was the contribution of the GATT's deployment to emerging trade patterns in manufactures and primary commodities. After an awkward start wherein post-war recovery in Europe had been slower than expected and had seen manufactured output fall below 1932 levels (leading to a concerted effort to highlight the need for liberalisation in these sectors to facilitate a revitalisation in production – GATT, 1953a; ITO Report, 1953: 587–588), the economic fortunes of the GATT's industrial contracting parties improved markedly. Fuelling this recovery was a GATT-facilitated increase in trade among their number. The picture for their developing counterparts was, however, much less rosy. The 1954 GATT report detailed what were to become worrisome trends – that a relative growth of trade within and among industrial areas had occurred; but that there had also been a relative decline in trade between the non-industrial and industrial states (GATT, 1955a; ITO Report, 1955c: 597). The report also noted that world production of raw materials between 1948 and 1950 was only 25 per cent higher than it had been before the war whereas the volume of manufactures had increased by 57 per cent. Moreover, by 1952 the differences between the increases in manufactures and in raw materials had widened still further: from 1948 to 1950 and to 1952, world manufacturing production had increased by 20 per cent, whereas raw materials production had risen by only 15 per cent (ITO Report, 1955c: 597–598).

The report argued that three factors combined to contribute to the relative decline in the trade between industrial and non-industrial states. First, the period had seen an increase in the production of natural raw materials and fuels in the industrial states themselves. Second, rapid increases in the production of substitute raw materials – initiated in response to wartime scarcities – coupled with rises in the relative price of natural raw materials had significantly reduced demand for the latter. The report estimated that the import requirements of the industrial states for natural raw materials would have been approximately 40 per cent larger than the actual imports in 1955 if those substitutes had not existed. And third, the relative decline of textile production in the industrial states (textile industries in the industrial states had risen, compared to the 1938 volume, by only about half as much as had all other manufacturing industries) had resulted in a decline in demand for imports of raw materials (ITO Report, 1955c: 515–516). 'It is obvious,' the report stated, 'that the problem arising from these divergent trends in the world's industrial activity and its raw materials production is one which is likely to loom large in the future course of economic development everywhere' (GATT, 1955a: 16). These trends continued nevertheless. A year later, the GATT report noted that trade among the industrial countries had accounted for the lion's share of the rise in the value of world exports, and that the relative importance of the non-industrial states had continued to decline. It also noted that the increase in the export trade of the industrial countries had been, in large measure, enjoyed by North America; and that this had been fuelled by a growing dependence among Western European states on supplies of raw material and fuels from the US and Canada (ITO Report, 1956a: 515).

Efforts to address these trends, and with it the declining performance of developing countries, were made, though they were rather lacklustre. In recognition of the importance of stimulating capital flows to developing countries (but also in an effort to slow the trend towards industrial protectionism therein – see ITO Report, 1955c: 598) on 4 March 1955 the contracting parties adopted a resolution on 'International Investment and Economic Development'. Yet, despite its laudable call for capital rich countries to take up investment opportunities in their developing counterparts and for underdeveloped countries to create a favourable investment climate (by providing 'appropriate methods of security for existing and future investment, the avoidance of double taxation, and facilities for the transfer of earnings upon foreign investments'), the resolution merely urged contracting parties to enter into consultations or participate in negotiations to these ends (GATT, 1955b: 49–50). There was no compunction.

Similarly, 20 months later the contracting parties adopted a resolution on the 'particular difficulties connected with trade in primary commodities'. As with the case of investment, the commodities resolution recognised that those contracting parties heavily reliant on exports of primary commodities as sources of income to fund imports and/or economic development were significantly disadvantaged by current trends in world trade. Yet the resolution offered little of substance: a commitment to review trends and developments in international commodity trade; a request to take account of the impact of problems in commodity trade on national balance-of-payments and the maintenance of any import restrictions arising therefrom; a call for consultations to be entered into; and a request for an intergovernmental meeting on this issue to include not only contracting parties to the GATT but also significant others not signatories thereto (GATT, 1957: 26–27). In what was by now becoming a familiar and established pattern, the trade in primary commodities resolution resulted in little action. As the November 1958 report on commodity trade noted, while 'the basic resolution could be regarded as satisfactory so far as its provisions are concerned . . . its implementation [was far from] effective' (GATT, 1959: 42). Of particular disappointment were the vagaries of the annual review of trends and developments in commodity trade and the small number of consultations that had been entered into between contracting parties (GATT, 1959: 43–46).

It was not, however, just in trade performance that developing countries were beginning to feel isolated. The negotiating machinery was also proving problematic. By 1956 the contracting parties had agreed to return to the negotiating table for what was to become the fourth round. They were not, however, able to reach a consensus on how to operationalise the previously adopted French plan (to assist low tariff countries) reducing tariffs by a fixed percentage and consequently reverted to the selective product-by-product basis and the five basic rules that had governed the first three rounds (GATT, 1956: 79–82). This had an important impact on the extent of the talks. Although the launch of the negotiations had been widely supported, in the end only 25 of the then 39 contracting parties agreed to participate (see Table 3.2). Notable, however, was the almost total absence of developing countries from this group. Moreover, only 22 of the participating countries offered concessions (Hoda, 2001: 25–26). Indeed, though the 1956 negotiations are known as a 'round' they in fact arose from a provision allowing for two or more contracting parties to engage in negotiations at any time under GATT rules. (The inclusion of over half of the contracting parties that were then signatories to the General Agreement accounts for the negotiations being termed a 'round'.)

Compounding developing country problems further, the early GATT negotiations were dominated by the three most economically and politically significant contracting parties – the US, UK and France – with Canada, Belgium and Luxembourg playing second order but nevertheless visible roles. The domination of proceedings by the US, UK and France was both obvious and subtle. It was obvious in that they set agendas and pursued the liberalisation of those areas important to their national interests, but it was also subtle in that they dominated all aspects of the GATT machinery. As Hudec (1990: 54–55) notes:

> Their [the US, UK and France] real influence came to bear in the smaller working parties and drafting groups. The Plenary Committee met in the afternoons. Ad hoc drafting groups then met the following morning to produce drafts or to try to work out compromises based on the plenary

Table 3.2 Contracting parties exchanging concessions during GATT rounds

Round	No. of contr. parties	No. and identity of contracting parties actually granting concessions*
Geneva (1947)	23	23 – Australia, Belgium, Brazil, Burma, Canada, Ceylon, Chile, China,** Cuba, Czechoslovakia, France, India, Lebanon,** Luxembourg, Netherlands, New Zealand, Norway, Pakistan, Southern Rhodesia, Syria,** South Africa, UK, US.
Annecy (1949)	33	33 – Australia, Belgium, Brazil, Burma, Canada, Ceylon, Chile, China, Cuba, Czechoslovakia, France, India, Lebanon, Luxembourg, Netherlands, New Zealand, Norway, Pakistan, Southern Rhodesia, Syria, South Africa, UK, US (contracting parties) and Denmark, Dominican Republic, Finland, Greece, Haiti, Italy, Liberia, Nicaragua, Sweden, Uruguay (acceding states).
Torquay (1950–1)	34	29 – Australia, Belgium, Brazil, Burma, Canada, Ceylon, Chile, China, Cuba, Czechoslovakia, France, India, Lebanon, Luxembourg, Netherlands, New Zealand, Norway, Pakistan, Southern Rhodesia, Syria, South Africa, UK, US (contracting parties) and Austria, West Germany, Korea, Peru, Philippines, Uruguay (acceding states).
Geneva (1956)	39	22 – Australia, Austria, Belgium, Canada, Chile, Cuba, Denmark, Dominican Republic, Finland, France, West Germany, Haiti, Italy, Japan, Luxembourg, Netherlands, Norway, Peru, Sweden, Turkey, UK, US.
Dillon (1960–1)	42	22 – Australia, Austria, Belgium, Canada, Chile, Cuba, Denmark, Dominican Republic, Finland, France, West Germany, Haiti, Italy, Japan, Luxembourg, Netherlands, Norway, Peru, Sweden, Turkey, UK, US.
Kennedy (1964–7)	76	37 – Argentina, Australia, Austria, Brazil, Canada, Chile, Czechoslovakia, Denmark, Dominican Republic, EEC (Belgium, France, Italy, Luxembourg, Netherlands, West Germany) Finland, Iceland, India, Ireland, Israel, Jamaica, Japan, Korea, Malawi, New Zealand, Norway, Peru, Portugal, South Africa, Spain, Sweden, Switzerland, Trinidad and Tobago, Turkey, UK, US, Yugoslavia.
Tokyo (1973–9)	85	44 – Argentina, Australia, Austria, Brazil, Canada, Chile, Côte d'Ivoire, Czechoslovakia, Dominican Republic, EC (Belgium, Denmark, France, Ireland, Italy, Luxembourg, Netherlands, UK, West Germany), Egypt, Finland, Haiti, Hungary, Iceland, India, Indonesia, Israel, Jamaica, Japan, Korea, Malaysia, New Zealand, Norway, Pakistan, Peru, Romania, Singapore, South Africa, Spain, Sweden, Switzerland, Uruguay, US, Yugoslavia, Zaire.
Uruguay (1986–1994)		The Uruguay round required every member to have a schedule of concessions – hence all participated. That said, concessions granted ranged from full schedules to ceiling bindings from the least developed countries.

Sources: Hoda (2001: 25, 67–68, 228, 232, 238); Healy *et al.* (1998: ch. 1).

* GATT negotiations also involved countries that were not signatories to the General Agreement but which had requested accession or were in the process of acceding.
** China (Formosa – 1950), Lebanon (1951) and Syria (1951) withdrew from the GATT under the provisions of the provisional protocol.

discussion. These smaller groups generally had five members, and each of the Big Three had a permanent seat. Moreover, they virtually monopolized all the technical work, a feat made possible by having much the largest and best equipped delegations there [see for example Table 3.3]. Other delegations invariably found themselves in the position of arguing with an existing text reflecting the Triumvirate's view.

By November 1957 the contracting parties had decided that the situation facing developing countries (in terms of the unfavourable trends in commodity trade, the widespread growth in agricultural protectionism, and the lack of inward investment but not their relative marginalisation from negotiations and the GATT's administrative apparatus) was sufficiently worrying to commission an 'expert examination of past and current international trade trends and their implications with special reference to . . . the general state and prospects of international trade . . . [and] the failure of the trade of less developed counties to develop as rapidly as that of industrialized countries' (GATT, 1958b: 18). The result was the production of the 1958 report on *Trends in International Trade* (GATT, 1958a) – known as the 'Haberler Report' (after the Chair of the panel of experts commissioned to produce the report, Gottfried Haberler).

Again, however, and in now established fashion, little was forthcoming (for a contrary view see Curzon, 1969). The Haberler Report concluded that,

Table 3.3 Size of contracting party delegations during the first round of GATT negotiations (1947)

Contracting party	Size of delegation
USA	128
UK	107
Australia	61
Netherlands	46
France	43
Czechoslovakia	36
India	36
Belgium-Luxembourg	34
Canada	31
Brazil	31
South Africa	23
New Zealand	20
Chile	10
Cuba	17
Norway	11
Lebanon	3
Syria	3

Source: Hudec (1990: 54–55)

although no evidence of a general tendency towards specific discrimination in trading relations with the developing world was found, factors did exist that were detrimental to the terms of trade of less developed countries (GATT, 1958a). In particular, it suggested that the high incidence of trade barriers faced by these countries, coupled with unfavourable price trends, had significantly affected the terms of trade performance of developing countries. The response of the contracting parties was to embark upon a programme of action designed to address these trends through the 'further reduction of barriers to the expansion of international trade'. Yet while the contracting parties committed themselves to exploring the 'possibilities of further negotiations for the reduction of tariffs', identifying the 'problems arising from the widespread use of non-tariff measures for the protection of agriculture, or in support of the maintenance of incomes of agricultural producers', and rendering visible other 'obstacles to international trade, with particular reference to the importance of maintaining and expanding the export earnings of the less developed countries' (GATT, 1959: 28), they did not seek to make alterations to GATT rules or their deployment as a vehicle for liberalisation. Moreover, some of the barriers identified as problematic by the committee established to look into the problems facing developing countries post-Haberler (such as tariffs on tropical products, tariff escalation, quantitative restrictions and internal taxes) were still in force 30 years later at the start of the Uruguay round (Srinivasan, 1998: 23). Ultimately, it was political will, not an absence of knowledge, that was proving to be the biggest obstacle to readjusting the way in which the GATT was deployed. As the Haberler Report put it:

> The only chance of a successful outcome is a negotiated settlement involving a gradual shift away from undesirable policies on both sides. This is without question to the long-term advantages of both sides [developed and developing countries]; but it requires on both sides a broad-minded approach as to the elements in their total economic and financial policies which they would be willing to make the subject of international discussion and negotiation.
>
> (GATT, 1958a: 127)

The problems facing developing countries resurfaced a year later. The report of the working party on commodity trade noted that as a group the export earnings of 43 primary producing countries had declined by 9.5 per cent in the period 1957 to 1958; and that, as a result of reduced export revenue, demand for imports from this group had been curtailed, levels of indebtedness had increased as countries had attempted to reduce their current account gap through foreign loans and credits, and holdings of gold and foreign exchange reserves had fallen 'to the lowest level of the decade' (indeed, the report estimated that reductions in these reserves as a whole was about

7 per cent) (GATT, 1960: 78–79). Again, however, the report recommended against any alteration of the GATT. Instead, it concluded that the problems facing these countries were better and more appropriately addressed by other intergovernmental organisations and international machineries (specifically the UN, the UN Commission on International Commodity Trade (UNCICT), UN regional economic commissions, the Interim Co-ordinating Committee for International Commodity Arrangements (ICCICA), the Food and Agri-culture Organisation (FAO), international commodity agreements, study groups and committees, the UN Administrative Committee on Co-ordination subcommittee on Commodity Problems and the IMF), and that the contribu-tion of the contracting parties was to pursue the further reduction of barriers to trade and to draw attention to GATT provisions for bilateral and multi-lateral consultations 'of which governments may avail themselves when difficulties arise in international commodity trade' (GATT, 1960: 84–5). A strategy of avoidance and an unfounded faith in the ability of negotiations to address the problems of developing and primary producing contracting parties was emerging. Importantly, the resistance to undertake even a modicum of reform locked the GATT tightly into a path-dependent trajec-tory arising directly from its original design. Those states not privy to the economic opportunities provided therein continued their association with the General Agreement only by dint of the 'prospects' offered by these reports and resolutions.

The Dillon round

By the time the Dillon round (1960–1961) – the fifth under General Agree-ment auspices – was launched, development, commodity trade, non-tariff barriers and agriculture had become staples of an increasingly heated GATT politics. Each had been the subject of lengthy discussion and the focus of numerous reports, though little had been forthcoming. The growing con-sternation that resulted therefrom was not, however, confined to those few developing countries that actively participated in the round. Hostility at the way in which the GATT was deployed was increasingly coming from middle-income agricultural exporting nations as well. In the run-up to the round, Australia lobbied hard, with reasonable success, to focus contracting party attentions on the need to address non-tariff barriers in the negotiations on agriculture and to include an acknowledgement of such in the negotiation's rules and procedures. The Australian delegation also proposed that the nego-tiating rules should explicitly recognise that negotiations could take place on subsidy levels including any form of price or support mechanism which 'operated directly or indirectly to reduce imports', though it only succeeded in securing a recognition that 'there was nothing that prevented negotiations on subsidies simultaneously with negotiations on tariffs' but that this would not be made explicit in the negotiation's rules themselves (GATT, 1960:

107). Again, the contracting parties – and in particular their dominant number – proved reluctant to legislate, particularly in those areas that threatened to curtail practices that were central aspects of their commercial behaviour (as price and support mechanisms were to the US and Europe).

In another effort to extend the remit of the negotiations in an attempt to address some of the emerging imbalances in the GATT's deployment (as well as to enact one of the Haberler Report's recommendations) India proposed (with strong support from Brazil) to put internal taxation on the negotiating agenda on the strength that internal duties were a significant factor hampering demand for imports of tea, coffee and tobacco. The Indian proposal, however, met with strong resistance from the US delegation and from representatives from the then newly formed European Economic Community (EEC) (GATT, 1960: 108–109). More generally, agricultural exporting countries bemoaned the growing nullification and impairment of tariff concessions negotiated during early rounds by the increasing number of non-tariff measures being implemented in importing (largely industrial) countries. Their concerns were, however, met with arguments that the removal of such protection would 'take many years and [would be] only possible if this took place parallel with improvements in the structure of agricultural markets in industrial countries' (GATT, 1960: 126). Again, the industrial countries refused to take any action.

At the behest of the US delegation (which had originally proposed the negotiations and was anxious to have them concluded before the expiration of US presidential authority at the end of June 1962) the contracting parties commenced negotiations on 1 September 1960. Along with the aim of seeking reductions in tariff levels and other charges on imports, the round's aims and objectives also recognised the desirability of negotiating reductions in non-tariff barriers (though this was stipulated in the by-now-typical GATT fashion of an assertion that contracting parties 'may' wish to engage in such an activity rather than by stating a requirement). Again, however, the negotiations were conducted around broad principles rather than an extensive set of rules. Of particular note was the decision to persist with the principal-supplier rule and the request-and-offer system as a (rather arcane bilateral) means of pursuing trade barrier reductions on a multilateral basis (GATT, 1960: 116; Wilkinson, 2000: 100–114), albeit that – subject to certain exceptions – the EEC and UK both tabled a linear offer to reduce tariffs by 20 per cent (Hoda, 2001: 30). Despite the stipulation that the negotiations were to be conducted on a mutually advantageous and reciprocal basis, the deployment of the principal-supplier rule muddied the waters, as it had in each of the previous rounds. Rather than resulting in reductions in barriers to trade that were to the benefit of all contracting parties, the principal-supplier rule ensured that the smallest and most vulnerable of the contracting parties were locked out of setting the tone and agenda of the negotiations as it structured the negotiations around the commercial interests of the dominant powers (Winters, 1990: 1291). As one observer noted:

[T]he real trouble with GATT [is] not the institution of bargaining for tariff reductions, but the techniques of bargaining and especially the procedure of bargaining between dominant suppliers on a basis of bilateral balancing of balance-of-payments effects. This technique [belongs] to the 1930s; if bargaining could be computerized, it could be made truly multilateral, on a basis of over-all balancing of balance-of-payments effects . . . this would enable the small countries to aggregate individually small concessions in the bargaining process.

(Johnson, 1968: 368)

The problems facing developing countries were compounded by a growing nervousness among their number regarding the commitment to reciprocate for concessions granted to them. In 1965, reviewing the requirement to reciprocate, Indian Ambassador Lall commented:

The developing countries of course [have] had no bargaining power, politically or economically. The rule of reciprocity has required them to give a matching concession, but clearly they were not in a position to give any. While over the last fifteen years, tariffs on industrial products of interest to industrial nations have been gradually brought down, those on products of interest to developing countries have remained at a high level.

(1965: 174–179)

It was not only the requirement to grant concessions in return for those received that was troubling, however. Many developing countries argued that should products of interest to them become the subject of negotiation (which, given that they were seldom principal suppliers, was in itself problematic), they were unlikely to be in a position to reciprocate. This was because reducing barriers to entry would (i) remove protection for infant industries put in place as a result of a commitment among developing countries to import substitution industrialisation (ISI) as a development strategy, and (ii) reduce valuable sources of government revenue. Otherwise, the industries in which developing countries were interested were in decline in the industrial states and as such their tariffs were not entered into the negotiations (Johnson, 1968: 367). Ironically, however, once pressure eventually resulted in the removal of the commitment for developing countries to reciprocate (with the introduction in 1965 of Part IV of the GATT – see below) this actually had the effect of further isolating developing countries from discussions over the shape and direction of negotiations (Srinivasan, 1998: 24).

Predictably, the focus on negotiating among principal suppliers combined with the *de facto* exclusion of agriculture from the GATT and the growing use of non-tariff barriers to protect agricultural markets in the industrial states saw disappointing results for developing and agricultural exporting countries during the Dillon round. The third report of Committee

II (Agricultural Protection – adopted 15 November 1961) found that in dairy products, meat, cereals, sugar, vegetable oils and fish 'there has been extensive resort to non-tariff devices involving protection to an extent and having consequences which were . . . not fully recognized earlier'. Fifteen days later at the 30 November 1961 meeting of ministers, it was noted that 'a number of contracting parties found that [the] recent negotiations had been disappointing, as they had produced no substantial results in respect of agricultural products because no significant concessions had been offered on these products in [the] negotiations' (GATT, 1962: 26). As a result of pressure from those contracting parties that were not primarily exporters of industrial goods, ministers agreed that conducting negotiations on a commodity-by-commodity and country-by-country basis was no longer adequate and required instead the adoption of new techniques, in particular some form of linear tariff reduction.

In recognition of the continuing plight of developing contracting parties, the meeting of ministers also adopted a declaration on the Promotion of the Trade of Less-Developed Countries. Yet, like previous declarations, it failed to commit contracting parties to substantive action. Instead it requested, among other things, that: (i) industrial contracting parties pay special attention to the reduction of barriers to trade for exports from less-developed countries; (ii) governments from less-developed countries expand their export portfolios; (iii) industrial states seek the speedy removal of quantitative restrictions (QRs); (iv) developed contracting parties seek to limit the use of export subsidies in products that compete directly with those from less-developed states; (v) industrial contracting parties remain mindful of the negative consequences of dumping surplus produce that competes directly with products from less-developed countries; (vi) a 'sympathetic attitude' on the question of reciprocity be kept in mind during negotiations for reductions in less-developed country trade barriers; (vii) less-developed countries seek to improve their marketing and production techniques; and (viii) less-developed countries endeavour to expand trade among themselves (GATT, 1962: 28–32).

Twelve months later a Nigerian-led Group of 21 (G21) developing countries proposed a programme of action urging the contracting parties to focus their attentions on targeting those barriers to trade identified as directly affecting the less-developed states (GATT, 1963: 204–206).[2] This programme was, in turn, adopted as a Resolution (Measures for the Expansion of Trade of Developing Countries as a Means of Furthering their Economic Development) at the May 1963 GATT ministerial meeting. The Resolution called for: (i) a standstill on the erection of new tariff and non-tariff barriers by industrial states; (ii) the elimination within one year of all QRs; (iii) duty-free entry into industrial markets for tropical products; (iv) the removal of tariffs on primary products; (v) the reduction and elimination of tariff barriers affecting exports of semi-processed and processed goods from developing countries; and (vi) the progressive reduction of internal taxes in developed states on products produced wholly or mainly in developing countries (GATT, 1964: 36–47).

Perhaps predictably, the Resolution's adoption came with the usual caveats from just those countries at which it was aimed: the industrial contracting parties. The standstill on new tariff and non-tariff barriers was generally accepted with the notable exception of the EEC (which was in the process of sorting out a common external tariff); Austria and Japan 'regretted' that while they were committed to the removal of QRs, they were unlikely to be able to meet the 31 December 1965 deadline; the US wished it to be noted that its national legislation required tariff reductions to be staged over a five-year period; and a number of primary producing countries, though welcoming the Resolution, suggested that they 'would have difficulty in accepting inflexible tariff commitments on certain products' (GATT, 1964: 38–39). Needless to say, these responses drew sharp criticism from the sponsoring developing countries.

The most concrete outcome of the 1963 Resolution was the decision to establish a committee to investigate the revision of the GATT with a view to 'safeguarding the interests of [developing countries] in their international trade and development programmes' (GATT, 1964: 45). Although there was far from widespread support for an amendment of the GATT (the suggestion was initially supported by only the 21 sponsoring countries and the six members of the EEC), there nevertheless existed a general acceptance that something had to be done beyond yet another report into the problems facing these countries. This proved to be the beginning of the closest the GATT was to come to a critical moment in which existed the potential for a fundamentally distinct shift in its evolutionary trajectory to occur. This moment emerged from the growing pressure to amend GATT rules to take account of the interests of developing countries that had evolved throughout the General Agreement's early years and culminated in the G21 proposal, and lasted through the annexation of Part IV to the GATT (below) and the challenge posed by UNCTAD (to which we return momentarily). Needless to say, a fundamentally distinct shift in trajectory did not occur. Rather, despite these challenges the GATT's evolution continued to track the path set out by its original design.

Despite some initial resistance, at a special session in Geneva in November 1964 the contracting parties drew up a protocol amending the GATT by introducing a fourth section (known as Part IV – in force on a *de facto* basis from 8 February 1965 and formally from 1966) dealing with trade and development. Part IV was not, however, the panacea the developing countries had hoped. As Evans notes, it 'was essentially a qualified, and at some points emasculated, version of a set of provisions submitted by the less developed contracting parties themselves to the drafting committee' (Evans, 1971: 121). For Srinivasan, under Part IV the 'less developed countries achieved little by way of precise commitments . . . but a lot in terms of verbiage' (Srinivasan, 1998: 24). In the end it committed developed countries (and their less developed counterparts in relation to trade among themselves) to: (i) give high priority to the reduction and elimination of barriers to trade for goods of export interest to their developing counterparts; (ii) refrain from introducing or increasing customs duties or non-tariff barriers on those goods; and (iii) refrain from imposing or making any adjustments in existing fiscal measures that would hamper demand for products from developing countries. It also removed the requirement for reciprocity for any concessions made during trade negotiations; and it put into place a reporting and surveillance mechanism under the auspices of a Committee on Trade and Development (GATT, 1965: 2–11). Yet, in by now classic GATT fashion, nothing in Part IV was compelling. As a result, it had little impact on the fortunes of less-developed countries. It did, however, serve to further entrench their growing hostility towards the shape and direction of multilateral trade regulation.

The decision to adopt Part IV was not only the result of a change of heart among the industrial contracting parties, however. It was a more overtly political decision that resulted from an emerging threat to the GATT from efforts to create an alternative trade machinery in the form of the UN Conference on Trade and Development (UNCTAD) (Whalley, 1990: 1320). But before we turn to this threat, we must first consider the plight of a final sector of interest to developing countries: textiles and clothing.

Textiles and clothing

The problems facing non-industrial contracting parties were compounded further by the exclusion of textiles and clothing from the GATT's purview. Whereas tariff reductions had been secured in most sectors in the early GATT rounds (albeit that protection of agricultural markets in the industrial states was ratcheted up by the introduction of non-tariff measures), levels of protection in textiles and clothing actually rose over the course of the 1950s. Moreover, much of the trade in textiles (initially cotton, but later a more extensive range of fibres) and clothing was governed by stringently enforced QRs. By 1955, for instance, while most of the QRs affecting trade in industrial goods had been dismantled, this was not the case with textiles and clothing. Indeed, QRs in textiles and clothing became known as 'hard core' restrictions (GATT, 1984). The perceived threat of competition emerging first from Japan and later from Hong Kong, Pakistan, India and others was so great that the US and UK broke with the GATT tradition of informality by seeking, and securing, the *formal* exclusion of textiles and clothing from the General Agreement's purview.

Textiles and clothing proved particularly troublesome for Japan and efforts to protect this sector by the industrial states compromised the benefits arising from its accession to the GATT (see Patterson, 1966: 272–300). Concerns about the consequences of Japanese involvement in the GATT were evident almost from the outset and frustrated its accession until 1955. Most of the worries regarding Japanese accession related to its low-wage, relatively high-skilled population and, as a result, its ability to out-compete European and North American textiles industries. Fear of the potential for market disruption caused by Japanese accession was such that upon becoming a contracting party approximately 40 per cent – some 14 countries[3] – of the signatures invoked Article XXXV (non-application of the Agreement between particular contracting parties) of the GATT with two more countries (Cambodia and Tunisia), indicating that they might wish to do so upon their accession (GATT, 1962: 69). The result was to nullify much of the preferential treatment that Japan could have accrued from its accession. Discrimination against Japanese exports did not, however, end with GATT provisions. In 1957 the US urged Japan to agree to a voluntary five-year limit on cotton textiles exports to the USA. It was only with the negotiation of the first of the formal measures by which textiles and clothing were extracted from the GATT's purview – the Short-Term Agreement on Cotton Textiles (STA) – that most of the 14 revoked Article XXXV.

Although the revoking of Article XXXV enabled Japan to enjoy greater normalisation in its trading relations with its counterparts – particularly important given the decreasing significance of its textiles and clothing industries and the spectacular advances in other sectors, most notably in shipbuilding and machine tool, pharmaceutical, iron, steel, ball-bearing, camera, radio and television production (Patterson, 1966: 301) – the negotiation of the STA merely generalised the kind of discrimination to which the Japanese textile and clothing industry had been subjected. The STA emerged from US concerns at the 'adverse effects of an abrupt invasion [by sharp increases in imports] of established markets'. This, in turn, prompted a GATT study into 'market disruption'. Although potentially related to the impact of *any* sharp increase in imports, the GATT study focused on textiles and clothing. Its conclusion was that irrespective of existing safeguards against situations of market disruption in the General Agreement, 'there were political and psychological elements . . . which render it doubtful whether such safeguards would be sufficient' (GATT, 1961: 106) making it unlikely that contracting parties would abandon the 'exceptional' measures they were employing (GATT, 1984: 64). The result, a year later, was that the contracting parties agreed an addendum to the General Agreement in the form of the STA. What became clear with the introduction of the STA was that the principal contracting parties were not only willing to, but that they *could*, amend GATT rules when it served their purposes. This, in turn, served to highlight the extent to which the leading industrial states remained firmly at the GATT's tiller.

For the purposes of the study, market disruption was generally taken to comprise the following elements 'in combination':

(i)   a sharp and substantial increase or potential increase of imports of particular products from particular sources;

(ii)   products offered at prices which are substantially below those pre-vailing for similar goods of comparable quality in the market of the importing country;

(iii)   instances where there is serious damage to domestic producers or threat thereof;

(iv)   when the price differentials referred to in paragraph (ii) above do not arise from governmental intervention in the fixing or formation of prices or from dumping practices.

(GATT, 1961: 26)

The study's definition of market disruption in turn became the fulcrum of the STA. The implications of this definition for exports of textiles and clothing were aptly summarised in a 1984 GATT report on trade in this sector. It was argued therein that the definition introduced three changes to the GATT's regular safeguard clause (Article XIX):

> First, it would not be necessary for the allegedly injurious increase in imports to have already occurred – a *potential* increase could be suffi-cient to justify additional restrictions. Second, imports of the production from *particular sources* could be singled out as the source of the problem, rather than imports of the product in general; the logical corol-lary was that . . . additional restrictions could be applied on a country specific (that is, discriminatory) rather than MFN basis. Third, the exist-ence (size) of a price differential between particular imports and goods of comparable quality sold on the domestic market could be used in determining the need for *additional* restrictions.
>
> (GATT, 1984: 65; emphasis added)

The introduction of the STA (which ran from October 1961 to September 1962 and was, in true GATT fashion, intended only to be a 'temporary' measure) and its successor – the Long-Term Agreement on Cotton Textiles (LTA – in force initially from October 1962 for five years (see GATT, 1963: 25–41) but extended three times to take it to the entry into force of the Multi-Fibre Agreement (MFA) in 1974) – were both presented in a disin-genuous fashion. Both recognised the need to expand trade to promote economic development, and both stated their purpose as providing 'oppor-tunities for exports of these products'. Indeed, one of the stated objectives of the LTA was to 'bring about an expansion of less-developed countries' export trade in cotton textiles' (GATT, 1966: 2). Yet both removed cotton textiles as a legitimate target of GATT-sponsored liberalisation and both facilitated an increase, rather than a decrease, in protectionism in this sector. Clearly neither was of benefit to those contracting parties, or those of their counterparts that had yet to accede to the General Agreement, that were exporters of such products. Invariably, these were developing countries.

As the 1960s progressed the industrial contracting parties increasingly began to view the LTA as inadequate. The use of synthetic fibres – largely polyester and acrylic – in the production of textiles and clothing began to rival cotton; and developments in knitting technology stimulated knitwear industries not only in South and Southeast Asia but also in Eastern Europe. The competition to textiles and clothing producers in the industrial states generated by these developments led to pressure for the imposition of restrictions on non-cotton products. Initially this took the form of attempts to obtain voluntary export restraints (VERs) from producing states but eventually the US took the whole textile problem to the GATT (GATT, 1984: 73). The result was the negotiation of the MFA.

Modelled on the LTA, the MFA authorised contracting parties to extend their discrimination against imports of textiles and clothing from developing world producers beyond cotton to include wool, synthetic fibres and blends thereof. As with its predecessors, the MFA was presented as a mechanism for the gradual increase in trade flows from developing to developed countries in textiles and clothing in a fashion that would minimise market disruption and facilitate structural adjustment in industrial sectors. Indeed, its role in facilitating an expansion of trade in this area was the principal reason why Japan and the developing countries agreed to its negotiation. It nevertheless contributed to a significant tightening of import restrictions facing developing countries. In so doing, it compounded the asymmetrical character of the GATT's deployment (GATT, 1984: 8).

By the mid-1960s, then, the manner in which the GATT had been deployed had contributed to two distinct experiences in international trade. For the industrial contracting parties, liberalisation under the GATT had seen the volume and value of trade in manufactured, semi-manufactured and industrial goods increase significantly. They had also managed to successfully protect both their agricultural, and textile and clothing sectors through a blend of formal and informal restrictions. This had not only assisted with post-war reconstruction but had also contributed to a sustained period of economic growth. For the developing contracting parties the story was quite different. The focus on the liberalisation of trade in manufactures, semi-manufactures and industrial goods came at the expense of the removal of barriers to trade in those areas of economic significance to the developing world. Indeed, between 1950 and 1960 the less-developed countries' share of world trade fell from 30 to 20 per cent (Gardner, 1964: 697). Moreover, there had been a marked difference in the way in which the problems of the industrial and developing states had been addressed. When faced with potentially disruptive economic situations to the industrial countries, the contracting parties either agreed or negotiated substantive exception clauses (such as with the number of waivers agreed to protect industrial agricultural markets and the exclusion of textiles and clothing); yet in those instances wherein serious economic problems threatened the developing countries, only limited action was forthcoming (normally taking the form of reports, decisions and non-binding provisions). These developments firmly established the parameters of the GATT's path-dependent evolution thereafter, but not before the industrial contracting parties had to confront the most significant challenge to the General Agreement's pre-eminence as the vehicle for multilateral trade liberalisation.

UNCTAD and the GATT

Inevitably, the developments of the GATT's formative years led many developing countries to view the General Agreement with derision and to consider their fortunes not only outside of the GATT but also outside of the Western Alliance. As academic and US Deputy Assistant Secretary of State for International Organization Affairs Richard Gardner put it:

> The collective security of the industrial countries of the North Atlantic Community and Japan and the defense of freedom in the less developed countries will be importantly influenced by the extent to which the free world can provide satisfactory alternatives to trade with the communist bloc. . . . The natural forces of interdependence have bound the United States, the industrial countries, and the underdeveloped countries of the noncommunist world into an intimate relationship. The weakness of that relationship is our weakness; its strength, our strength. The health of the other free world economies affects the health of our foreign markets and sources of supply – and therefore our prosperity. It affects the capacity of our allies to defend themselves as well as the political stability of the newly independent nations – and therefore our security. It affects the material basis for the development of freedom abroad – and therefore our own freedom.
>
> (1964: 686–687)

One consequence of the growth of frustration among developing countries and the strategic implications this could have was the adoption of a more conciliatory approach by the US within the GATT. In the run-up to the Kennedy round, for instance, the US passed the Trade Expansion Act authorising the President, among other things, to reduce the majority of US tariffs by 50 per cent, eliminate tariffs of 5 per cent or less and negotiate reciprocal reductions in trade barriers on those tropical products produced in the US in negligible amounts. More worrying, however, was the potential for an alternative trade machinery to emerge in the form of UNCTAD.

UNCTAD emerged out of growing developing country dissatisfaction with their trade performance and a desire to see tangible efforts to correct this during the UN's first development decade. It also resulted from pressure by the Soviet Union and its satellites to consider the problem of development in a UN forum rather than just among contracting parties to the Western-dominated GATT (Wells, 1969: 72). However, UNCTAD failed to produce an institutional challenge to the GATT. While debate during the Conference covered market access, preferences, commodity policy and financial matters as well as some discussion of the possibility of subsuming the GATT into a radically different trade machinery developed under UNCTAD auspices (Wells, 1969: 74), it proved not to be a forum for negotiations between participating states seeking reductions in impediments to trade or a vehicle for reversing the relatively poor trade performance of developing countries. UNCTAD proved too unwieldy for that purpose, particularly when compared with the relatively streamlined (albeit acutely asymmetrical) fashion in which the GATT had approached the liberalisation of trade. What the Conference resulted in instead was the creation of a formal and permanent presence for UNCTAD along with a Secretariat to oversee its functioning; a decision to initiate detailed fact-finding exercises on issues of economic development; and an agreement that the Conference should be reconvened at regular intervals with a Trade and Development Board meeting twice a year in between. It did not result in powers to go beyond the issuing of recommendations.

UNCTAD was nevertheless successful in consolidating growing solidarity among developing countries, particularly among the Group of 77 (G77) (though this solidarity was deemed by the US a 'transient phenomenon that should not be taken too seriously' but which should nevertheless be viewed as undesirable – Johnson, 1968: 358–359), providing a periodic high-profile forum for the discussion of trade issues of interest to developing countries, and instigating a mechanism for monitoring and reporting on development issues. Yet its lack of significant powers and the lacklustre participation of the developed states served to secure the GATT's role as the primary international trade body. It also served to take developing country eyes off the GATT for a significant period during which the asymmetry in the General Agreement's deployment was both consolidated and amplified. Needless to say, this was done at their peril.

The Kennedy round

While talk of development, the 1963 programme of action, the introduction of Part IV and the emergence of UNCTAD may have framed the negotiations, and despite an agreement that the negotiations should cover 'all classes of products' and that 'every effort should be made to reduce barriers to ... exports of less-developed countries' (Wells, 1969: 71), the Kennedy round proved to be business as usual. Although some differences did emerge – particularly relating to the way in which negotiations were governed – the round nevertheless fell into an all-too-familiar pattern. The run-up to the round witnessed extensive debate over the agreement of rules governing the negotiations. Indeed, the debate was such that the May 1963 Geneva meeting which preceded the launch of formal negotiations nearly broke down as the EEC and US failed repeatedly to agree a tariff-cutting formula (Preeg, 1970: 7–10). In the end they agreed to move away from the relatively simple procedures that had governed the previous rounds, to a more complex across-the-board (linear) approach. The agreement to move to a linear approach did not, however, put an end to the debate. Tensions over how to apply such an approach continued in each of the negotiating groups, leading to significant delays. It was, for instance, six months into the round before rules were finally agreed for negotiations to begin on industrial products. Other sectors – notably agriculture, non-tariff barriers and the participation of less-developed countries – were even more rigorously debated and subject to further delays (Evans, 1971: 184).

In the case of agriculture, disagreements among the contracting parties unfolded across several axes. New Zealand, Canada, Australia and the US initially favoured treating agricultural tariffs in the same manner as those affecting industrial goods through 50 per cent reductions across the board. Japan, the UK and the EEC (the position of which was complicated by the slow progress made in developing its Common Agricultural Policy – CAP) opposed such an approach, seeking instead to distinguish between different products. In an effort to move the negotiations forward, the Executive Secretary[4] proposed that a distinction be made between tariffs and other forms of protection and support. This was countered with suggestions that the elimination of non-tariff barriers should be a supplement to, but not a substitute for, tariff reductions. Various proposals were tabled for exemptions to a linear approach, the negotiation of margins of support, the binding of tariffs, and the binding of minimum import prices (which included debate over a reference price) among many others.

Thereafter, tensions between members of the EEC, most notably France and Germany, complicated matters further, resulting in the lack of a common position. An agreement was only reached after a bout of brinkmanship on the part of France forced the other contracting parties to consider continuing with the negotiations in the absence of the EEC, thereby withholding any concessions from which the Community may benefit. Ultimately, proceeding without the EEC was deemed impossible. France and Germany finally reached an agreement enabling the EEC to re-enter the negotiating fray. It was, nevertheless, two and a half years after the Kennedy round's official start that the negotiations on agriculture began (Evans, 1971: 203–217). In the end, a linear tariff cut was sporadically applied. Notable anomalies were the EEC's reduction of its tariff by less than the target of 50 per cent on items wherein its existing duties were significantly lower than those in the US and UK; and the exemption of Canada, New Zealand, South Africa and Australia from the linear approach (Canada because of its 'special economic and trade structure' and the other three by virtue of 'their very large dependence on exports of agricultural and other primary products') allowing them to engage in the negotiations on an item-by-item basis (Hoda, 2001: 31).

Needless to say, the Kennedy round had an important impact on the development of the GATT. Not only did it signal the onset of a new era in the way in which negotiations were conducted (in terms of the approach to tariff cutting adopted) and the heightening of political tensions among the contracting parties resulting therefrom, GATT rounds were further politicised by the onset of (what are now perennial) tensions between the US and the then EEC resulting from: (i) the growing significance of the EEC as a political force in trade; (ii) a relative decline in US influence in the GATT; and (iii) markedly different approaches to the liberalisation of agriculture (Lee, 1998: 516–520). As Ernest Preeg put it, the 'Kennedy Round was in fact the first major negotiation . . . across the Atlantic in which neither side was more equal than the other' (Preeg, 1970: 262).

The Kennedy round was also notable for the manner in which it was concluded. Donna Lee's (2001) meticulous account of the last months of the round (from January to May 1967) is instructive in this regard (see also Evans: 1971: 265–279). Lee notes that it was not until the last five months of the round that meaningful negotiations got underway once it became clear that the round's deadline (set at 30 June 1967 by the date of the expiry of US presidential authority) was firm and non-extendable. However, the conclusion of the round was compromised in April 1967 when a potentially insurmountable problem arose over the balance of concessions between the US and EEC wherein 'the total balance of offers between the US and the six [the EEC] was $318 million in the Community's favour' (Lee, 2001: 123). In an effort to overcome the deadlock, USTR William Roth announced that 'in his judgement the way to make progress with the Community was . . . to create a "crisis atmosphere" and adopt brinkmanship tactics' (Lee, 2001: 123). Roth's intention was to encourage the EEC to make meaningful concessions on agriculture (the key axis of contention between the two players) through the combination of a threat to withdraw from the round and the enticement of US acceptance of EEC demands on industrial tariffs. In the highly tense period that followed, in which the US delegation 'did all the running', an agreement was finally reached. Yet, although the US was successful in extracting further concessions from the EEC, this did not stretch to agriculture. As Lee notes:

> Whatever negotiating style and technique the Americans tried – threatening to walk out of the talks, proposing to raise the level of the talks to include senior executive figures, or offering generous concessions and reasonable exchanges – they were unable to entice the Community into a more cooperative negotiating position. In the end, the US had to accept a Kennedy Round agreement void of meaningful agricultural offers from the EEC. They did so because of overriding national security interests. . . . Without some agreement with the six, however minimal, the Community, [the US] believed, would turn inward and become an independent anti-American force in world politics, upsetting the balance of power in the Soviet's favour. For the sake of improved political

security in Europe, the Americans chose to swallow significant trade losses in its relations with the Community in the late 1960s.

(2001: 134)

Crisis thus played a significant role in the conclusion of the Kennedy round, first as a strategic ploy by the US to engineer a moment of tension that would lure the EEC into making further concessions, and second, in encouraging the US to accept a deal without securing what it deemed to be concessions roughly equivalent to that exchanged. For the US, the round had been far from successful.

More generally, the round's conclusion saw the further peripheralisation of less-developed countries in the negotiations. While the round's conclusion was notable for establishing a pattern wherein success hinged on agreement between the US and EEC, the provisions of Part IV and the removal of the requirement for less-developed countries to reciprocate further eroded their role in the negotiations. Although the round had opened with a general agreement that all sectors should be covered by the negotiations – including agricultural and primary products, as well as tariffs and non-tariff barriers – the results fell far short of these aspirations. Of the 76 contracting parties to the GATT in 1967 only 31 (plus the EEC six) granted tariff concessions. Of these, only 11 were developing countries (Argentina, Brazil, Chile, Dominican Republic, India, Jamaica, Korea, Malawi, Peru, Trinidad and Tobago, and Turkey – see Table 3.2). Little progress was made on market access; agricultural support programmes remained highly restrictive; the production of synthetic fabrics in the industrial states continued to replace demand for natural products; attempts to create commodity agreements for cocoa and sugar were unsuccessful; the terms of trade of primary producing countries in 1967 were less favourable than they had been in 1958; the price of rubber, tropical oils and oil seeds, jute and sugar continued to fall; developing countries continued to face relatively high tariffs on finished and semi-finished products (Wells, 1969: 75); and the practice of negotiating side agreements to the General Agreement that had been established under the STA and LTA was consolidated with the negotiation of the Agreement relating principally to Chemicals and the Memorandum of Agreement on Basic Elements for the Negotiation of a World Grains Agreement effectively separating these sectors from normal GATT business (and enabling the US and EEC to reach an agreement – GATT, 1968: 8–24). As Sidney Wells (1969: 71–72) put it:

On the whole the results of the three years' negotiations were disappointing to less developed countries . . . the largest cuts [were] made in tariffs on products like machinery, transport equipment and goods of greater interest to developed than to less-developed. . . . Quantitative restrictions and other tariff barriers [were] hardly affected, and there [was] no improvement of access through the modification of internal support policies.

After Kennedy

Problematising the results of the round further, the immediate aftermath of the Kennedy round saw much pressure exerted on the value of the concessions negotiated therein. Currency speculation in the autumn of 1967 forced the UK to devalue sterling thereby reducing the value of its concessions. The year 1968 opened with a warning from US President Johnson that a crisis faced the US dollar, triggering heated debate about the need for the US to introduce protectionist measures to alleviate the situation (Evans, 1971: 301–307); a dispute broke out between Congress and the executive branch over the failure of the former to ratify a Kennedy round negotiated side agreement relinquishing the American Selling Price System (ASPS) for certain goods for customs purposes in exchange for EEC concessions principally on chemical goods (see GATT, 1968: 8–18; also Winham, 1986: 70–71); and tensions erupted within Congress over the negotiation of, and US entry into, an agreement on antidumping duties (Jackson, 1987: 380). Social unrest in France placed pressure on the government to raise wages; the Franc increasingly became the subject of speculative attacks; and export subsidies and import quotas among others were introduced as a consequence.

More widely, the period between the conclusion of the Kennedy round and the launch of the Tokyo round brought with it a rapid deterioration in the global economic climate. Throughout the late 1960s and early 1970s much of Western Europe and North America saw the onset of high levels of inflation, rising unemployment, industrial stagnation, declining profitability and low rates of growth and investment. Inflation in the US underpinned several oil price rises by members of OPEC in an effort to offset dollar devaluation (Strange, 1997: 71–72). Rather than tightening monetary and fiscal policy to combat an overvalued dollar and excessive Vietnam War-driven government expenditure, on 15 August 1971 US President Nixon chose instead to suspend the convertibility of the dollar into gold and placed a 10 per cent surcharge on all imports, effectively ending the Bretton Woods system. In moves that resonate loudly with the current US-led 'war on terror', the US emphasised the need to open up European and Japanese markets to American goods and the necessity of these countries accepting a larger share of the costs of global security. In pressing for further market openings – and ultimately the launch of what was to become the Tokyo round – the US also sought to resist growing domestic pressure for greater protectionism while at the same time rectifying perceived imbalances arising from previous GATT rounds in which it was deemed that EEC and Japanese concessions had been less valuable than those offered (Ostry, 1997: 74–75).

At the same time, however, the US sought to offset Japanese (and increasingly other East Asian) challenges to its domestic competitivity. The US also sought to develop a unilateral machinery to overcome the lack of compliance with, and indeed *de facto* abandonment of, the GATT's dispute settlement procedures by drawing up the 1974 Trade Act (and with it the notorious Section 301 – see Bhagwati and Patrick, 1990; and Curzon and Curzon, 1989). More generally, protectionist urges surged. One commentator has suggested that by the end of the 1970s 'as much as one-fifth of OECD manufacturing imports were affected by quantitative restrictions . . . a quadrupling over the decade' and grew from a prevalence only in agriculture, textiles, footwear, iron and steel to include 'consumer electronics and automobiles' as well (Ostry, 1997: 76–77). The result was the onset of a second twin crisis – this time monetary and commercial – which generated a broad diagnosis that a radical overhaul of the post-war economic settlement was necessary. A key feature of this diagnosis was reform of the way in which international trade was regulated. What resulted was not, however, a critical juncture signalling a qualitatively distinct shift in the GATT's trajectory (as Chapter 4 clearly demonstrates); what was produced instead was a substantive leap forward in that system's development firmly in keeping with the evolutionary trajectory established by the General Agreement's formative years.

The argument so far

The conclusion of the Kennedy round marked the end of the GATT's formative years. By that point all the practices and procedures that combined to structure the relations of its participants were in place. What was to occur thereafter was a consolidation of and a building upon this foundation. This foundation was not, as is now obvious, one that was symmetrical or one that afforded each of the contracting parties an equal say in its construction; nor was it a machinery affording each an equity of economic opportunity. How could it be when it was deployed as a means of liberalising trade in manufactures, semi-manufactures, other non-agricultural produce and capital goods, and not those areas of primary importance to its developing contracting parties (principally agriculture, and textiles and clothing)? What the GATT's formative development had produced was an instrument tuned and refined in accordance with its original objectives. The only caveat had been the need to accommodate the rising economic power of the EEC and its challenge to US pre-eminence. What happened hereafter was a process of further consolidation of the GATT's character and the entrenchment of its mode of operation in international trade law. More importantly, the emergence and entrenchment of asymmetry in GATT rules coupled with the growing disenchantment of less-developed countries with their trade performance generally and their influence in the General Agreement more specifically and the use of *ad hoc* operating procedures fuelled tensions over the direction of the trade agenda. In the absence of appropriate remedial action it was inevitable that trade politics would become an ever more charged affair – as what was to happen subsequently proved. The seeds of a propensity for ministerial meetings to break down were about to bear their first fruit.

4 Fashioning the WTO

Formalising multilateral trade regulation

While most accounts of the creation of the WTO begin with the Uruguay round, the run-up to Uruguay, or at best the end of the Tokyo round, the momentum for a significant deepening and widening of multilateral trade regulation had actually been gathering since the Kennedy negotiations. This momentum was accelerated by the political response to the monetary and commercial crises of the late 1960s and early 1970s (Winham, 1986: 3–14), though other factors were also important: the relative decline of the US as the dominant force in international trade; escalating tensions over agricultural liberalisation; a sharp increase in non-tariff barriers; and the continuing growth of frustration among developing countries.

What emerged from this gathering momentum was not, however, a fundamentally distinct shift in the GATT's institutional trajectory. Rather, what resulted was a consolidation and extension of existing ways of operating very much in keeping with the parameters of multilateral trade regulation as they had been established. This consolidation and extension was most notable in the outcome of the Tokyo negotiations. The General Agreement continued to operate and regulate international trade in accordance with those practices and procedures developed during its formative years. The primary difference was that the negotiations codified these ways of operating to generate what Sylvia Ostry calls 'detailed legalisms' (Ostry, 1997: 89) and what Alan Winters characterises as a preoccupation with constitutional issues (Winters, 1990: 1288; also Hoekman, 1993: 1528; Esty, 2002: 12). With this codification came an extension, consolidation, amplification and, most importantly, entrenchment of the asymmetries of opportunity arising from the way in which GATT rules had been deployed.

The main difference between the GATT's formative years and the period it now entered was the interests the General Agreement now came to serve. Whereas the GATT had very much been fashioned as a means of enabling the US to realise the economic opportunities and address the strategic realities of the post-war era, the Tokyo round reflected changing configurations of global economic power. The GATT had also become an important tool for a nascent EEC to realise its commercial ambitions; ambitions that were, and remain, often in conflict with those of the US. It also involved

– rather nominally, as we see below – a growing number of developing countries.

Tokyo did not, however, address many of the GATT's defects. Although progress was made on non-tariff barriers, the round resulted in the negotiation of a clutch of side agreements that applied to only a handful of (largely) industrial signatories. Little movement was made in liberalising agricultural markets: the US continued to dish out lavish export subsidies to domestic producers and impose quotas on imports of dairy produce; and European discrimination in the sector was exacerbated by the further development of the CAP. Similarly, the round oversaw the continued exclusion of textiles and clothing from the GATT's remit, first with the negotiation of the MFA and then with the extension of discrimination under MFA II. More generally, as the round closed recession hit and much of the bullishness of the developing world that had continued to grow in the wake of the OPEC oil price rises was evaporated by the debt crisis. Moreover, the late 1970s and early 1980s saw the emergence and gradual entrenchment of a new economic ideology, one that eschewed the state building and public welfare projects of the post-war era in favour of ever greater market freedoms. It is upon this basis that the Uruguay round was launched, and the bargain ultimately struck that lay the foundations for the WTO.

This chapter explores the development of the GATT in its later period. It begins with an exploration of the Tokyo round and its outcome. Thereafter it focuses on the institutional developments, negotiations and political tensions played out in the run-up to and during the Uruguay round. The chapter then explores the shape of multilateral trade regulation at the point of the WTO's creation. As with the preceding chapters, emphasis is placed on better understanding those developments that built upon the GATT's existing mode of deployment and attendant practices and procedures, and highlighting those instances of departure that together combine to explain the current propensity of WTO ministerials to collapse.

Tokyo – consolidation and evolution

The idea of a further bout of negotiations was aired by the US almost as the ink was drying on the Kennedy round accords. The marked upsurge in protectionism that followed the Kennedy round brought with it a resurgence of fears of a breakdown in the global economy that again served as a frame for the new negotiations. Rather than succumbing to a fall back into national insularity, these fears proved sufficient in encouraging a return to the negotiating table. In the US, President Johnson nurtured support for a new round through the convening of a Public Advisory Committee on Trade Policy (comprising leading private and labour groups) and by commissioning a study on the future of US trade policy led by USTR Roth. The Roth study proved instrumental in the production of a report which highlighted the continuing frustration of American exports by foreign trade barriers and the need for a further round of negotiations (Winham, 1986: 73). Support for a new round was further garnered by the creation of a Commission on International Trade and Investment Policy bringing together private, labour and academic interests. The Commission (known as the Williams Commission after its Chair Albert L. Williams) in turn produced a report which emphasised the need for the US to meet the challenges of the early 1970s not by falling back into protectionism but by pursuing further liberalisation. The momentum generated by the Commission's report was, in turn, picked up and taken forward by the Organisation for Economic Co-operation and Development (OECD) which established a study group to consider the state of the global economy (known as the Rey Group after its Chair Jean Rey). The group's deliberations resulted in a report that further highlighted the need: (i) to strengthen the GATT as a measure of halting any slippage into protectionism; (ii) for a major effort to liberalise trade through further negotiation; and (iii) to combat the use of non-tariff measures as instruments of trade policy (Winham, 1986: 74–76).

Despite Jean Rey's (then President of the European Commission) role as Chair of the OECD study group, European support for a new round was not initially forthcoming. In the period following the Kennedy round the EEC had become absorbed with internal happenings, notably facilitating greater unification of the Community's monetary policy, the renegotiation of a trade and aid relationship with the continuing and former colonies and dependent areas of the member states (under the Yaoundé Agreement and later the Lomé Convention), and the accession of Denmark, Ireland and the UK. Indeed, it was only with the deepening of the international monetary and commercial crises in the early 1970s and mounting US pressure that European attention was diverted towards the need for a new round of negotiations. Shortly thereafter further liberalisation became a formal goal of both powers, and in February 1972 the US and the EEC issued a joint declaration highlighting the need for a new trade round and the necessity of such action to promote greater stability in international monetary relations (Winham, 1986: 5, 15, 78–79).

On 14 September 1973 the Tokyo round formally began. True to form the negotiations overran. Originally intended to be concluded 'in 1975' (GATT, 1974: 22), the round lasted until 12 April 1979 (albeit that the US and EEC disagreed over whether the signing ceremony actually represented the end of negotiations) with the tariff reductions negotiated during the round being adopted in the following November. The negotiation of the Tokyo Declaration setting the tone of the negotiations was a terse affair. The wording of the Declaration was more a statement combining diametrically opposed views than a text arrived at by consensus (Winham, 1986: 92–100). The negotiations themselves focused largely on those areas of economic interest to the industrial states, despite the by-now-familiar calls to secure additional benefits for developing countries and to address barriers to trade in agriculture (GATT, 1974: 19–22). The round presided over the

1977 renegotiation of the MFA. However, rather than relaxing restrictions on imports of textiles and clothing from the developing world, the second incarnation of the MFA resulted in a significant tightening of discriminatory measures in the industrial states (GATT, 1984: 8, 80). The US and EEC clashed continually over agriculture injecting a stasis into the negotiations until mid-1977. The negotiations over an appropriate tariff-cutting formula were tense and protracted (largely the result of another US–EEC conflict over the latter's desire to address tariff peaks rather than just pursue a linear formula) and were agreed only once a heavy list of exceptions had been worked out; the result was the general acceptance of the so-called Swiss formula (Balassa, 1980: 98) albeit that Canada, New Zealand and South Africa were again anomalous (with Canada applying a different formula, and New Zealand and South Africa along with Iceland adopting an item-by-item approach) (Hoda, 2001: 32). It took four years for the US and EC to agree on the Swiss formula and an additional year-and-a-half to settle on a mutually acceptable exceptions list (Winters, 1990: 1294). Despite the participation of ninety-nine countries in the round, most of the major decisions were made by the US, an expanded EEC and Japan with some input from Canada (Jackson, 1997: 70). A crisis (in this case over countervailing duties) threatened the round's completion (see Winham, 1986: 213–219). Many developing countries opposed the round's results, believing that they were not sufficiently in their interests; and an UNCTAD report admonished the Tokyo accords for their role in perpetuating a trading system that better reflected the interests of the industrial states (UNCTAD V, 1979).

In contrast to previous rounds the negotiations witnessed the emergence of a more abrasive and forceful US. The growth of Western European and Japanese competitivity and an increasing American trade deficit coupled with the poor unbalanced results of the Kennedy round (as the US saw them) generated dissatisfaction within the US about the post-war trading system. Part of this dissatisfaction was manifest in increasing support for greater protectionism, but it also emerged in the development of a much more robust trade negotiating machinery. The negotiation of the 1974 Trade Act (which gave the executive authority to negotiate during the Tokyo round) brought with it a stouter means of dealing with, and penalising, subsidised and dumped imports. It also gave the President 'broad and unconstrained authority' to deal with trade policies deemed unfair, unreasonable and/or unjustified (Ostry, 1997: 85–86).

More generally, quad (and in particular US and EC) domination of the proceedings was made all the more possible by the preoccupation of developing states with events outside of the GATT – principally a growing interest in and preoccupation with UNCTAD and the solidarity nurtured through membership of the G77, the pursuit of a common development strategy in the form of Import Substitution Industrialisation (ISI) (Srinivasan, 1998: 27), and an (ill-founded as it turned out) perception of shifting hemispheric power in the wake of the OPEC driven oil price rises and the 1974 General

Assembly issued Declaration of the Establishment of a New International Economic Order (NIEO). Developing country attentions were further diverted by the creation of the Generalised System of Preferences (GSP) under which industrialised countries could grant trade preferences to all developing countries. Yet rather than a multilateral and evenly applied scheme, this authorised the establishment of *individual* GSP schemes allowing the industrial states to pursue the political, military and economic linkages such bilateral agreements normally entail. As the GSP was inconsistent with the GATT's principle of MFN, to get the system up and running a waiver had to be secured. This was initially granted in 1971 for a period of ten years.

Developing country participation was further hampered by perennial problems relating to a relative lack of technical and legal expertise, a shortage of appropriately qualified personnel and a lack of awareness of the significance of, or commercial interest in, the sectors under negotiation. Tigani Ibrahim noted that less than a quarter of the 78 developing countries officially declared as participants were actively taking part in the negotiations. Most inactive were the African states of which only Egypt, Nigeria and 'occasionally' Ghana were engaged in any way (Ibrahim, 1978: 15). Moreover, those developing countries which were engaged during the Tokyo round invariably came from that élite group of countries able to meet the logistical costs (in terms of number of personnel, requisite knowledge, legal expertise and financial resources) of participation. They were also those that stood to gain the most. The concentration on the liberalisation of industrial goods inevitably meant that this élite group comprised states with established industrial sectors – particularly Argentina, Brazil, South Korea, India, Yugoslavia, Egypt and Nigeria – but which nevertheless professed to speak on behalf of the developing world (albeit that they had differing economic interests). Indeed, this perennial feature of trade politics remains: that developing countries are treated as a largely homogeneous group in which, with very few exceptions, the largest and most powerful speak for the poorest and least capable – a state of affairs that has and continues to cloak and compound the problems faced by the poorest.

The round was not, however, without its concessions to developing countries – though they were largely lacklustre. The contracting parties adopted a declaration – entitled 'Differential and More Favourable Treatment, Reciprocity and Fuller Participation of Developing Countries' – that empowered contracting parties to accord differential treatment to developing countries without according such treatment to other contracting parties, thereby removing the need for an extension to the GSP waiver – the so-called 'enabling clause' (Golt,1978: 29; Jackson, 1997: 323). The conclusion of three other agreements also sought to pacify developing countries in the negotiations: (i) the Declaration on Trade Measures Taken for Balance-of-payments Purposes enabling contracting parties to use QRs to protect against poor balance-of-payments situations; (ii) the Safeguard Action for

Development Purposes which, subject to the approval of affected parties and the contracting parties as a whole, empowered developing countries to implement trade restrictions to encourage the growth of particular (so-called infant) industries; and (iii) the Understanding regarding Notification, Consultation, Dispute Settlement and Surveillance codifying the practice of using panels to settle trade disputes.

The outcome of the round saw some significant reductions in (largely industrial) tariffs, but almost no movement on agricultural market access. Moreover, efforts to address non-tariff measures were only relatively successful; the EEC managed to block US efforts to reform the GATT's dispute settlement mechanism; no agreement was reached on safeguards or the elimination of quantitative restrictions; and differences between the US and EEC over subsidies politicised the issue, ensuring it would emerge again during the Uruguay round (Ostry, 1997: 86–88).

The Tokyo codes

The round did, however, produce two outcomes that are crucial to understanding the GATT's development. First, the Tokyo discussions resulted in the negotiation of a series of side agreements. In large measure these related to issues on which widespread agreement could not be reached but wherein negotiation was deemed to be crucial to the conclusion of the bargaining and as such were agreed to by only a subset of contracting parties. And second, the growing complexity of the negotiations in terms of content and number of participants produced a shift away from the *ad hoc*-ery and broad statements of principle governing the conduct of the round that characterised the early GATT years towards the pursuit of detailed legalisms (Ostry, 1997: 89). This move brought with it a heightening of tensions over rule negotiations as each contracting party sought to ensure that their interests were adequately reflected. This inevitably favoured those contracting parties whose delegations comprised personnel with a requisite level of understanding of, and familiarity with, international trade law, and it resulted in the consolidation and further entrenchment of asymmetries in economic opportunity arising out of GATT rules.

The negotiation of the ASPS and anti-dumping side agreements during the Kennedy round set a worrying precedent for the Tokyo round: that future rounds would result in the negotiation of more issue-specific agreements which applied only to particular contracting parties but which were concluded at the behest of the industrial states to protect or advance an area of economic interest. In an attempt to stop such developments occurring, the Tokyo ministerial declaration contained a provision stating that the negotiations should 'be considered as one undertaking, the various elements of which shall move forward together' (GATT, 1974: 22). The ministerial declaration proved not to be enough however, as the Tokyo round resulted in the negotiation of nine side agreements dealing with non-tariff measures as well as in four understandings (relating to the interpretation of aspects of GATT rules) (see Table 4.1). Of the nine side agreements seven were sufficiently coherent to be known as 'codes'. These covered anti-dumping, government procurement, subsidies and countervailing measures, import licensing, technical barriers to trade, customs valuation and trade in civil aircraft. Negotiations on an eighth code – dealing with safeguards – failed (see Winham, 1986: 240–247). It is also noteworthy that the round witnessed some discussion, though no action, on the relationship between trade liberalisation and the protection of certain worker rights (Haworth and Hughes, 1997: 184); in addition, the EC and US tabled a draft agreement on intellectual property protection (and pursued unilateral measures to shore up what were perceived to be inconsistencies in the intellectual property protection of third countries – Hoekman, 1993: 1531) – two issues that became important sites of contestation in the Uruguay and post-Uruguay era.

The negotiation of the Tokyo side agreements was significant for three reasons. First, they resulted in an appreciable broadening of the commercial coverage of the GATT, extending coverage beyond trade in goods and dealing with aspects of agriculture to include trade-related issues such as government procurement. But second, they did so in a highly selective and uneven fashion. Only a small number of contracting parties – principally the leading industrial states – agreed to be bound by the agreements. The result was to enable the industrial signatories to exploit the advantages afforded by these agreements. And third, their existence brought into being a pick-and-mix approach to multilateral trade regulation (often referred to as GATT *à la carte*) whereupon contracting parties were at liberty to adhere only to those agreements that served their national interest.

Table 4.1 Tokyo round side agreements and understandings

Side agreements
- Arrangements regarding bovine meat
- Arrangements regarding dairy products
- Government procurement
- Implementation of Article VI (anti-dumping duties)
- Implementation of Article VII (customs valuation)
- Import licensing procedures
- Interpretation and application of Articles VI, XVI, XXXIII (subsidies and countervailing measures)
- Technical barriers to trade
- Trade in civil aircraft

Understandings
- Declaration on trade measures taken for balance-of-payments purposes
- Differential and more favourable treatment, reciprocity and fuller participation of developing countries
- Safeguard action for development purposes
- Understanding regarding notification, consultation, dispute settlement and surveillance

This selectivity, and the fragmentation that it generated, resulted in a push for the unification of GATT-negotiated trade law under a single body in the wake of the round's conclusion. Yet this created another problem. The extension in the GATT's commercial coverage established by these side agreements set a precedent for that coverage to be universalised across all contracting parties in future negotiations. And although the means by which much of this extension in commercial coverage was formalised during the Uruguay round – the so-called 'single undertaking' – and was agreed in exchange for the negotiation of agreements that appeared to be in the interest of developing countries, it nevertheless brought a widening of multi-lateral trade regulation in through the back door. It is unlikely that such a widening would have been agreed by the membership as a whole during the Uruguay round had the Tokyo side agreements not already existed.

From Tokyo to Uruguay

As had been the case in the wake of the Kennedy round, the period immediately following the conclusion of the Tokyo negotiations saw a sharp increase in protectionist sentiments and a resurgence of fears of a breakdown in the global economy. These fears were fuelled by a crisis that threatened the entire international financial system. The extent of the crisis was such, however, that US pressure for yet another round of negotiations went unheeded until 1985. Food shortages in the early 1970s had fuelled massive increases in food grain prices. The price of oil had also increased significantly following OPEC's restriction of supply in the wake of the 1973 Arab–Israeli conflict. These two events combined to increase levels of indebtedness among developing countries as they sought to finance current account deficits. Much of this indebtedness was funded by the 'petro dollars' that had been accumulated by the OPEC countries and deposited in commercial banks. Levels of indebtedness were increased further by a second oil price rise in 1979. The inflationary pressure caused by the second oil price rise combined with strong demand for credit from the US government to service the federal budget deficit to fuel huge increases in interest rates. This, in turn, put ever greater pressure on those developing countries that had borrowed at variable rates of interest. The result was to place the international financial system in a state of extreme precariousness. Eventually the system was thrown into crisis when, in August 1982, Mexico announced that it could no longer service its public sector debt obligations (see Cohn, 2005: 182–184). Not surprisingly, in this climate few contracting parties were keen to embark upon a new round of negotiations.

The period between the Tokyo and Uruguay rounds was also notable for the growing consolidation of changes in the relative power capabilities of the GATT's key protagonists. Japan's position as a major player in international trade was consolidated by its continued economic performance. Other challenges to the trade hierarchy were beginning to emerge led, in the main, by the newly industrialising countries (NICs) of East Asia. The dynamic economic performance of the NICs further undermined ISI as a development strategy among the developing contracting parties. This, in turn, had a marked impact upon the solidarity of developing countries as a group. The mid-1980s also saw European economic might continue to increase, first through the extension of EEC membership to Greece (1981) and then to Portugal and Spain (1986). Prompted in part by continuing European expansion and, in part, by a desire to build upon and pursue economic opportunities in the region, talk of various East Asian and Pacific regional initiatives proliferated, leading most notably to the establishment of Asia Pacific Economic Co-operation (APEC) in 1989.

In the US the late 1970s and early 1980s saw a steadily increasing hostility towards the results of the Tokyo round generally, and the growth of European agricultural protection and closed Japanese markets in particular. The burgeoning hostility generated early support for a further trade round designed to recover some of the ground perceived to have been lost. This comprised not only securing further market access (particularly on agriculture and manufactured goods) but on services, investment and intellectual property (all areas in which the US had significant comparative and absolute advantages and which had, to this point, been outside of the GATT's remit). It also led to a significant change in and diversification of US trade policy. The mid-1980s saw the US begin negotiating regional trade agreements, most notably the North American Free Trade Agreement (NAFTA). The period also witnessed a resurgence of interest in unilateralist measures and the use of Section 301 of the 1974 Trade Act to pursue US trade objectives; and a growing trade deficit, an overvalued dollar and a perception that US markets were more open than those of its major competitors coupled with frustrations at the delay in launching a new round of GATT negotiations (what was to become the Uruguay round) ignited calls for a swathe of protectionist measures.

The Uruguay round

Despite limited success in addressing non-tariff barriers in the Tokyo round (albeit in the form of side agreements), the negotiations had left several areas of the GATT untouched and in need of reform. Two areas in particular required attention: the way in which disputes between contracting parties were settled; and the uneven and incomplete extent of the GATT's remit. With the exception of Dutch retaliation (by imposing an import quota on wheat flour) against US restrictions on dairy products in 1952, the GATT's dispute settlement procedures had relied on collective moral suasion and the good nature of a contracting party to take corrective action. As a result, they had proven ineffectual. Contracting parties were able to disrupt the process of dispute settlement and could block any action eventually arising therefrom. As a result, compliance with GATT obligations depended on the commercial consequences of any costs to a contracting party's reputation and its ability to weather any unilateral retaliatory action that may be forthcoming.

A second source of frustration was the way in which the incomplete commercial coverage of the GATT frustrated the ability of contracting parties to take advantage of the economic opportunities therein. Not only was the exclusion of agriculture, and textiles and clothing a hindrance to economic development in the South, but pressure was also increasing among the industrial states for a multilateral code on services as well as on aspects of intellectual property protection and investment (Jackson and Sykes, 1997: 3). In addition, the manner in which the Tokyo round had dealt with non-tariff barriers ensured that they continued to be a problem. Developing countries continued to bear the brunt of the QRs imposed by their industrial counterparts and, set against an ever worsening global economic situation for the most vulnerable of their number, pressed repeatedly for greater special and differential treatment. In addition, the momentum generated by the Tokyo round on the codification of trade rules established an expectation that constitutional issues would remain on the agenda. Inevitably the Uruguay agenda was burgeoning.

Much like the previous round, efforts to encourage a return to the negotiating table took place within the context of, and were framed by, global economic depression and fears of a slide back into protectionism. At the behest of the US, and arranged at the suggestion of the Consultative Group of 18 (CG18),[1] the contracting parties met to discuss the possibility of a new round in Geneva at the November 1982 ministerial meeting. For the US, the meeting was to be an opportunity to drive the trade agenda forward as well as to seek ways in which to unpick growing agricultural protection in the EEC. For many developing countries, it was an opportunity to discuss growing protection of industrial markets and their greater participation in world trade (*SUNS*, 29 June 1981).

The meeting, however, failed to nurture a consensus on a new round. The US pushed hard for a work programme that would not only open up European agricultural markets but would also expand the GATT's remit to include services, investment and intellectual property (the so-called new issues) under a threat of congressional action should agreement not be forthcoming. The EC was lukewarm to the idea of further negotiations (and initially opposed US pressure to include services, intellectual property and investment on the agenda). Japan favoured a new set of talks as a means of relieving increasing pressure from the US to open up its markets further to American goods. Support for a new round also came from an alliance of medium-sized industrial states keen to push forward the codification of trade rules in an effort to cajole the US and EC into greater compliance with the GATT and developing states anxious to begin unpicking discrimination in industrial, agricultural, and textile and clothing markets as well as to increase levels of special and differential treatment (Winters, 1990: 1297). The majority of developing countries were, however, opposed to a new round, preferring instead the pursuit of a standstill on the further introduction of protectionist measures in markets of economic interest to them, the dismantling and phase-out of existing impediments, full implementation of Part IV of the GATT and of special and differential treatment, better dispute settlement, and an effective safeguards agreement (*SUNS*, 26 November 1982). As Narlikar puts it, their arguments were simple: 'the voluminous backlog of pending issues (liberalisation in agriculture, textiles, tropical products, removal of NTBs such as VERs, ADDs [anti-dumping duties] and CVDs [countervailing duties]) had to be dealt with' before any extension of the GATT's remit could be considered (Narlikar, 2003: 69).

Not surprisingly, the ministerial meeting proved to be a terse affair. Both the industrial and developing countries complained of excessive US pressure and the outcome was, as Ostry put it, 'near-catastrophic' (Ostry, 1997: 105). In what has since become established practice, the meeting was extended on a rolling basis in an effort to reach agreement. Moreover, a number of the delegates, particularly from developing countries, left early, dismayed at pressure to accept an agenda that clearly was not in their interests; complaints were heard about deals done in corridors; and the appointment of the 'friends of the President' (now known as 'Chair') as facilitators of the discussion was seen by many as designed to push through an 'agreed' text for which there existed little support. As Raghavan (1982) describes:

> the paper put forward by chairman Allan Maceachen was adopted by consensus. No one liked it, almost everyone had serious problems about one part or another, and yet no one wanted to even record them before it was put and declared adopted by consensus. It was both because the document could not be taken seriously, and even more because no one wanted to be blamed for a breakdown, and everyone was afraid of the consequences they were being daily warned about, namely a trade war. No one knows whether there was such a danger (apart from implying trade peace now), and no one can predict that a trade war will not come with the document either.

In the end the contracting parties agreed to a work programme that included the improvement of dispute settlement procedures, developing an understanding on safeguards and bringing agriculture, and textiles and clothing more firmly under GATT rules. More importantly, the US was successful in setting in motion a work programme on services with a view to future negotiations in the area. The meeting's outcome was, however, anomalous and two interpretations prevailed. On the one hand, the majority of developing countries presumed that the work programme would instigate a process *independent* of the GATT; whereas, the US understood the outcome to be broad preparation for a *new* round. Inevitably, the lack of a single interpretation proved frustrating. What followed was a concerted effort on the part of the US to drum up support for a new round (Narlikar, 2003: 72).

By July 1985 acute US pressure had resulted in contracting party agreement to begin negotiations and to the creation of a Preparatory Committee to begin work on establishing the round's aims, objectives and negotiating modalities. In an effort to sustain momentum for a new round and cajole the EC, India and Brazil into action, the US announced on 23 September 1985 that it would pursue a three-pronged trade strategy: unilaterally through Section 301; bilaterally with key trade partners; and multilaterally through the GATT (Ostry, 1997: 107–108). Thereafter the familiar pattern of GATT negotiations began to unfold. Preliminary work on setting the agenda for the new round was carried out in the run-up to the Punta del Este, Uruguay ministerial meeting (from which the round took its name – 15–20 September 1986) by a Preparatory Committee (Prepcom) chaired by Arthur Dunkel (the GATT DG). Predictably, the differences of opinion that had been evident in the run-up to the July 1985 agreement re-emerged reflecting diametrically opposed views on the purpose of the negotiations. Much of the tension took on a North/South flavour, though in reality it was more complex. These differences saw the content of the ministerial declaration launching the negotiations become the subject of much debate. A group of nine industrial contracting parties (G9) called for a broad approach to the negotiations both in terms of the extent of the commercial terrain to be covered (including bringing in new issues) and the further codification of GATT rules; whereas a proposal tabled by a group of ten developing countries (G10) led by Brazil and India advocated a much less extensive agenda focusing largely on agriculture, and textiles and clothing. In the end, with input from the G10, a modified version of the G9 proposal was adopted (Winters, 1990: 1298). The result was the formalisation of an understanding that had prevailed during the Kennedy and Tokyo rounds but which had yet to bare fruit: that if the talks were to be successfully concluded linkages would inevitably be made between old (agriculture, textiles and clothing, trade in goods) and new (services, intellectual property and investment measures) issues (Hoekman, 1993: 1533). This was to form the basis of a single undertaking.

Given the anomalous fashion in which a linear across-the-board approach to tariff negotiations had been applied during the Kennedy and Tokyo rounds it was unsurprising that the Ministerial Declaration launching the Uruguay round omitted to specify the tariff-cutting formula to be deployed. Instead, it merely specified that the negotiations 'aim, by appropriate methods, to reduce or, as appropriate, eliminate tariffs, including the reduction or elimination of high tariffs and tariff escalation' (GATT, 1986). The vagaries of the Declaration reflected the differing views as to how the negotiations ought to be conducted. The US, for instance, pushed for the negotiations to be conducted on a request-and-offer basis, arguing that adoption of a linear approach in the previous two rounds had liberalised trade to the extent that an across-the-board method would do little to address remaining barriers to trade. Japan initially proposed the complete elimination of all tariffs on industrial products, though its position was subsequently modified to exclude developing countries from a blanket removal requiring that they make proportionate cuts in tariff levels. The EC's approach was more complex. It proposed a three-tier approach. For industrial contracting parties tariffs of 40 per cent or more should be cut to a ceiling of 20 per cent; duties of 30 to 39 per cent should be reduced by 50 per cent; and tariffs between 0 and 29 per cent should be reduced by a percentage based on the base rate of customs duty for that produce plus 20. For developing (but not least developed) countries, EC proposals were more forgiving: a tariff ceiling of 35 per cent on high duties and bilateral negotiations designed to reduce and harmonise all duties below that level was proposed. In the case of the least developed countries, the EC proposed 'that contributions would be made within the limits of their capabilities' (Hoda, 2001: 34). Canada proposed that all rates of 3 per cent and below should be eliminated (a view strongly opposed by the EC); that remaining tariffs should be cut by a formula which set 38 per cent as the maximum rate of reduction; and that the linear method be supplemented with request-and-offer balancing. And Switzerland, with the support of most of the developing countries, offered a variant of the formula it proposed and had been adopted during the Tokyo round (Hoda, 2001: 33–35).

On 28 January 1987 the Group of Negotiations on Goods (GNG) set up 14 negotiating groups, each of which was to be chaired independently and treated as a separate entity. Thirteen of the groups covered a particular aspect of the negotiations: tariffs; non-tariff measures; tropical products; natural resource-based products; textiles and clothing; agriculture; GATT articles; safeguards; MTN agreements and arrangements; dispute settlement; subsidies and countervailing measures; trade-related aspects of intellectual property rights; and trade-related investment measures. A fourteenth group was convened to address the Functioning of the GATT System (FOGS) with a view to its improvement and further codification (Reif, 1995: 6). The creation of FOGS was particularly important, not only because of its role in the decision – later in the round – to establish the WTO, but also because it reflected a concerted effort on the part of middle power-contracting parties to curtail the domination of the GATT by the US and EC. As Ostry puts it, the 'middle powers recognized that the alternative to a rule-based system would be a power-based system and, lacking power, they had the most to lose' (Ostry, 1997: 192–193).

Despite this level of organisation, by the Montreal mid-term review (5–9 December 1988) the negotiations had reverted to form and the meeting ended in deadlock. Although agreement had been reached on the immediate implementation of improved dispute settlement procedures, some concessions on market access for tropical products, and the Trade Policy Review Mechanism (providing for the periodic review of national trade policies), the contracting parties failed to agree on whether the negotiations would be conducted via a formula or a request-and-offer basis. Instead, four broad principles guided the negotiations: (i) tariff reductions and/or eliminations at least as ambitious as those achieved during the Tokyo round; (ii) more extensive binding of tariffs; (iii) that appropriate credit be given to the binding of tariffs as well as any liberalisation implemented since the beginning of the round; and (iv) the phased reduction of tariffs over specified periods (Hoda, 2001: 35). Moreover, in spite of much background work and an intervention by the Chair of the group, the negotiations on natural resource-based products stalled and talks in this area were transferred into the tariffs group; and disagreements persisted in the negotiations over safeguards and on textiles and clothing.

The Montreal meeting was perhaps most notable for the deadlock generated by the agriculture negotiations. The US opened the negotiations with a demand for all agricultural subsidies and all ORs on agricultural imports to be phased out over a period of ten years, and a harmonisation of health and safety measures – the so-called 'zero-zero' option. Whereas, the EC sought to negotiate on an item-by-item basis focusing on a perceived need to 'rebalance' tariffs on agricultural produce, thereby targeting US tariff peaks (but which also enabled it to reintroduce tariffs – which had previously been eliminated – on non-cereal animal feed in exchange for improved access to EC cereal markets). Japan also showed reluctance in the opening stages of the negotiations, stressing the need to protect its rice producers on the grounds that rice plays a unique role in Japanese culture and diet (the so-called multifunctionality argument). Japan nevertheless strongly supported measures to reduce export subsidies. The opening positions of the major players proved insurmountable. In the end the meeting failed to complete the review and the negotiations were thrown into crisis. Indeed, it was not until the following April that the mid-term review was completed.

Despite the glimmer of hope provided by the US negotiators dropping their demand for the zero-zero option during the resumed mid-term review in April 1989, by July 1990 'serious fears' that a deal was unlikely to be struck and the round concluded by the December 1990 deadline had begun to emerge (see Winters, 1990: 1300). Adding further to the tension was the Cairns group's[2] stated position that their agreement to the inclusion of, and liberalisation in, all of the 13 other negotiating groups was contingent upon significant reductions in agricultural protectionism (Healy *et al.*, 1998: ch. 1).

Tensions again came to a head at the December 1990 Brussels ministerial meeting. The meeting had been intended to mark the conclusion of the Uruguay round. Yet, while the limited progress so far achieved had called this into question, few had expected that the meeting would collapse. Most newsworthy were the disagreements between the US and EC that caused the round to stall; but the meeting also witnessed demonstrations (some violent) by 30,000 largely European farmers over proposed cuts in the EC's subsidy regime (Jackson and Sykes, 1997: 3; Sampson, 2001: 5).

In what has become a familiar pattern, the Brussels meeting collapsed due to deeply entrenched positions on agriculture. Not only were there significant differences between, on the one hand the EC, and on the other the US and the Cairns group, over the extent of cuts in export subsidies and domestic support, but disagreements also raged over: the base year to be taken for calculating subsidy reductions; the exact process by which quotas, import bans and other trade-distorting measures were to be converted into tariffs (the so-called tariffication process); and the extent to which tariff levels could be 'rebalanced' prior to the entry into force of the Agreement on Agriculture. Rival positions were further entrenched by the inability of the EC to show any flexibility in its position. The EC's position was bound from within by a move to the Right on farm issues during Germany's first post-reunification general election and from outside by the demonstrations that plagued the ministerial. Matters were made worse by an awkward political climate caused by the shadow of the Iraqi invasion of Kuwait and a looming US-led response. Instead of a conclusion to the round, the meeting produced what at the time looked to be its most difficult moment (see Ungphakorn, 1994). A solution was, however, at hand.

The Dunkel text and the concept of a 'single undertaking'

In an attempt to revive the negotiations in the wake of the Brussels meeting, Arthur Dunkel oversaw the drafting of a working text intended to navigate between the US and EC positions. The intention was to break the Brussels impasse by bringing together a series of concessions across various sectors and binding them together in a single undertaking. As Odell and Eichengreen put it, '[b]y obtaining a credible commitment on services and intellectual property, the United States might be willing to compromise on agriculture. By obtaining concessions from Europe on agricultural trade, the Cairns Group might be willing to compromise on services' (Odell and Eichengreen, 1998: 188; see also Odell, 2005: 437).

Significantly, the Dunkel text (as the draft became known) also comprised a charter for a new trade organisation (Jackson and Sykes, 1997: 4). In April 1990 Canadian trade minister John Crosbie tabled a proposal arguing that the GATT no longer offered a sufficient means of administering the what-looked-at-the-time-to-be the likely results of the Uruguay round and that a Multilateral Trade Organisation (MTO) be established for that purpose. The idea was not that the GATT would cease to exist – it was envisaged that the General Agreement would remain the cornerstone of multilateral trade regulation; merely that the operationalisation of Article XXV (Joint Action by the Contracting Parties) would no longer serve as the means by which the burgeoning array of agreements would be administered.

The Dunkel text was strongly opposed by a number of developing countries. Summarising the G77 position, Chakravarthi Raghavan argued that the 'concept of a "single undertaking" had been introduced at a "very late stage" and was tantamount to "breach of good faith". It was not part of the basis of negotiations and had been introduced to force Third World countries to accept all the results of the Round or opt out of the system' (Raghavan, 1991). Most considered that the introduction of these new areas would be of greater benefit to the industrialised countries than their developing counterparts; that a move in this direction was incommensurate with the GATT's traditional focus on 'at-the-border' measures and thus threatened to affect domestic political-economic organisation to an unprecedented and unacceptable degree; and that, with the exception of services, these issues had little place in a *trade* agreement. Instead, it was argued, the GATT should focus on resolving those issues that remained anomalous: namely agriculture, and textiles and clothing. Suspicions also reigned as to the motives behind the introduction of trade-related disciplines. Regulations to counter intellectual property piracy through the codification of international standards were interpreted by some as an attack on the economic base of many developing countries as well as a means by which discriminatory activity could be hidden behind the dispute settlement process. Moreover, the negotiation of an agreement on trade-related investment measures was deemed by some to be a precursor for wider investment liberalisation (Sauvé, 2000: 85) leading ultimately to its future incorporation as a key feature of a significantly extended system of trade regulation.

Nor was the text sufficiently persuasive to bridge the transatlantic divide. While EC negotiators were willing to make some concessions they remained unconvinced that any new undertaking would be sufficiently robust in ensuring US compliance with the rulings of GATT panels. Moreover, the European position on services was complicated by French charges that extensive liberalisation of the sector posed cultural risks, particularly in cinematography. In the end a combination of internal EC pressure and a deal brokered for the reform of the CAP (via the implementation of the MacSharry plan – see Patterson, 1997) proved sufficient to break the deadlock. The result was the infamous Blair House Accord (named after the US President's official guest-house where the talks took place) amending aspects of the Dunkel text (which the EC had rejected just three days after it had been tabled albeit that the text continued to structure the negotiations).

Agriculture was not, however, the only obstacle that needed careful navigation during the Uruguay round. Disagreements among the quad on industrial tariffs also contributed to the round's protraction. By January 1990 it had become clear that agreement on the negotiating modalities for industrial products could not be reached. Thereafter the negotiations limped along in piecemeal fashion and were eventually halted by the failure of the Brussels ministerial meeting. A breakthrough in the negotiations was finally reached in Tokyo in July 1993 when the US, EU, Japan and Canada agreed (via the so-called Tokyo accord) to eliminate tariff and non-tariff barriers in pharmaceuticals, construction equipment, medical equipment, steel, beer, furniture, farm equipment and spirits; the harmonisation of tariffs among the group in chemical products, a target of 50 per cent on tariffs over 15 per cent (subject to exceptions); and tariff cuts of at least one-third in all other products (Hoda, 2001: 37).

Concluding Uruguay

The final days of the Uruguay round played out in crisis-laden fashion. As had been the case in the Kennedy round, the deadline of 15 December 1993 was dictated by the date at which US fast-track authority was set to expire (itself the result of a two-year extension), and heightened political contestation resulted from the absence of clear and precise rules governing the round, and the brinkmanship, grandstanding, and issue linkage that had come to characterise GATT negotiations. Agriculture was once again the fulcrum of disagreement, though services, textiles and clothing, and market access in industrial goods continued to play a role; and the threat that the US would withdraw from the round and pursue its trade objectives bilaterally and regionally in the context of NAFTA and APEC added additional drama (Odell and Eichengreen, 1998: 188, 191–192; Kapoor, 2004: 528).

By the autumn of 1993 the EC was pressing hard for the Blair House Accord to be reopened. This prompted a second, much wider round of hostility. The Group of Rio[3] stated that '[t]he Blair House Accord represents a weakening of the Final Draft Act and takes us further from the agricultural liberalization that our nations seek' (*UPI*, 18 September 1993). A joint press release by the US President and the Australian Prime Minister 'strongly urge[d] the European Community not to reopen the Blair House Accord on agricultural trade. . . . We need to move forward not backward, to complete the Round and to give the world economy a much-needed boost' (Office of the Press Secretary, 14 September 1993). And the Cairns group (1993) warned that:

> The negotiations on agriculture cannot be completed without the full involvement of the Cairns Group and all the other parties concerned. As major stakeholders in world agricultural trade the Group insists that agriculture is not simply a trans-Atlantic affair. Successful completion of the task in agriculture will require the negotiation of commitments which expand market access. It will also require rapid and final acceptance of all the Draft Final Act provisions to liberalise agricultural trade. . . . The immediate task in reaching a successful conclusion to the negotiations is to secure a substantial market access package which expands trading opportunities for all participants. . . . The Draft Final Act remains the basis for concluding the negotiations. The Cairns Group is not party to the Blair House accord, containing proposals which would dilute the

Draft Final Act. The Group can only take a final position on the Blair House accord in appropriate multilateral negotiations when it has been tabled and all of the market access outcomes are known and can thus be evaluated. Notwithstanding this, it is with alarm that we note the further efforts to weaken the Draft Final Act disciplines on agriculture [by reopening the Blair House accord]. Clearly such efforts seriously jeopardise an overall acceptable outcome on agriculture.

Tensions were heightened further by French Prime Minister Edouard Balladur's announcement that France could not sign the Uruguay round accords on the basis of the negotiations thus far, and that changes had to be made to (principally) the agreements on agriculture and services (to enable France, on the grounds of cultural security, to restrict imports of foreign – primarily American – films and television programmes), as well as to the agreements on trade in civil aircraft, and textiles and clothing. Instead, France proposed that agriculture be temporarily excluded from the negotiations so that the round could be concluded on time. Not surprisingly, this proposal was flatly rejected by then GATT DG Peter Sutherland (*Trade News Bulletin*, 18 October 1993).

Adding to the sense of urgency and contributing to the impending sense of doom surrounding the negotiation's final outcome, in a letter to USTR Kantor, the American Corngrowers Association, the Farmers Union Milk Marketing Cooperative, the Georgia Peanut Commission, the Institute for Agriculture and Trade Policy, the League of Rural Voters, the National Farmers Organisation, the National Farmers Union, the National Family Farm Coalition and the Rural Coalition urged the US to pursue changes to the agreement on agriculture, warning of congressional rejection should they not be undertaken (*Trade News Bulletin*, 9 November 1993); EC foreign ministers issued a joint statement supporting France's position and encouraging a reopening of the Blair House Accord; deadlines for the conclusion of each of the agreements were continually missed despite acceptance of the draft texts for the MTO and the dispute settlement procedures (*Financial Times*, 17 November 1993); the conclusion of NAFTA and suggestions that APEC represented a 'fall-back option' for the US should the Uruguay round fail placed additional pressure on the negotiations; France continued to hold out for further concessions on agriculture (*Financial Times*, 22 November 1993); and a series of bilateral talks in the last week of November 1993 between the US and EC failed to produce an agreement.

A breakthrough finally emerged when the US announced that it may be willing to make two minor changes to the Blair House Accord, increasing the flexibility for the implementation of export subsidy reductions and an extension of the peace clause (*Wall Street Journal*, 1 December 1993). Predictably, the prospect that the agreement on agriculture would be watered down further was met with derision from developing and agricultural producing countries alike. The breakthrough was, however, short-lived. In classic GATT fashion, a crisis emerged one week prior to the 15 December deadline during which talks between the US and EU on agriculture, services and civil aircraft were suspended, 'upsetting' nearly all of the other negotiating parties (*Trade News Bulletin*, 7 December 1993) before an agreement was finally brokered whereby modifications would be made to the Blair House Accord (Blair House II) but wherein a decision was taken to hold remaining disagreements over until the new Organisation was established (*Financial Times*, 15 December 1993). Needless to say, the further watering down of the agreement on agriculture was met with much consternation.

As had been the case with the Tokyo round, the conclusion of the Uruguay talks failed to draw a line under the negotiations. Although Peter Sutherland, Chair of the TNC, formally closed the round on 15 December 1993, negotiations still continued. Mindful of this, Sutherland declared that any additional agreements reached could only add to the bargain struck and that there would be no withdrawals. Prior to the April 1994 Marrakesh ministerial meeting withdrawals, nevertheless, occurred. Notably, in tit-for-tat fashion the EC withdrew from its commitment on non-ferrous metals and trucks on the basis that the US had retreated from its position on tariff offers (Hoda, 2001: 50).

Negotiations within the round were not, however, the only slice of drama surrounding the WTO's creation. As important was the debate that unfolded in the US over American membership of, and participation in, a trade organisation. This inevitably raised the spectres of the ITO and OTC. While the failure of the US to ratify a third trade institution may have seen the contracting parties fall back on the GATT, the General Agreement's utility as a vehicle for dealing with trade issues beyond tariff barrier reductions was limited. Moreover, the GATT's narrow focus, though once of key importance to the US, offered little long-term commercial benefit. Rather, US economic opportunities lay in the liberalisation of services and the global codification of patent law among others. Yet, these opportunities would remain unrealised if the GATT had become the fall-back option since, in much the same way as the Tokyo codes, being a signatory to the General Agreement did not require that contracting parties be bound by additional agreements. As a result, the realisation of US trade opportunities lay in the WTO's ratification; and Congress duly obliged (Odell and Eichengreen, 1998: 186, 192, 195; see also Jackson, 1997; Pigman, 1998).

Codifying asymmetry: the Uruguay bargain

With Congressional approval came the further development of post-war trade regulation. But it resulted not just from the successful creation of a trade organisation and the deepening, widening and codification of international trade law. It also resulted from the further consolidation and amplification of asymmetries of opportunity in the WTO's legal framework. This was made possible by the conclusion of a single undertaking that bound together movement forward in new areas with remedial action in existing provisions. Intrinsic to this single undertaking was the extension of certain developmentally sensitive provisions. These included: a reduced level of obligation; a more flexible approach to the implementation of timetables; the empowering of developing countries to contribute their 'best endeavour'; a greater degree of favourable treatment for the least developed; and a renewed emphasis on technical assistance and training.

Yet these measures were mere window dressing. At its core the political bargain that underpinned the round's conclusion was not of equal opportunity. Uruguay saw the inclusion of agreements on agriculture, and textiles and clothing within a wider umbrella of trade agreements administered by the WTO and the inclusion of a range of provisions throughout the Organisation's legal framework designed to ease some of the pressure for reform generated by the new rules. It also resulted in the adoption of agreements on services (the General Agreement on Trade in Services – GATS), intellectual property (the Agreement on Trade Related Intellectual Property Rights – TRIPs) and investment measures (the Agreement on Trade Related Investment Measures – TRIMs). While the inclusion of agriculture, and textiles and clothing rectified a modicum of an existing imbalance and the sprinkling of development-sensitive provisions was a step forward from the old era, the introduction of new rules in services, intellectual property and investment measures simply generated additional asymmetry. Whereas under Uruguay rules developing states could finally hope to benefit from a measure of liberalisation in agriculture and in textiles and clothing, their lack of capacity and resources ensured that this was not to be the case in the new areas. However, the potential fruits of Uruguay were much larger for the industrial states. Not only were they existing beneficiaries of trade liberalisation in areas covered by GATT rules, their economic make-up ensured they would be the principal beneficiaries of the market opportunities presented by the liberalisation of services and investment measures, and the codification of trade-related intellectual property rights in international trade law. What Uruguay clearly did, then, was to further divide up the arenas of economic activity in which member states could specialise and, in so doing, accentuated the problems facing developing countries seeking to diversify their export portfolios. Moreover, not only were the industrial states better suited to take advantage of these new rules, their ability to use the market opportunities presented therein enabled them to develop a competitive advantage over future market entrants. The creation of the WTO had brought with it an extension of core privileges peppered with a sprinkling of measures designed to mollify the periphery.

It is also important to note that the sheer extent of commercial coverage achieved by the Uruguay round resulted from the deployment of a quintessential trade policy strategy – agenda overload. One tactic used by the quad (and the EC and US in particular) was to pad out the negotiating agenda by adding an ever greater number of issues (the signalling of labour standards and investment issues during the Uruguay round are just two of a number of examples of this). Although it was widely acknowledged among sponsoring delegations that these agenda items would not result in negotiations, they nevertheless created a perception among the wider membership that successes in removing these items were victories in whittling down the extent of the agenda. In this way, these 'superfluous' items – though they might be treated as desiderata by their proponents – played a key role as negotiating levers; and their ejection encouraged the perception that concessions had been given. This, in turn, increased pressure on the wider membership to agree to what remained. Even before the conclusion of the Uruguay round, for instance, then EC Trade Commissioner Leon Brittan suggested that the next round should include restrictive business practices and cartels on its agenda in the likely knowledge that negotiations on these issues, within the context of the GATT or WTO, would be unlikely (see Hoekman, 1993: 1536). Likewise, EU and US support for the inclusion of what were to become known as the four Singapore issues (investment, government procurement, competition policy and trade facilitation) in the DDA was eventually whittled down to just one (trade facilitation) in the wake of the Cancún meeting. And during the Tokyo round contracting parties debated at length the relative merits of beginning negotiations on government procurement (see Winham, 1986: 138–141).

Four other facets of the Uruguay bargain are noteworthy – (i) the continuing presence of the Tokyo codes; (ii) the reform of the GATT's dispute settlement procedures; (iii) the Organisation's decision-making procedures; and (iv) the WTO's contribution to global economic governance – since they illustrate the extent to which the conclusion of the Uruguay round resulted in the significant deepening and widening of post-war multilateral trade regulation and the locking in of asymmetries of economic opportunity therein.

The Tokyo codes/plurilateral agreements

A secondary but nevertheless important dimension of the Uruguay bargain lay in the continuation of four of the Tokyo codes in the form of 'plurilateral' agreements. These were the agreement on trade in civil aircraft; the agreement on government procurement; the international dairy agreement; and the international agreement on bovine meat. Both the international dairy agreement and the international agreement on bovine meat were phased out by the end of 1997 whereupon both areas became the subject of more general WTO rules (under the agreement on agriculture). However, both the agreement on trade in civil aircraft and the agreement on government procurement remain in force albeit that they are not subject to the single undertaking and are only binding on their respective signatories.

Dispute settlement

Much celebrated was the creation of the Dispute Settlement Mechanism (DSM). Yet, as with the WTO's legal framework more widely, the Organisation's creation merely codified and built upon GATT provisions. Not surprisingly, in so doing, it also preserved a measure of the power-orientated approach to dispute settlement that prevailed under the GATT. As Donna Lee puts it, reform of the GATT's dispute settlement procedures did:

> little to alter the politics of dispute settlement. . . . The political issues that tested the credibility of the GATT dispute settlement – the lack of transparency in procedures, the dominance of powerful states, the weakness of developing countries, the marginalisation of the least developed members, the relative lack of domestic legislative input, and the absence of civil society contribution – remain. Dispute settlement is still an opaque intergovernmental process, dominated by developed states. While there are much lauded claims of a shift from a power-orientated diplomacy towards a rule-orientated diplomacy . . . in the WTO the rules, norms and practice of dispute settlement are still largely determined by power politics.
>
> (Lee, 2004: 121–122)

Rather than departing wholesale from the GATT, the Uruguay provisions sought only to build upon the 'consultation' (Article XXI) and 'nullification and impairment' (Article XXIII) procedures of the General Agreement in an effort to approximate more closely a formal system of dispute settlement. The first of these provisions – consultation – merely established a convention that when in dispute contracting parties would first engage in bilateral negotiations designed to reach an amicable solution. This was complemented by the nullification and impairment provision empowering a contracting party to ask the contracting parties to preside over the settlement of a dispute and, under certain conditions, authorise the implementation of sanctions. As these provisions alone proved insufficient for settling disputes between the contracting parties, the GATT's dispute settlement procedures evolved through time.

Until the early 1950s disputes were handled by means of establishing working parties. These working parties were designed to move towards the settlement of a dispute by bringing together the parties to a dispute with other contracting parties in a process of negotiation. However, from 1952 onwards working parties were replaced by a practice of establishing 'panels' to examine the substance of a dispute. Thereafter the GATT's dispute settlement procedures were codified through a series of decisions and understandings. Significant among these was the November 1979 Understanding Regarding Notification, Consultation, Dispute Settlement and Surveillance, and the accompanying annex relating to the Agreed Description of the

Customary Practice of the GATT in the Field of Dispute Settlement (see Petersmann, 1997: 71; Jackson, 1998: 166).

The GATT dispute settlement procedures were, however, plagued by the inability of the contracting parties to enforce the recommendations of the panels. The main problem was that contracting parties were not bound by panel decisions. Rather, they were able to exercise a right of veto over panel recommendations; and they were not obliged to implement the recommendations within a specified time period. This absence of compunction provided fertile ground for the rise of two kinds of unilateralism. First, contracting parties frequently ignored or omitted to implement panel recommendations, and thus continued to pursue a course of illegal action. Second, and perhaps as a consequence of the first, certain states sought to use, and indeed strengthen, particular aspects of national legislation in an effort to provide an *ad hoc* sanctioning mechanism designed to persuade acting contracting parties to comply with what these states deemed to be 'correct' interpretations of GATT rules. Most notable in this category was Section 301 of the US's 1974 Trade Act (amended 1988).

The evolution of GATT dispute settlement procedures culminated in the incorporation of the Understanding on Rules and Procedures Governing the Settlement of Disputes (known as the Dispute Settlement Understanding – DSU) into the WTO's legal framework. The DSU provides for the establishment of panels designed to mediate disputes arising between or among members; to refer disputes to an Appellate Body; and to survey the implementation of rulings and recommendations. The DSU also enables members to take retaliatory action against illegally acting states, or to request compensation for such action (see Wilkinson, 2000: 118–121).

However, the DSM also has a second function. It binds together the various aspects of the WTO's legal framework. Violations of any of the WTO's rules may be subject to a DSB investigation. This in itself, and any action forthcoming therefrom, serves to lock in modes of behaviour given rise to by WTO rules. This, in turn, further entrenches the asymmetries in the WTO's legal framework. Thomas Brewer and Stephen Young, and Robert Hudec also argue that the plight of developing countries has been further compounded by their relative deficiencies in legal expertise and by the sheer volume of complaints brought against them since the Organisation's establishment (Hudec, 1998; Brewer and Young, 1999; also Lee, 2004).

Decision-making in the WTO

The conclusion of the Uruguay round left much of the GATT's decision-making structure (and culture) in place. Although the Establishing Agreement set out voting procedures in three instances – relating to changes proposed to the core principles of the WTO (wherein unanimity is required); the implementation of the specific provisions or in respect of a waiver (requiring a three-quarters majority); and an amendment to the *Final Act* in cases relating to issues other than its core principles (requiring a two-thirds majority) – and put into place a one-member-one-vote system, governance by consensus has remained the order of the day. Moreover, the Uruguay round did not result in the *formalisation* of the GATT's ruling number. A proposal that an executive committee be created, much along the lines of that proposed for the ITO and OTC, was flatly rejected. That said, the remnants of great power domination live on in the residue of the GATT-era CG18 (formally inactive since 1987 albeit morphed into other groups of like-minded states), the continued domination of the quad (plus India and Brazil, depending on how entrenched and intractable movement forward with the trade agenda is – see their role during the negotiation of the July 2004 package and the Hong Kong ministerial meeting discussed in the next chapter) and the industrial states generally.

Global economic governance

Although much of the legal framework of the WTO deals with the detail of trade regulation, it also contains important provisions which locate the Organisation at the heart of the system of global economic governance (see Wilkinson, 2002a). The stillbirth of the ITO not only put paid to the first attempt at formalising international trade regulation, it also inhibited the establishment and functioning of a system of global economic governance. The GATT's contribution to the development of such a system was relatively small, providing for co-operation with the IMF in instances relating to 'exchange questions within the jurisdiction of the Fund and questions of quantitative restrictions and other trade measures within the jurisdiction of the Contracting Parties' (GATT, 1947: Article XV, Paragraph 1) – though of course behind-the-scenes co-ordination took place with other Organisations. In this respect, the creation of the WTO proved more than just about the regulation of international trade. It also has a major role in the governance of the global economy and, in many ways, it fulfils as well as expands upon the role envisaged for the ITO.

The blueprint for the WTO's role in this system of governance is set out in the Declaration on the Contribution of the World Trade Organisation to Achieving Greater Coherence in Global Economic Policy Making annexed to the Establishing Agreement, though the full extent of the system is realised only when provisions scattered throughout the Agreements administered by the Organisation are drawn together. The central and primary feature of this blueprint is the development of mutually supportive policies and the removal of 'cross-conditionality' among the WTO, IMF and World Bank. The purpose of this co-operation is to harmonise the conditions under which members and prospective members deal with each Organisation, as well as to consolidate the character of global economic governance.

The drawing together of the work of these organisations is supplemented by other provisions in the WTO's legal framework establishing linkages with particular bodies deemed intrinsic to the general goal of achieving greater coherence in global economic policymaking, but which relate to specific aspects of the WTO's remit. For instance, the TRIPs empowers the WTO to nurture a closer relationship with the World Intellectual Property Organisation (WIPO). Similarly, the GATS contains a set of provisions enabling the WTO to strengthen links with the International Telecommunications Union (ITU) and the International Organisation of Standards (IOS). Moreover, since commencing operations the WTO has begun to develop limited relationships with the United Nations Environment Programme (UNEP), the Office International des Epizooties (The World Organisation for Animal Health), and UNCTAD. The development of these more limited relationships has been made possible by a set of provisions empowering the WTO to establish relations with unspecified organisations. It should be noted, however, that the WTO's legal framework, unlike that of the ITO, does not contain provisions for the development of a co-operative and meaningful relationship with the ILO (see Stigliani, 2000; Wilkinson *et al.*, 2001).

The result of these provisions has been to develop a formal system of global economic governance centred on a core of three institutions – the WTO, IMF and World Bank – supplemented by a supporting cast of the WIPO, ITU and IOS and a host of other organisations with which relations are established on an *ad hoc* basis. This is not, however, the extent to which the WTO's establishment has nurtured the development of a system of global economic governance. The WTO's legal framework requires that all regional free trade areas and customs unions in which its member states participate register with the Organisation; and it also requires that the rules of these regional arrangements do not contravene WTO rules, but rather that they are broadly complementary with the goal of trade liberalisation. The result has been the emergence of a coherent set of relations among international and regional organisations organised into a multi-layered system of economic governance that further locks in the asymmetries in the WTO's legal framework.

The argument so far

The processes of reform put in place during the Tokyo round and continued in the Uruguay negotiations resulted in the production of a much consolidated, significantly more robust and considerably extended system of multilateral trade regulation under the WTO. Importantly, however, this system does not significantly depart from the manner in which trade was regulated in the preceding era. Rather, the new system retains, and indeed builds upon, much of the GATT's character. The WTO's legal framework remains an instrument created to serve the economic interests of its dominant members albeit peppered with provisions created to ensure the acquiescence of middle-income, developing and least developed states. The new institution retains the absence of clear, precise and detailed rules governing negotiations or ministerial meetings. In addition, while formal decision-making procedures exist, much is decided outside of official fora of which green room meetings and mini-ministerials are but the most notorious and attention-grabbing of venues. Most important of all, crisis continues to play a key role in the institution's development. Not only were the monetary and commercial crises of the late 1960s and early 1970s an apposite backdrop to the GATT's reform, the collapse of ministerial meetings (as in 1982, 1988 and 1990) and the sense of fear generated by perceptions of their consequences has encouraged the continuous driving forward of the trade agenda. Moreover, the causes of deadlock and collapse during ministerial meetings are the result of inevitable political contestations generated by opaque decision-making procedures, great power domination and asymmetries of opportunity (and, in extension, vastly differing trade performances) that have emerged and become entrenched features of multilateral trade regulation throughout its development. Somewhat ironically, it is these crises combined with a fear of what might happen should the trade bicycle be allowed to stall and the lack of an alternative machinery through which trade objectives might be realised, which give rise to moments of reflection and renewed energy that result in the further extension of the trade agenda and the amplification of asymmetries of opportunity therein. It is to the perpetuation of these asymmetries under the current DDA that we now turn.

5 Perpetuating asymmetry

The collapse of ministerial meetings and the Doha Development Agenda

The WTO's first three years of operation appeared to contain much to celebrate. The Organisation's very creation represented a triumph over the discordant politics of the Uruguay round and the narrow and élitist fashion in which trade had been liberalised in the post-war era. Its legal framework was seen by many as a celebration of this new, more certain, predictable and equitable era: the extension of trade rules to include agriculture and textiles and clothing, the conclusion of the GATS, the revision and extension of the GATT, and the adoption of disciplines on trade-related intellectual property rights (under the TRIPs) and trade-related investment measures (under the TRIMs), overseen by a much revised, and more importantly contractually binding dispute settlement mechanism (DSM) all bound together in a single undertaking combined to support this view. The Organisation's establishment also marked the completion of a post-war economic architecture nearly fifty years in the making, bringing greater coherence to global economic policymaking by drawing together the work of the WTO with that of the IMF and World Bank, as well as with other cognate institutions: the WIPO, ITU, the Office International des Epizooties, and IOS among others (see Wilkinson, 2002a). Moreover, the end of the Cold War and the notification of intentions to commence accession negotiations by many of the states of the former Soviet Union, its Central and East European satellites and their socialist brethren in East Asia promised to bring former enemies into the fold; and the possibilities presented by finally securing China's re-entry to the multilateral trading system caused much excitement among those hoping to benefit from the possibilities presented by this gigantic emerging market.

However, the euphoria that accompanied the WTO's creation and its first few years of operation belay a more turbulent picture and one that pointed more to politics as usual than a new era in multilateral trade regulation. Just five months into the WTO's life cycle, a dispute broke out between the US and Japan over the latter's import régime for cars and automotive components. This was followed in quick succession by disputes between, variously, the US, EU and Japan over alcoholic beverages, grain, bananas, beef, photographic film, aircraft 'hush-kits', foreign sales corporations, anti-dumping, steel and aircraft subsidy régimes. Tensions flared between India and the US, Australia, New Zealand and the EU over India's refusal to shorten its phase-out period for import restrictions implemented to ease balance-of-payments difficulties. Concerns began to be raised that developing countries were structurally disadvantaged in using the WTO's dispute settlement mechanism not only as a result of basic asymmetries in legal expertise and resources but also by a decision to allow *amicus curiae* submissions from private individuals and organisations (see Smith, 2004).[1] The US Congress began raising questions over the ratio of 'losses' to 'wins' in disputes mediated by the DSM. In addition, although it was eventually settled through bilateral consultations, the US threatened to boycott a WTO dispute settlement panel in response to an EU complaint over the possibility for discrimination against goods produced by third parties using materials of Cuban origin following the passing of the Helms-Burton act in 1996 (*Inside US Trade*, 21 February 1997; US State Department, 11 April 1997).

True to form, the WTO's first experience of negotiations saw collapse and heightened political contestation prior to the conclusion of agreements on financial services and basic telecommunications. A US walk-out in 1995 designed to 'send a message that nations must submit meaningful market-opening commitments if they want negotiations to bear fruit' caused a two-year interruption in the financial services negotiations (*Bridges*, 24 March 1997; see also WTO, 1995b); and the basic telecommunications negotiations were marred by a Canadian stance limiting the percentage of foreign ownership of its telecommunications firms (a move which saw Mexico and Korea follow suit). Although individually hailed as major successes, the agreements were more indicative of a turn back towards 'Tokyo *à la carte*' than 'Uruguay single undertaking'. Each agreement sought only to bind its individual signatories (70 in the case of the financial services agreement and 69 for the basic telecommunications agreement – WTO, 1997a, 1997b) rather than the membership as a whole. Moreover, their conclusion raised concerns that the pursuit of single-sector negotiations would mitigate the gains that could be made from cross-sector trade-offs available during more general negotiations; give industrial lobby groups a stronger voice in the negotiating process; and actively disadvantage members (largely developing countries) whose national telecommunications industries were comparatively underdeveloped (and competitively disadvantaged as a result) (see Simpson and Wilkinson, 2002). Of course, they also paved the way for WTO-wide regulation of these sectors as part of a future single undertaking.

The WTO's creation could of course do little to alter the marked differentials in the human resources that were apparent across the member states, inevitably calling into question the ability of the smallest and most vulnerable to participate in the staffing of the Organisation's councils, committees and working groups and, in so doing, have an influence therein. As late as April 1997, only 97 of the WTO's then 131 members had one or more full-time representatives in Geneva. Of these, many had to deal with business at other international organisations as part of their portfolio, thereby reducing the amount of time they could spend on the WTO's various and burgeoning committees. The remaining 34 covered business at the WTO via embassies elsewhere in Europe. This contrasted sharply with permanent delegations of ten or more from Brazil, the US, the EU, Thailand, South Korea and Japan (Blackhurst, 1998: 36).

More damaging perhaps was the 1997 Human Development Report's (HDR) estimation that, despite projected gains of between $212 to $510 billion resulting from the Uruguay round for the period 1995 to 2001, 'least developed countries [stood] to lose up to $600 million a year and Sub-Saharan Africa $1.2 billion'; 'three-quarters of the World's people [would] get only a quarter to a third of the income gains generated'; and the persistence of 'bad' trade rules (identified as WTO rules on tariffs, non-tariff barriers, textiles and clothing, agriculture and trade-related intellectual property rights) offered the world's poorest little prospect of change (UNDP, 1997: 82, 85–87).

Yet the WTO's problems were not confined to the reappearance of, and growth in, tensions among the member states, a return to Tokyo *à la carte* negotiating, persistent asymmetries in human resources, or the forecasting of markedly different economic experiences. Questions about the Organisation's democratic accountability and apparent lack of transparency, its utility as a forum for determining commercial policy and its refusal to deal with social and environmental issues began to be asked by a rapidly expanding and increasingly vociferous number of civil society organisations (see e.g., LeQuesne, 1996; Hale, 1999; McGrew, 1999; Wallach and Woodall, 2004; also Wilkinson, 2005). This criticism was manifest most notably in demonstrations during the WTO's Geneva and (more spectacularly) Seattle ministerial meetings but it also became a central feature of less visible debt relief campaigns and other grassroots initiatives.

What the veil of the WTO's honeymoon period obscured, then, was a return to trade politics as usual blended with the emergence of a measure of public disaffection. Yet each of these sources of tension did not by themselves, or in combination, rekindle turbulence in trade politics; rather they all resulted from the way in which multilateral trade regulation was fashioned and has developed through time. As the previous chapter clearly shows, what the Uruguay round had produced was not actually a more equitable framework governing international trade; nor had it resulted in the creation of an institution distinct from the GATT in its practices and ways of operating as well as the kinds of behaviour that its rules, norms and decision-making procedures gave rise to. Although important developments did occur, they served to consolidate and entrench the marked asymmetry evident at the creation of the GATT and extended throughout its tenure. This, in turn, has fuelled political contestation and imbued (as we see below) WTO ministerial meetings with a propensity to collapse (as in Seattle and Cancún) and embedded this propensity in the institution's evolutionary trajectory. The principal difference was that in the post-Uruguay era trade regulation was now much grander in scale.

This chapter explores the major developments in trade politics since the creation of the WTO. It illustrates throughout how the nature of the GATT's creation and subsequent development has been carried through into the WTO and how that institutional evolution profoundly affects the way in which member states interact and the bargains that have been produced as a result of their negotiating. In so doing, the chapter also illustrates how the collapse of ministerial meetings and a post-crisis politics in the later GATT years has come to play a unique role in the development of multilateral trade regulation; and how this pattern of development promises to perpetuate if not amplify the asymmetries of opportunity given rise to by WTO rules during the DDA. As broad chronological markers, the chapter tracks these developments by focusing on the politics of trade across the WTO's first six ministerial meetings (see Table 5.1) – the most visible instances of political contestation – but crucially it does this in an historical institutional context.

Singapore (December 1996)

Tensions among WTO members were much in evidence in the run-up to the WTO's first ministerial meeting in Singapore. Debate centred initially on the purpose of such meetings with members agreeing that they should comprise sessions devoted to ministerial speeches as well as set-aside time for ministers to discuss pressing trade issues. Thereafter, discussions focused on the content of the Singapore agenda with debate centring on the relative merits of various 'non-papers' (documents intended as food for thought) putting forward arguments for possible agenda items. The most prominent among these included a proposal by the ASEAN countries on issues relating to the full implementation of the Uruguay round agreements and difficulties arising therefrom; US and Korean proposals on government procurement; a Canadian proposal on investment; a Hong Kong proposal on 'WTO rules in a globalising world' dealing with, among others, anti-dumping and rules of origin; EU and Japanese proposals on competition policy; US and Norwegian proposals for an investigation of the relationship between trade liberalisa-

Table 5.1 WTO ministerial meetings

Singapore	9–13 December 1996
Geneva	18–20 May 1998
Seattle	30 November – 3 December 1999
Doha	9–13 November 2001
Cancún	10–14 September 2003
Hong Kong	13–18 December 2005

tion and the protection of core labour standards (see Table 5.2); an Australian proposal on services; Canadian and Australian proposals on tariff liberalisation; and a Korean proposal on regionalism (*SUNS*, 18 July 1996).

Each of the proposals was hotly debated. Much of the developing world pressed for implementation to be the key issue at the ministerial, though they did not share a consensus on the so-called 'new issues' (government procurement, competition policy, investment, trade facilitation, trade and the environment, and labour standards), and many warned against overloading the trade agenda. India strongly opposed suggestions that a working party be set up to explore the issue of investment; the ASEAN countries rejected any WTO involvement in labour issues (citing the ILO as the appropriate forum in which to deal with the issue) and supported an acceleration of the implementation of the provisions of the Agreement on Agriculture; Peru saw implementation as the core issue and showed a willingness to support an exploration of investment. Likewise, the Brazilian delegation saw implementation as key; it supported an examination of investment as a potential WTO issue by a working party; and it was hostile to any involvement by the Organisation in worker rights. Hong Kong also favoured a move on investment. Pakistan and Argentina came out against the labour standards issue; Uruguay and Tunisia indicated lukewarm support for an investigation of the relationship between trade liberalisation and worker rights; and Japan came out strongly in favour of the labour standards issue. Attempts to use the meeting as the precursor to the launch of yet another round of trade negotiations – dubbed by the then EU Trade Commissioner Leon Brittan the 'millennium round' (Brittan, 1996) – so soon after the conclusion of the

Table 5.2 Core labour standards and the relevant ILO conventions

Labour standards	*Relevant ILO conventions*
Freedom of association	No. 87 – The Convention on Freedom of Association and Protection of the Right to Organise (1948)
Right to collective bargaining	No. 98 – The Convention on the Right to Organise and Collective Bargaining (1949)
Prohibition of forced labour	No. 29 – The Convention on Forced Labour (1930)
Restrictions on the usage of child labour	No. 105 – The Convention on the Abolition of Forced Labour (1957) No. 138 – The Convention on Minimum Age (1973)
Non-discrimination in employment	No. 111 – The Convention on Discrimination (Employment and Occupation) (1958) No. 100 – The Convention on Equal Remuneration (1951)

Uruguay round also proved contentious, initially splitting the quad and generating acrimony in middle- and low-income countries.

These emerging tensions were exacerbated by a growing perception that WTO DG Renato Ruggiero was moving beyond the neutrality expected of his position and supporting proposals to extend the Organisation's remit to include worker rights, investment, government procurement, trade facilitation and competition policy (*SUNS*, 5 March 1996). The number of preparatory meetings also drew criticism that they disadvantaged those delegations with insufficient human resources (namely small developing countries) and conspired to forge a consensus on the Singapore agenda in their absence. As Raghavan (1996a) put it:

> [O]nly the Quad countries [have been] able to field bodies to be present at every meeting. . . . While the meetings of the General Council and the three Councils under it (the Goods, Services and TRIPs Councils), take place with full attendance and don't meet simultaneously, meetings of subordinate bodies are quite different. . . . The large number of almost simultaneous meetings . . . has forced the meetings to be scheduled at another conference centre in Geneva, about a kilometre away, complicating the problems of the small delegations of developing countries who have to keep running, not only from one room to another inside the WTO, but from one building to another. Even [those] developing country delegations with several diplomatic personnel have been finding it hard to cope.

In the month preceding the meeting divisions among the members hardened – though they were not as clear-cut as the North/South split portrayed by many. Debate focused on both the draft text of the Singapore ministerial declaration (prepared by the Secretariat and introduced by Ruggiero at an informal Heads of Delegation meeting on 2 November 1996) and on the process by which it was constructed. With regard to the text, three issues proved particularly thorny: (i) the tone of the declaration; (ii) the inclusion of new issues, particularly investment and government procurement; and (iii) labour standards – though the relationship between the WTO's legal framework and Multilateral Environmental Agreements (MEAs), the acceleration and full implementation of commitments made under the Agreement on Textiles and Clothing, the built-in negotiations on agriculture and services, the plight of the least developed countries, and the prospect of a new round were also much debated.

India and the US held diametrically opposed positions on the way in which the declaration sought to frame the contribution of the multilateral trading system to the growth of the world economy. India pressed for the removal of overly rosy language regarding the contribution of the GATT/WTO to world prosperity; while the US demanded the removal of all references to difficulties encountered with the implementation of WTO rules. On new issues, Egypt, Ghana, Haiti, India, Indonesia, Malaysia, Tanzania and Uganda tabled a motion to remove investment from the negotiations due to a lack of consensus despite Ruggiero's assertions that the divisions over this issue 'should be easy to bridge' (*SUNS*, 4 November 1996). In the face of growing hostility (particularly from Malaysia, but also with notable opposition from Thailand, Egypt, Hong Kong and Indonesia), the US delegation made it clear that it would block the entire text of the ministerial declaration if it did not include a reference to labour standards. Australia, Canada, Korea, Morocco, Chile, Argentina, Brazil and the Czech Republic indicated that they were willing to go along with a formulation of words that supported the principle of core labour standards, but which would not put into place a post-ministerial process. The EU delegation, though strongly supporting a WTO investigation of the relationship between trade liberalisation and worker rights at subsequent ministerials, was sharply divided on the issue, with notable opposition to any WTO involvement therein coming from Ian Lang, Head of the UK's Department of Trade and Industry (Lang, 1996).

With regard to the process of drafting the text, three aspects were at issue: (i) the lack of transparency in the consultation process underpinning the refinement of the text, particularly with regard to green room meetings; (ii) the persistent inclusion of controversial issues (particularly investment, government procurement, trade facilitation, labour standards and competition policy) in the text on which there was not a clear consensus; and (iii) the perception that Ruggiero's involvement in the construction of the text favoured the positions of the US and EU.

Not surprisingly, the Singapore meeting opened without a consensus on labour standards, investment, competition policy, government procurement and trade facilitation. Indeed, divisions on the labour standards issue were such that in the immediate run-up to the meeting ILO DG Michel Hansenne's invitation to speak at the ministerial was revoked at the behest of India and Pakistan (*SUNS*, 6 December 1996). More significantly, the meeting witnessed a step-change in the degree to which differences between member states were openly paraded. Media reports attributed this development to anomalies in the preparatory process coupled with a growing confidence among non-Western (and particularly Asian) members to voice their concerns (see Raghavan, 1996b). Yet, while these were no doubt factors in the growth of discord, the politics of the meeting were the inevitable result of the way in which the institution and its development had come to structure member –state interaction. What Singapore produced was a struggle between those seeking to consolidate existing agreements and rectify imbalances therein and those pressing to drive the agenda forward.

The labour standards issue provoked particularly strong feelings. Of the 128 ministerial statements made to the meeting 58 per cent chose to voice an opinion on the issue. Of these, 67.5 per cent registered their lack of support for or outright hostility to a WTO investigation of the issue; and 28.5 per cent were, to varying degrees, supportive of such an initiative.

The remainder merely registered non-committal opinions (see Wilkinson, 2002d). The extent of the negativity towards the labour standards issue at Singapore was reflected in the ministerial declaration. The declaration attempted to settle the issue by declaring the membership's commitment to core labour standards and by identifying the ILO as the appropriate administrative body, but stopped short of any WTO involvement therein. The statement was not, however, without contention. The declaration committed members of the WTO to the observance of core labour standards; it attempted to put an end to suggestions that the WTO have any responsibility in this area; it rejected the use of labour standards as a veil for protectionism; it sought to safeguard the comparative wage advantage of developing countries; and it pointed to the continuation of 'existing collaboration' between the WTO and ILO secretariats (Hughes and Wilkinson, 1998). As the declaration put it:

> We renew our commitment to the observance of internationally recognized core labour standards. The International Labour Organization (ILO) is the competent body to set and deal with these standards, and we affirm our support for its work in promoting them. We believe that economic growth and development fostered by increased trade and further trade liberalization contribute to the promotion of these standards. We reject the use of labour standards for protectionist purposes, and agree that the comparative advantage of countries, particularly low-wage developing countries, must in no way be put into question. In this regard, we note that the WTO and ILO Secretariats will continue their existing collaboration.
>
> (WTO, 1996: paragraph 4)

Most contentious was the assertion that the WTO and ILO would 'continue their existing collaboration'. Although intended merely as a 'throw away line' (Stigliani, 2000: 188), this appeared, to supporters of WTO involvement in the area, to open up an avenue for a future discussion of the issue. Indeed, the potential for further investigation by the WTO drew hostile comments from the Chair of the Singapore Ministerial Conference – Yeo Cheow Tong – who, in his concluding statement, strongly denied that the declaration constituted grounds upon which future discussions could ensue and emphatically shut the door on any further deliberation (Yeo, 1996).

More generally, the Singapore ministerial reflected a patchwork of comprises resulting from political contests thrown into sharp relief in the run-up to and during the meeting; though, true to form, the balance of those compromises was uneven. The declaration was framed in the language of economic development comprising commitments to: (i) address the problems of marginalisation among the least developed; (ii) improve the availability of technical assistance for developing countries; and (iii) put in place a plan of action to facilitate the integration of the least developed countries into the world economy. The text was only moderately congratu-latory about the contribution of the multilateral trading system to world prosperity; and it pointed to, but did not propose action on, the challenges and opportunities of growing global interdependence. The declaration offered textile-exporting members little beyond a restatement of the importance of 'full and faithful' implementation of the Agreement on Textiles and Clothing. It, nevertheless, saw members agree to a work programme designed to drive the trade agenda forward and, by so doing, amplify further the asymmetry of opportunity entrenched in the WTO's legal framework. The declaration committed members to revive the built-in agenda on services, hold future negotiations on agriculture and aspects of the TRIPs agreement, and to review and conduct work on anti-dumping, customs valuation, dispute settle-ment, import licensing, pre-shipment inspection, rules of origin, sanitary and phyto-sanitary measures, safeguards, subsidies and countervailing measures, technical barriers to trade, textiles and clothing, trade policy review, TRIPs and TRIMs (WTO, 1996: paragraphs 17–19). More importantly, the decla-ration made provision for the establishment of working groups on investment, competition policy (both of which were agreed 'on the understanding that the work undertaken shall not prejudge whether negotiations will be initi-ated in the future' – WTO, 1996: paragraph 20), government procurement and trade facilitation.

Geneva (May 1998): dress rehearsal

By the time of its second ministerial meeting in Geneva in May 1998 tensions among WTO members over the shape and direction of the trade agenda were reaching new heights. The financial crisis in East Asia had seriously affected the economic health of member states in the region and threatened those in Latin America and the former Soviet Union; and public disquiet over the social consequences of neoliberalism was rapidly increasing. EU pressure for the launch of a millennium round was proving divisive. Concerns were raised by many developing countries that a new round of negotiations could be embarked upon only once the Uruguay commitments had been fully implemented. Even then the negotiation of new issues (investment, govern-ment procurement, competition policy and trade facilitation – now increas-ingly known as the Singapore issues after their inclusion in the Singapore work programme) would have to be carefully balanced against existing 'built-in' negotiating commitments (particularly in agriculture), and that any negotiation would have to be mindful of the pressure of a new round on the infrastructure of the smallest members.

Unease at the launch of a new round was not, however, confined to the developing world. Of the other quad members, only Japan had come out strongly in favour of a new round prior to the ministerial. Canada had raised serious reservations. Australia came out in favour of a new round with the caveat that agriculture had to figure prominently in any negotiations.

The US was remaining non-committal, arguing that it was too early to make such a decision (*Inside US Trade*, 1 May 1998); the Clinton administration's autumn 1997 failure to achieve the necessary fast-track authority upon which to negotiate saw the US adopt a position congruent with the pursuit of the existing in-built agendas alone (particularly in agriculture and services – for which it needed no such authority) (*Inside US Trade*, 11 November 1997); and Washington exuded unease at the possibility of any comprehensive new round that might enable the EU and Japan to shelter from making meaningful concessions on agriculture through cross-sector trade-offs. Even the European position was itself far from consensual. Much of the pressure for the new round was attributed to the personal ambitions of EU Trade Commissioner Brittan and not to a unanimous commitment among the then 15 member states – a position that had reputedly led Brittan into direct conflict with French President Jacques Chirac (*Business Recorder*, 28 April 1998).

Tensions were exacerbated a week before the Geneva meeting during a debate over the draft ministerial statement. During the debate EU, Australian and New Zealand delegations urged other representatives to include a call for the start of a new round in the text; US, Canadian and Japanese delegates pressed for a formulation of words that was flexible enough to work towards negotiations 'without alienating other members'; and India, Pakistan and Egypt, among others, proposed that the ministerial statement deal mainly with problems relating to the implementation of the Uruguay round accords and include an acknowledgement of the disproportionately greater benefits accrued to the industrial states from the trade liberalisation so far facilitated by the WTO (*Bridges*, 11 May 1998).

An extra dimension to the meeting was added by the demonstrations during the Birmingham G8 summit that preceded the ministerial, as well as those that took place during the Geneva ministerial itself. Whereas the G8 summit saw upwards of 50,000 people voice concern at the persistence of Third World debt, the Geneva demonstrations were much smaller in scale – numbering a mere 2,000. Moreover, they proved newsworthy only for some minor vandalism (*Wall Street Journal*, 18 May 1998). The lack of media attention, however, belay much NGO activity. Indeed, the significance of growing public interest in, and criticism of, WTO activities (among others) was such that WTO DG Renato Ruggiero along with ILO DG Michel Hansenne and UNCTAD Secretary-General (SG) Rubens Ricupero all saw fit to attend an International Confederation of Free Trade Unions' (ICFTU) conference on the impact of trade liberalisation on worker rights (*ICFTU Online Bulletin*, 28 May 1998). Moreover, in his opening address to the ministerial conference Ruggiero talked candidly about financial instability, development, marginalisation, the environment, social conditions, employment, public health and cultural diversity, and the need for the WTO to divert attention towards improving information and communications channels with civil society (Ruggiero, 1998). US President Bill Clinton issued a call for the creation of a WTO forum wherein 'business, labour, environmental and consumer groups [could] speak out and help guide the further evolution of the WTO' and made clear his support for a closer working relationship between the WTO and the ILO and the possibility of a commitment to core labour standards finding its way into the WTO's remit (Clinton, 1998); while British Prime Minister Tony Blair and the then European Commission President Jacques Santer, among others, voiced similar sentiments (Blair, 1998; Santer, 1998).

Yet this courting of civil society fuelled already simmering tensions within the meeting. Many developing country members raised concerns that comments such as these were the prelude to a concerted push to open up the WTO's agenda to a host of trade-related issues. Once again, of particular concern was the proposed extension of the WTO's remit to include core labour standards and its potential to serve as a Trojan horse for the greater protection of industrial markets. Although the issue was deemed by many to have been settled during the Singapore meeting, Egypt, Pakistan, Mexico, Nicaragua, Myanmar, Brazil and the members of the South Asian Association for Regional Co-operation (SAARC)[2] all chose to restate their opposition to any movement of WTO activities into this area. As the then Brazilian President Fernando Henrique Cardoso put it, 'it would seem to us unjust and senseless, given the very philosophy that inspires the . . . [WTO], to seek guarantees for the improvement of working conditions through punitive trade measures whose only consequence would be to aggravate the social question' (Cardoso, 1998: paragraph 7).

The Geneva ministerial declaration was itself a rather limp document, reflecting a lack of clear consensus among the membership as to the future of the trade agenda. The document celebrated the fiftieth anniversary of the multilateral trading system, welcomed the conclusion of the basic telecommunications and financial services agreements, warned against succumbing to protectionist urges in times of financial crisis (particularly pertinent to Asia at the time), recognised the need to enhance 'public understanding of the benefits of the multilateral trading system in order to build support for it' (WTO, 1998: paragraph 4), renewed the commitment to trade-led growth as a model of development, expressed concern about the marginalisation of small and least developed countries, welcomed new members, and reinforced the need to facilitate (as well as put in place a mechanism to review progress in) the full implementation of the Uruguay round commitments. It was to prove to be the calm before the storm.

From Geneva to Seattle

Geneva was followed by a growing confidence among civil society groups, particularly in the wake of the withdrawal of the French government from the Organisation for Economic Co-operation and Development's (OECD) negotiation of a Multilateral Agreement on Investment (MAI) following a concerted NGO campaign (see Wilkinson, 1999b). Events such as these, and the pandering to civil society concerns that resulted therefrom (of which the launch of the UN Global Compact was perhaps the most high profile), drew sharp criticism from developing countries. Of particular note was (i) a concern that civil society interests threatened to obfuscate or obscure those of developing countries; and (ii) a perception that by courting civil society groups (and thereby lending a measure of legitimacy to their concerns) support would seem to be developing for the introduction of various trade-related provisions into the WTO's legal framework – provisions that contained within them the potential for discriminatory action to be undertaken.

Growing North/South tensions were also evident in, and exacerbated by, the election of a successor to Ruggiero as WTO DG. After a protracted debate in which all but two candidates – former New Zealand Prime Minister Mike Moore and Thai Finance and Deputy Prime Minister Supachai Panitchpakdi – fell by the wayside, Moore was put forward as the majority choice. However, Moore's majority was slim – just 62 compared with 59 for Supachai. Although Moore's candidature was endorsed by the EU, Peru, Panama and Brazil (all of which had supported Supachai) the ASEAN group, Japan, Mexico and a number of African states rejected the proposition, claiming that the process had lacked transparency and was riddled with unfairness. What followed was 'the most unexpected and horrible quarrel . . . ever witnessed at the WTO' (*Bridges*, 3 May 1999). The dispute was finally resolved by a joint Bangladeshi and Australian proposal that both candidates share the post for two consecutive non-renewable terms of three years (*Financial Times*, 19 June 1999; *Bridges*, 28 June and 19 July 1999; *Inside US Trade*, 23 July 1999). Nevertheless, the disagreement left the WTO without a formal DG from 30 April to 1 September 1999 (during which time David Hartage, then Director of the WTO's Trade in Services Division, stood in as acting DG).

The 'battle' in Seattle (November/December 1999)

Darker clouds were, however, on the horizon. Just 18 months after the Geneva meeting 30,000 demonstrators descended on the WTO's Seattle ministerial to protest about the impact of trade liberalisation on working conditions, economic development, the global environment, national sovereignty as well as issues of transparency and democratic accountability. Whereas the Geneva demonstrations had been obscured by (and had originally and mistakenly been perceived to be part of, rather than related to) the Birmingham G8 protests and had managed only a few column inches in selected broadsheets, Seattle thrust the WTO upon a global public most of which had previously been unaware of the Organisation's existence (though the GATT was not quite as obscured from public view as a number of commentators have suggested – see, for instance, Marceau and Pedersen,

1999). However, the media attention generated by the demonstrations, the imposition of a curfew and the heavy-handed reaction of the US National Guard combined to obscure another conflict: the political contestation among the Organisation's members over the possible launch of a new round of trade negotiations.

The tenor of the meeting had been set in the immediate run-up to the ministerial. Serious divisions had emerged among the members in the wake of the Geneva meeting. The members took varying and seemingly entrenched positions on what the core focus of a new round ought to be. India again championed the issue of implementation. The US and the Cairns group favoured commencing agricultural negotiations beyond those mandated in the built-in agenda. The EU sought to expand the negotiations to include the Singapore issues and, along with the US (albeit marginally different in form), to include worker rights. Brazil and Cuba objected strongly to any suggestion that the WTO become involved in employment issues and opposed the launch of negotiations on investment and competition policy. India pressed for the full implementation of the Uruguay commitments by the industrial states prior to any new negotiations; and Malaysia suggested that any new round be postponed to 2001 to enable Asian countries to concentrate on recovery in the wake of the financial crisis.

The fall-out from the election of a successor to Ruggiero provided little opportunity for the new DG to bridge these divisions and left Moore scant time to begin nurturing a consensus among the membership. The appointment of DDsG on 3 November 1999 just short of four weeks before the Seattle meeting (WTO, 1999) further hampered the building of a consensus, as did the last-minute announcement of the chairs of the respective negotiating groups (just the day before the meeting began). To make matters worse, the construction of the draft text of the Seattle Ministerial Declaration was poorly handled. Instead of beginning from a low base and slowly piecing together the framework for a new round, General Council Chair Ali Mchumo sought to allay tensions by overseeing a formulation of words that, as Odell puts it, 'was a compilation of opposed positions rather than a true single negotiating text thought to express a possible consensus' (Odell, 2002: 417). The text's only saving grace was that it at least incorporated ideas from all quarters, rather than reflecting the interests of only a few. Nevertheless, given the shortness of time, the cluttered, complex and fraught nature of the agenda, and the hangover from the appointment of Ruggiero's successor, the Geneva process failed to lay the foundations for, let alone produce, a consensus.

The divides that had emerged in the run-up to the meeting were further entrenched as the meeting opened. Although frequently finessed with pointers to the language of development and set against various commitments to extend duty-free access to the least developed countries under GSP, the industrial states proved unwilling to address those issues of primary concern to their developing counterparts. Canada, Australia, New Zealand, the US and the EU, for instance, proved reluctant to discuss exemptions to existing

Uruguay round obligations or to renegotiate extensions to the deadlines for implementing any of the accords; the US delegation refused to discuss anti-dumping measures and any acceleration in its textile liberalisation commitments; it also resisted pressure to open up the TRIPs agreement in relation to generic pharmaceuticals or to discuss probing questions about the patenting of life forms; and the EU firmly opposed any renegotiation of the WTO's basic rules (*Bridges*, 30 November 1999).

The positions of many of the developing countries proved comparably entrenched. Egypt and Zimbabwe were vociferous in their opposition to any discussion of the relationship between trade and labour standards in the WTO; a group of 28 South and South East Asian, Caribbean, African, Middle Eastern and Pacific countries opposed the commencement of negotiations on the Singapore issues;[3] the African group reiterated its reluctance to agree to engage in negotiations beyond those specified in the built-in agenda, despite some support within the group from, most notably, South Africa; and the attentions of the African, Caribbean and Pacific (ACP) states were focused squarely on the renegotiation of the waiver for the Lomé (now Cotonou) Convention.

Tensions were also apparent in the mechanics of the meeting's organisation. The ministerial was initially organised around five negotiating groups, with a sixth (on labour standards) being added part-way through the meeting: (i) agriculture; (ii) market access; (iii) new issues (including but not limited to the four Singapore issues); (iv) implementation; and (v) systemic issues, transparency and relations with civil society. Each group was charged with crafting a portion of the ministerial text that would form the basis of any new round of negotiations. These pieces of text would then be considered in various green room discussions (comprising 15 to 20 members supposedly sensitive to geographic representation and levels of economic development), and final approval would be sought from the ministerial conference as a whole.

The allocation of the chairs for each of the negotiating groups was refined in an effort to mitigate some of the tension despite their much delayed announcement. The group on agriculture was chaired by Singapore (originally identified as the likely sole chair) and Bangladesh; Lesotho chaired the market access group; Hong Kong was originally lined up to provide the chair for the new issues group but the strength of hostility to the commencement of negotiations in this area saw the offer withdrawn and New Zealand assume the role; Brazil refused to chair the implementation group, eventually resulting in joint chairs coming from Canada and Jamaica; and Chile (though originally touted as chairing alone) co-chaired the systemic issues group with Fiji (*Bridges*, 30 November 1999; *Bridges*, 1 December 1999).[4]

However, complaints about the process were heard from the very outset. Delegates found themselves unable to attend meetings either because demonstrators barred their way, or they were not invited to (or precluded from) green room sessions. Smaller delegations found it difficult to attend all of the meetings, particularly those held concurrently. Complaints were heard about the lack of time available for delegates to take stock of developments in the negotiations and prepare national responses. This was compounded by the loss of time resulting from the disruption of the demonstrations. Matters were made worse by an absence of provision for the extension of the meeting beyond its official end (despite a well-established GATT/WTO culture of doing just that). There were significant problems with the conference infrastructure – telephone systems failed, accommodation was scarce, the provision of and access to food and drink was limited, and rooms lacked adequate soundproofing. And USTR Charlene Barshefsky was severely criticised for the partisan way in which she chaired the ministerial meeting (Odell, 2005: 432; see also Moore, 2003: 98).

Within the negotiations themselves, although tensions over the Singapore issues, labour standards and the appropriate content of a new round grabbed most of the headlines, traditional differences of opinion emerged, albeit that some progress was also made. In the agricultural group disagreements emerged over the appropriate interpretation of Article 20 of the Agreement on Agriculture (on the continuation of the reform process). At the outset, the EU, supported by Korea, Hungary and Japan, offered a version of the text that suggested the negotiations should be 'based on' Article 20; whereas the US and the Cairns Group preferred a formulation wherein the Article should be taken 'into account'. Beneath this apparently semantic tussle lay differing interpretations of the goal of the negotiations. By seeking to base the discussions on the Article, the EU sought to interrupt the purpose of the negotiations as the pursuit of 'substantial reductions' in (rather than the complete eradication of) agricultural support. For the US and the Cairns group, however, a formulation that sought to take account of Article 20 provided for (i) recognition of non-trade concerns and (ii) abandoning the measured reduction implied in the Article. A US/Cairns group draft issued in response proposed the elimination of export subsidies and substantial reductions in domestic support, though no movement on the indirect subsidy mechanisms favoured by the US. It also sought to generate support among the developing countries by including an extended section on special and differential treatment including taking 'fully into account all of [the developing countries'] ... needs, including food security, and agricultural and rural development' (*Bridges*, 1 December 1999); but in so doing, it also sought the full participation of developing countries in the negotiations on agriculture – that is, in terms of commitments undertaken and concessions offered. Needless to say, the text was widely criticised by developing countries.

As the discussions progressed, various attempts were made to reach a consensual position. The US/Cairns group text was modified in an attempt to address both EU and developing country concerns by including a reference to the multifunctional role of agriculture under non-trade concerns; inserting square brackets in the text outlining the reduction – as opposed to elimination – of all forms of assistance to exports under the section on export subsidies; and modifying the section on special and differential treatment based on text 'distilled' from a 19 October 1999 Indian submission (*Bridges*, 2 December 1999). Thereafter, the reference to multifunctionality was replaced by a reference to the need to take account of non-trade concerns such as food security and rural development; the EU hinted that it would forego explicit reference to multifunctionality if the US were to give up on its demand to bring trade in agricultural products under the normal GATT rules; and attempts were made to navigate between the US/Cairns group and EU positions on the elimination of substantial reductions in export subsidies.

Elsewhere in the negotiations, the EU sought to appease developing countries by reworking large sections of the ministerial declaration, though it clung resolutely to the inclusion of investment and competition policy. Almost no movement of substance was noted in the group on implementation. Developing countries called for action relating to difficulties with their implementation of certain WTO agreements, the need for extensions in deadlines in TRIPs, TRIMs and Customs Valuation, and the necessity for imbalances across the range of WTO agreements to be rectified. The US and EU sought to allay developing country concerns with the offer of a capacity building package (including, from the EU, a substantial contribution to the WTO technical co-operation programme). Japan sought to place reform of WTO anti-dumping measures at the core of a new round, and Iceland argued for the commencement of negotiations designed to remove subsidies on fisheries.

Elsewhere, debate in the market access group centred on the relative merits of different negotiating formulas and modalities; and a gulf quickly emerged in the new issues group, with very few members lending support to the inclusion of the Singapore issues in the new round (*Bridges*, 3 December 1999). In a near comical turn, confusion reigned within the EU delegation over an apparent change in its stance on the establishment of a working group on biotechnology. The EU's prior position had been that the Biosafety Protocol negotiations were the appropriate forum for deciding a multilateral approach to biotechnology issues. However, a version of the draft ministerial declaration circulated on 30 November suggested that the EU would agree to the establishment of a WTO working party on the issue with a 'fact-finding mandate on the relationship between trade, development, health, consumer and environmental issues in the area of modern biotechnology' (*Bridges*, 2 December 1999). The inclusion of this text was followed by strong denials from the French, British, Italian, Danish and Belgian environment ministers.

Tensions were particularly acute in discussions surrounding the labour standards issue and were visibly expressed in ministerial statements to the meeting. Indeed, labour standards became *the* site of contestation over the direction of the trade agenda during the meeting. Of the 141 statements available from the meeting, 75 chose to comment on the issue (53 per cent). Of these, 49 (65 per cent) were unsupportive, 23 (31 per cent) were supportive, and the remainder were non-committal. Moreover, over 68 per cent of the statements given either perceived the Singapore Ministerial Declaration to be the definitive word on the issue, or demonstrated outright hostility. Regionally, the picture proved more acute. Among the statements from East and South Asia, Central America, the Caribbean, and North Africa there was no support for a WTO examination of the relationship between trade and labour standards. A similarly negative picture may be found in the statements from South America, Sub-Saharan Africa, Eastern Europe, the former Soviet Union, the Middle East and the Pacific (including Australasia). Only Western Europe and North America registered support for a degree of WTO involvement in the issue (see Wilkinson, 2001, 2002d).

Fears that US and EU proposals to explore the relationship between trade liberalisation and the protection of certain basic worker rights were merely a prelude to discriminating against products from countries with a comparative advantage in labour costs were exacerbated by an interview given by US President Clinton to the *Seattle Post-Intelligencer* (Clinton, 1999; see also Nyhan, 1999; Paulson, 1999), in which he argued that:

> I think that what we ought to do first of all is adopt the United States's position on having a working group on labor within the WTO ... then that working group should develop these core labor standards, and then they ought to be part of every trade agreement ... ultimately I would favor a system in which sanctions would come for violating any provision of a trade agreement.
>
> (Clinton, 1999)

USTR Charlene Barshefsky's efforts to qualify Clinton's comments as merely a long-term policy goal and not part of the proposed working group's mandate failed to mitigate any of the hostility. EU Trade Commissioner Pascal Lamy tried to resuscitate the debate by distancing the EU's proposal for a joint ILO/WTO standing forum on trade from US attempts to establish a working party and by expressing his belief that trade sanctions were not an appropriate means of promoting respect for core labour standards. His efforts, however, failed to bear fruit. The debate in the labour standards working group lasted just 45 minutes. During this time, nearly four-fifths of WTO members opposed any extension of the Organisation's remit into this area (*Bridges*, 3 December 1999).

The meeting was not without signs that important concessions would be forthcoming. The EU, for instance, was prepared to give way to developing country demands for adjustments to the WTO's legal framework, to renegotiate aspects of the anti-dumping and subsidies agreements and to address issues relating to the implementation of the agreement on agriculture in exchange for an agreement to begin negotiations on two of the Singapore issues (investment and competition policy). These, however, proved to be insufficient to overcome the acrimony that had developed throughout the course of the meeting generally and over the labour standards issue more specifically. Inevitably, and despite the continuation of meetings through the night of 2 and 3 December 1999, delegates failed to reach agreement on the content of a ministerial declaration launching a new round of negotiations. Ultimately the meeting collapsed and the WTO was thrown into a crisis from which few thought it could easily recover.

After Seattle

Although the collapse of a ministerial meeting was not an unheard of occurrence, the dramatic fashion in which events unfolded in Seattle surprised many and had a marked impact upon the post-crisis politics that unfolded. Crucially, the collapse of the Seattle ministerial produced a concerted effort to identify the sources of the meeting's breakdown and to put in place a plan of action designed to stop a recurrence of the discord within and outside of the conference. It also generated myriad suggestions for reforming the way in which relations among the member states were governed. This included a Canadian resurrection of the idea of an executive committee to steer the Organisation's operations akin to that proposed for the ITO and OTC (and floated during the Uruguay round) as a means of overcoming breakdowns in the WTO's consensus-based decision-making. However, as Raghavan notes, ideas such as these were 'met with resistance from developing countries which [saw] them as attempts to continue . . . "undemocratic decision making" by legitimizing the non-transparent, "green-room" processes, through some kind of representational constituency system'. As he points out, '[i]f all . . . rules and obligations apply to all members equally, then arguments about "efficiency" cannot be used to exclude any country from the decision-making processes, whatever its trade or economic weight' (Raghavan, 2000: 497).

The second response to the collapse of the meeting was the Organisation's engagement in a public confidence-building exercise, and an accompanying effort to improve and increase the WTO's general profile (see Wilkinson, 2002c: 131–134; Odell, 2005: 435–436). This comprised not only an increase in the usage of the WTO's website as the Organisation's principal medium in response to accusations of poor transparency, but also the development of a public relations strategy designed to mollify civil society hostility by bringing key NGOs into the fold while preserving the Organisation's intergovernmental character. Less obvious were the behind-the-scenes efforts of the DG, Secretariat, notable international public officials (including UN Secretary-General Kofi Annan) and key member states to rebuild the image of the WTO among developing countries. This was not intended merely to rehabilitate the Organisation's image; it was also intended to generate support for a second effort to launch a new trade round.

The chosen strategy for nurturing a new consensus was to place 'development' at the heart of any new negotiations, thereby pacifying what were seen to be the most hostile elements of the membership, but nevertheless maintaining a commitment to extend WTO rules into new areas (with the exception of labour standards). What followed was a 20-month period of intense confidence building and behind-the-scenes negotiations with a view to relaunching the millennium round (albeit subsequently rebranded as the Doha Development Agenda – DDA) at the Organisation's fourth ministerial meeting in Doha in November 2001. One dimension of this saw DG Moore concentrate on courting the African group and their Caribbean and Pacific counterparts in an attempt to gain their trust and encourage support for the launch of a new round (Moore, 2003: 113). A second dimension saw the inclusion of key developing countries in previously closed WTO-related fora. This was most notably the case with the involvement of Tanzania (as co-ordinator of the LDC group) and Nigeria (as co-ordinator of the African group) in the August (Mexico) and October (Singapore) 2001 mini-ministerial meetings – gatherings of the most prominent member states designed to discuss key issues and build consensus that, for Jawara and Kwa, operate as a '*de facto* executive council' (Jawara and Kwa, 2003: 280). The purpose of Tanzanian and Nigerian involvement was, as Anthony Payne puts it, to 'deliver' their support and that of their constituencies (Payne, 2005: 181). A third dimension saw the launch of various publications designed to emphasise the need for a successful conclusion to the Doha meeting as well as to highlight the consequences of a second failure. This included, among others, the Secretariat's production of *The WTO . . . and why it matters* resource handbook (WTO, 2001d).

Efforts to build a consensus in the wake of Seattle were not, however, couched entirely in terms of the contribution of a new round to the plight of the world's least developed countries. In what was by now quintessential GATT/WTO fashion, they were also firmly situated within the context of crisis aversion. As Jawara and Kwa (2003: 271-272) put it:

> From the beginning of the process leading up to Doha, the shadow of Seattle hung over the negotiations. . . . There was a widespread fear, among Secretariat staff and delegates alike . . . that a second successive 'failure' would seriously undermine the WTO and the multilateral trading system itself, and could even lead to the organization's demise. The major powers did not want this, and in their anxiety to put the WTO train back on its tracks, exerted a huge amount of pressure on developing countries to reach some kind of agreement. While many developing countries regarded this apocalyptic view as mere rhetoric . . . it raised the stakes, and made ministers still more cautious about the risk of being singled out for blame by the powerful countries and the Western media as the villain jeopardizing the multilateral trading system by blocking an agreement.

Yet the spectre of Seattle and the accompanying apocalyptic rhetoric about the imminent collapse of the global economy was not the only crisis that served as a frame for the Doha meeting. The Doha ministerial took place just two months after the terrorist attacks of 11 September 2001. Inevitably, this cast proceedings in a different light (and initially threatened the meeting's cancellation with Singapore being touted as a likely alternative). Few states wished to be seen to be offering opposition in such a tender political climate. The security crisis nevertheless placed further pressure on developing countries to agree to the launch of a new round. It was also used opportunistically by the round's leading proponents. As Stuart Harbinson, then Chair of the GC, reflected:

> [there was] a certain amount of feeling that the events of September 11 were a bit of a threat to the world and to the established way of doing things. . . . And it was important for multilateral institutions, not just the WTO, to be seen to be operating successfully. So I think that put a bit of extra pressure on people to have a result. It was a positive effect in getting an agreement.
>
> (Harbinson, quoted in Kwa, 2003: 32–33).

Others were less persuaded that the twin crises of Seattle and 11 September had a positive effect. As Jamaican delegate Richard Bernal put it:

> We have been approached bilaterally in capitals. We are approached in Geneva. We are made to feel that we are holding up the rescue of the global economy if we don't agree to a new round. . . . In addition we feel that this meeting has no connection with the fight against terrorism . . . all these things have been put to us in a way that if we don't agree, we are not committed to those goals, which is certainly not the case.
>
> (Bernal, quoted in Kwa, 2003: 22)

It was not just pressure on negotiators resulting from the changed security environment that had an impact on arriving at a consensus to launch a new round at the Doha meeting. Aileen Kwa argues that the launch of the 'war on terror' presented opportunities for key developing countries to be bought off. While these seldom required recipients to withdraw their opposition to the launch of a new round, it nevertheless eroded the solidarity of prominent developing country coalitions such as the Like Minded Group (LMG).[5] She notes a softening of the positions of Pakistan and Malaysia as the most significant, with discernible alterations also occurring in the stances of Nigeria, Kenya and Tanzania (Kwa, 2003: 32; see also Bello, 2002: 276).

The preparatory process leading up to the Doha meeting was also different from its Seattle counterpart in another respect – a change that led then Zimbabwean ambassador to the WTO Boniface Chidyausiku to comment that 'Seattle was actually much more democratic in terms of the process of producing a draft text [than Doha as] at least all opposing views were presented in the draft declaration' (Chidyausiku, cited in Jawara and Kwa, 2003: 75). Whereas the Seattle process had been driven primarily by the submission of proposals, the Doha process was, as Stuart Harbinson puts it, 'chairman driven' (Harbinson, 2002: 4). This process involved the drafting of a text by the Chair of the GC (in this case by Harbinson) that reflected the overall balance of opinion, as he saw it, garnered from a process of consultation.

Inevitably, the Harbinson text was widely criticised. Concerns were raised about the degree to which the consultation process reflected the views of the whole membership; the appropriateness of using 'confessionals' to extract bottom lines from delegates; the manner of the text's revision; the utility of adopting a procedure that allowed Chairs to shape debate and ultimately outcomes in such a significant fashion; and the precedent that such a procedure set for future negotiations (it is worth remembering that such a text was used by Arthur Dunkel in an effort to break the deadlock during the Uruguay round – see Chapter 4). These criticisms notwithstanding, the text was adopted and formed the basis of the discussion that unfolded during the Doha meeting.

Doha and the DDA (November 2001)

Discussions during the Doha ministerial were organised into six streams, with a seventh being added during the closing stages. They were: (i) intellectual property and public health/access to medicines; (ii) implementation; (iii) agriculture; (iv) environment; (v) Singapore issues; (vi) rule-making; and, later, (vii) other issues.[6] The choice of streams reflected those areas wherein significant divisions remained among the membership. Yet despite some effort to improve the transparency and manageability of the ministerial, including a conscious effort not to run meetings concurrently (thereby enabling smaller delegations to spread themselves across all sessions) and a widespread acknowledgement that the process was more transparent than in Seattle, concerns were nevertheless raised. These centred on: the decision to organise the discussions into the six streams (the addition of the seventh was the result of developing country pressure to isolate particular issues such as labour standards, TRIPs and biodiversity, and dispute settlement reform); the appointment by Conference Chair Youssef Hussain Kamal, apparently without widespread consultation, and of the six facilitators (friends of the Chair) from countries known to be sympathetic to the launch of a new round (Payne, 2005: 182); the reported partisanship of at least one of the facilitators; a lack of information about the time, place and existence of meetings; the degree to which bargaining was taking place outside of the official meetings and the exclusion of delegates therefrom; and the selection of member countries represented in the green room sessions.

The negotiations themselves were predictably contentious. The three documents released in the run-up to the meeting as the basis upon which discussions would proceed – a draft ministerial declaration designed to launch a new round (WTO Document JOB(01)/140/Rev.1); a separate declaration on intellectual property rights and [Access to Medicines][Public Health] (WTO Document JOB(01)/155); and a draft ministerial decision on implementation-related issues and concerns (WTO Document JOB(01)/139/Rev.1) – were decried by developing countries as an attempt to force an agenda. The Indian, Nigerian and Malaysian delegations were among the most vocal. The degree of criticism to which the drafts were subjected prompted WTO DG Moore and GC Chair Harbinson to release a covering letter defending the process by which they had been constructed. They also explained that the texts did 'not purport to represent agreed elements in any way at this stage', but were rather 'the best possible basis for Ministers to build upon at Doha' (Moore and Harbinson, 2001; see also WTO, 2001e). They did not, however, reopen the texts ahead of the meeting.

The agricultural discussions saw the US and the Cairns group press for a form of words that identified the elimination of export subsidies and the full integration of agriculture into WTO rules. EU Trade Commissioner Pascal Lamy, despite repeated proclamations that the EU had very little room for manoeuvre (and much to the surprise of many delegations), agreed to reductions in export subsidies with a view to their eventual elimination; and developing countries pressed for the creation of a 'development box' to enable their agricultural subsidies and other forms of support that address food security and rural development to be treated separately from agricultural negotiations. In the implementation consultations Pakistan led a developing country push for an acceleration in the liberalisation of textiles, a move that was strongly resisted by the US and Canada; and discussions on the mechanisms for extensions under Article 27.4 of the Agreement on Subsidies (dealing with the period in which developing countries are required to phase out export subsidies) split the Latin American countries. The EU resigned itself to the absolute lack of movement on labour standards in the Other Issues group, adding weight to efforts to address the protection of worker rights under the mantle of pursing greater coherence in global economic governance that has since emerged (see Supachai, 2003; World Commission on the Social Dimension of Globalization, 2004). A North/South split emerged over the two main options for the text on TRIPs and public health (see Sell, 2002: 514–519) but was eventually resolved by a Brazil/ US brokered paragraph. The rule-making consultations were dominated by pressure from developing countries (with some support from Korea and Japan) for stricter anti-dumping measures and US resistance thereto, and a tussle between the US and Iceland on the one hand and the EU on the other to isolate and address fisheries subsidies in the new round (the consultations resulted in both the US and EU softening their respective positions). The environment consultations saw the EU press hard (with the support of

Switzerland, Japan and Norway) for a clarification of WTO rules and an examination of the relationship between those rules and Multilateral Environmental Agreements (MEAs).

Yet again, the Singapore issues proved the most contentious. The consultations began with strong opposition to any examination of these issues from the South Asian and African delegations (with Latin American members also voicing reservations); whereas the EU, Chile, Costa Rica, Japan and Korea called for more ambitious language on investment as well as on government procurement, competition policy and trade facilitation. The stand-off that emerged was finally broken when it was agreed that negotiations would only commence in these areas after the Cancún ministerial meeting *if* an 'explicit consensus' was forthcoming. Aware that this statement was nevertheless ambiguous, in a move comparable to Yeo Cheow Tong's attempt to clarify paragraph 4 of the Singapore Ministerial Declaration on labour standards, Conference Chair Kamal stated in his concluding remarks that 'in my view, this would give each Member the right to take a position on modalities that would prevent negotiations from proceeding after the Fifth Session of the Ministerial Conference [Cancún] until that Member is prepared to join in an explicit consensus' (Kamal, quoted in *Bridges*, 14 November 2001). However, as Payne notes (and again much like the Singapore discussion on labour standards), although Kamal's statement was appended to the ministerial declaration it did not have the same legal standing as the declaration itself. 'In other words, although the Chair's clarification was itself quite clear in its interpretation of the wording, the argument about the incorporation of the Singapore issues into the Doha "round" had not been resolved' (Payne, 2005: 186).

The meeting was of course not without moments of high drama. Tensions erupted between the EU and the ACP on the one hand, and Latin American countries (joined by the Philippines and Thailand) on the other over the request for a waiver for the former's Cotonou agreement (the revised version of the Lomé Convention) to be considered at the ministerial. Suspicions reigned that, although the request for a waiver was separate from the ministerial process (and had only been raised at the ministerial because of the difficulties in reaching an agreement at the pre-ministerial CTG meeting), efforts to deal with it in Doha were merely intended as a sweetener to secure ACP agreement for the launch of a new round. In addition, the meeting was not without what has now become legendary arm-twisting and heavy-handed consensus 'generating' tactics. Rooms selected for green room sessions were chosen, in one instance, because they held no more than 23 delegates; in the final session of the meeting DG Moore was heard instructing Conference Chair Kamal on who should be allowed to speak and who should not (Wade, 2004: 150–151); threats were made to secure the agreement of key states (the US, for instance, was accused of threatening to cancel its preferential trade agreement with Haiti and the Dominican Republic unless they reversed their opposition to the inclusion of government procurement in the ministerial declaration) (Bello, 2002: 276); telephone calls were made to the capitals of developing countries by, among others, USTR Zoellick to ensure their acquiescence, thereby circumscribing delegations present in Doha; and the success of the conference was linked to the conclusion of various bilateral deals (such as, in the case of the US, the African Growth and Opportunity Act – AGOA) (Jawara and Kwa, 2003: 86).

The meeting was nevertheless concluded (after the now obligatory round-the-clock negotiations and slippage in the deadline) resulting in the adoption of a ministerial declaration launching a new round, a decision on implementation, a declaration on TRIPs and public health, and two waivers (one dealing with the Cotonou agreement and a second dealing with the EU's revised banana régime). It also witnessed the completion of accession procedures for China and Chinese Taipei.

The DDA

From the point of view of the developing states, agreeing to the DDA was a fundamental error. There were undoubted successes in tailoring the work programme towards areas of interest to the developing world: the Ministerial Declaration was steeped in the language of development; the Ministerial Decision on Implementation-related Issues and Concerns (WTO, 2001b) and the Ministerial Declaration identified implementation issues as an integral part of the work programme – albeit that either lacked real compunction; the agricultural negotiations set out to pursue substantial improvements in market access, reduce (and eventually eliminate) export subsidies and trade-distorting domestic support systems; the negotiations on non-agricultural market access were structured such that the reduction and elimination of tariff peaks, high tariffs, tariff escalation, tariffs affecting the export interests of developing countries and non-tariff barriers sat alongside a more traditional focus on the reduction of barriers to trade; and the Declaration on TRIPs and public health offered members greater flexibility in adhering to the TRIPs agreement in times of national health crises (WTO, 2001c). The Ministerial Declaration promised to explore the relationship between trade, debt and finance, the plight of small economies, the transfer of technology, technical co-operation and capacity building, and a commitment to review and strengthen special and differential provisions; and paragraph 8 consolidated the Singapore decision on labour standards and placed the issue firmly at the door of the ILO (see Haworth *et al.*, 2005). However, the balance of potential gains from the work programme remained firmly in the interest of the industrial states. In addition to the benefits resulting from the full implementation of the Uruguay accords, improvements in non-agricultural market access, aspects of the negotiations on agriculture, and a further extension of the TRIPs, the DDA added a commitment to begin (albeit on the basis that an 'explicit consensus' should be forthcoming) negotiations in investment, government procurement, trade facilitation and competition policy (and possibly a fifth, e-commerce) (WTO, 2001a). Moreover, the DDA put in place a specific timeframe in which negotiations would commence on the Singapore issues (subject to minor clarification, after the mid-term review of negotiations in Cancún) and stipulated that the results would form the basis of a second single undertaking.

Despite the obvious asymmetry, the launch of the DDA nevertheless generated a sense of relief that the problems of Seattle had been overcome and the multilateral trading system was back on track. Steve Charnovitz echoed many in his comments that 'failure at Doha would have pummeled the WTO . . . [The Organisation] has now recovered from the institutional and political failure that occurred in Seattle' (Charnovitz, 2001: 13). But the aversion of a further crisis, or at least the perpetuation of the last, was short-lived. Almost as soon as the ink had dried on the Doha Declaration familiar fractures began to reappear. Questions were raised about the substance of what had been agreed in Doha; much of the work programme appeared vague and insubstantive; concerns were aired over the precise substance of the DDA's 'development' content; questions were raised about DG Moore's style and his perceived bias in favour of the quad (Payne, 2005: 188); the US engaged in a bout of protectionism, first by raising tariffs on steel imports, then by increasing farm subsidies; the EU's plans to reform the CAP proved remarkably unambitious, much to the displeasure of the Cairns group. Most contentious of all, ambiguity reigned over whether negotiations would commence on the Singapore issues after the DDA's mid-term review at the Cancún ministerial meeting and what precisely was meant by the term 'explicit consensus'.

The post-Doha period also saw members fail repeatedly to agree on how to proceed with strengthening special and differential provisions in existing WTO agreements; acrimony engulfed the TRIPs and public health nego-tiations; discussions on the agricultural negotiating modalities collapsed; deadlock pervaded the Trade Negotiations Committee's (TNC) discussions on implementation issues; deadlines in the negotiations were consistently missed; and the negotiations were overshadowed by (and their priority plum-meted among the quad because of) the 20 March 2003 invasion of Iraq and the negotiations underway for the Central American Free Trade Agreement (CAFTA) and the FTAA.

That said, immediately prior to the Cancún meeting important movements on key issues did emerge: the deadlock over intellectual property protection and public health was finally broken by a 30 August 2003 agreement empow-ering countries to import generic pharmaceuticals in emergency situations (WTO, 2003b); and key officials within the US delegation were hinting that it would concede to pressure and put forward its agricultural export subsidy régime for liberalisation. This small build-up of momentum was not enough however. As Bridges put it, members disagreed 'on practically all items on the agenda' (*Bridges*, 10 September 2003). It was unsurprising then that for the second time in four years a WTO ministerial should collapse.

Crisis in Cancún (September 2003)

Despite the collapse of the meeting, Cancún was quite different from Seattle. While demonstrations were evident in Cancún – the most harrowing aspect of which was the suicide of Korean farmer Lee Hyung Hae – their impact on the meeting was negligible. Apart from a few minor happenings within the conference centre, a conflict between press and NGO delegates that saw the latter banned from the conference centre at the former's request (see Wilkinson, 2003), a naked protest on the beach, and a bit of street theatre, the demonstrations took place in a now well-practised fashion: beyond the *cordon sanitaire* established around the meeting's perimeter.

Cancún also differed from Seattle in another regard. Although the North/South split that underpinned the meeting's collapse proved newsworthy (albeit that the fault lines between delegations were much more complex in reality), the tensions were not exacerbated by irritations with conference facilities, the inability of delegates to get to meetings because of the demonstrations, or the consequence of ill-conceived comments by the host nation's president and the partisan behaviour of its conference chair and chief negotiator as they had been in Seattle. The political contestation that ensued resulted directly from the asymmetry of opportunity embedded in the WTO's legal framework and the way in which this has structured relations among the participating states. This asymmetry, and more significantly the prevailing perception that little had been done to address the concerns of developing countries since Doha, heightened political contestation to the point where it was inevitable that the meeting would collapse. But the collapse was far from producing what the International Gender and Trade Network (IGTN) and the Africa Trade Network (ATN) interpreted at the time as 'a major political shift in the power dynamics of the WTO with developing countries successfully resisting power in the face of extreme pressure and bullying' (IGTN and ATN, quoted in *Bridges*, 15 September 2003). Rather, as we see below, its consequence was to generate a *perception* of adjustment set against the creation of an environment in which the further extension of the asymmetry of opportunity is likely.

Underpinning the heightened political contestation that caused the meeting's collapse were the usual suspects. Though improvements were noted by some of the developing country delegates attending the meeting, particularly with regard to access to information, the Cancún meeting was conducted in time-honoured fashion. The meeting was run in the absence of a well-established set of rules; green room meetings among those deemed to be the most significant players constituted the meeting's core decision-making fora; some meetings, including those of the five negotiating groups, were run concurrently (thereby disadvantaging members with small delegations);[7] members were 'encouraged' to reveal their negotiating bottom lines in a series of confessionals; and the obligatory strong-arming and telephoning of developing country capitals took place in an effort to 'nurture' agreement.

More controversially, the meeting's agenda was organised around a text (and seven accompanying annexes) put together in a fashion that purportedly reflected the general balance of opinion and issued on the responsibility of Carlos Pérez del Castillo, Chair of the WTO's General Council (in close co-operation with WTO DG Supachai), but which was neither bracketed (indicating moments of divergence in opinion or alternative formulations) nor agreed by the members (it is important to note that Castillo and Supachai stressed that the text did 'not purport to be agreed in any part at this stage ... and is without prejudice to any delegation's position on any issue' in a covering letter (see Castillo and Supachai, 2003); but it is also important to note that no attempt was made to secure that agreement). As Amrita Narlikar and I put it:

> by providing the basis for discussions at Cancún, the Chair's text played an important role in agenda-setting to the detriment of developing countries. [W]hile the text provided an Option 1 (to start negotiations) and an Option 2 (to continue work on clarification of the issues without starting negotiations) on the Singapore issues married to a version of how to move forward with the agricultural negotiations, the annexes attached to the text weighted the draft heavily towards Option 1 (thereby placing it closer to the stated positions of the US, EU and Group of 9 – later 10) than the majority of developing countries.
>
> (Narlikar and Wilkinson, 2004: 449)

Of course, though deeply troublesome, this process of agenda-setting by text was not without precedent. As we noted above, the Harbinson text introduced in the run-up to the Doha ministerial also purported to be a vehicle for forging consensus. As we also noted, it too was subject to severe criticism, particularly from developing countries. Worryingly, the shaping of agendas through the introduction of what are purported not to be, but which in reality are, settled texts, appears now to have become an embedded cultural trait. Similarly, the old GATT predilection for improvisation was much in evidence during the selection process of the 'Friends of the Chair' or the so-called 'Facilitators' – persons appointed to organise discussion in identified areas. Although attempts were made to keep geographical representation in mind, the lack of transparency in their appointment nevertheless proved controversial, particularly among developing country delegates (Narlikar and Wilkinson, 2004: 450).

The meeting was also notable for its display of the perennial inequalities between developed and developing members. In purely human terms, the size of the delegations of the industrial countries dwarfed those of their developing counterparts. While the US and EU delegations were estimated to number in excess of 800 and Japanese officials put theirs at somewhere between 'three and four hundred', the Malawian delegation numbered 30 (and was only this high because it had 'learnt' to its cost from previous ministerials the problems facing a small delegation in attempting to cover all of the meetings), the Central African Republic contingent comprised three and Barbados managed eight. These differences in size of course hid some of the more qualitative imbalances in human resources that were evident in Cancún. While the size of the delegations from the industrial states enabled them to have at their disposal considerable specialist expertise in all potential areas of trade and related law as well as for them to be generously populated by representatives from the private sector and a few super-privileged NGOs, the size of the delegations from the developing states ensured that their coverage was much less extensive. As a consequence, rather than bringing in specialists in individual fields, each developing country delegate was compelled to have a broad grasp of all the issues. Moreover, unlike their industrial counterparts, many developing country representatives were also central bankers, only loosely related government officials, diplomats with remits greater than just the WTO, heads of local chambers of commerce and the like. As a result, each was able to dedicate less time to trade issues than their developed counterparts. The problems of overstretch also led to misunderstandings over key technicalities. This was the case, for instance, when one developing country delegate mistook 'export subsidies' as potential funds to be used by developing states to assist in getting their produce into international markets rather than the payment by (largely industrial) national governments of a subsidy to make domestic produce competitive in world markets.

Alliance warfare

While the politics of text and the relative deficiencies in human resources were to play a crucial role in the breakdown that followed, it was the formation of and contestation between competing alliances that proved the most notable aspect of the politics of Cancún's crisis (see Narlikar and Tussie (2004) for an excellent account). In the immediate run-up to Cancún two developing country coalitions set out positions that were to prove instrumental in the meeting – the Group of 20 (G20 and later G21 and G22) and the Strategic Products and Special Safeguard Mechanism alliance (SPSSM) originally comprising 23 countries (which later morphed into the Group of 33 – G33).[8] The G22 put the conference on notice that the success of the meeting depended on the need for significant movement in agriculture. The coalition had emerged in response to fears that the US and the EU were attempting to negotiate a bilateral deal at the exclusion of the interests of developing countries; as one delegate put it, they feared that the US and EU would 'pull another Blair House Accord' (Narlikar and Tussie, 2004: 950). Yet the G22 was significant for more than just its stance. It brought together some surprising allies – advocates of agricultural liberalisation with those seeking to protect various aspects of their markets – whose co-operation proved all the more significant given the degree of bilateral (largely EU and

US) pressure exerted in an effort to split the coalition. Most striking perhaps was that the G22 combined Cairns group countries like Brazil and Argentina with countries like India that had a defensive interest in agriculture (Narlikar and Wilkinson, 2004: 456). Also significant was G22 support for the SPSSM group/G33 – a coalition of much smaller, economically more vulnerable developing countries. Rather than substantive movement on agricultural liberalisation the SPSSM group/G33 sought the negotiation of special measures designed to improve food security and protect the rural livelihoods of resource-poor farmers; measures that would invariably witness an *increase* in the degree of protectionism among the poorest. These were joined by a small coalition that emerged in the run-up to and during the ministerial of four West and Central African countries (Mali, Benin, Chad and Burkina Faso, the so-called C4) – organised around a proposal for a complete phase-out of subsidies on cotton and the provision of financial compensation for the least developed countries prior to that phase-out – whose significance lay not in sheer weight of numbers or percentage share of world trade but, as it transpired, as a *cause célèbre* for much of the membership.

The G22, G33 and the C4 were not, however, the only gatherings of note; nor was coalition formation confined to developing countries (though the activities of the latter were perhaps the most noteworthy). An 8 July 2003 communiqué from Bangladesh, Cuba, Egypt, India, Indonesia, Kenya, Malaysia, Nigeria, Pakistan, Venezuela, Zambia and Zimbabwe provided a point of coalescence for those African, Asian, Middle Eastern and Latin American countries strongly opposed to EU pressure to commence negotiations on the Singapore issues, and the notion that negotiations in this area were 'part and parcel' of the DDA (WTO, 2003c). The least developed (LDC), the ACP and the African Union (AU) countries (collectively the ACP/LDC/AU and later known as the Group of 90 – G90)[9] also came together pressing for movement in agriculture, non-agricultural market access, special and differential treatment, and cotton while rejecting the launch of negotiations on the Singapore issues. The Group of ten (G10 – though originally the G9)[10] net food-importing (largely) middle-income countries added further depth to the building tension by refusing to make meaningful concessions on agriculture, arguing that a measure of protection was necessary to preserve rural lifestyles and the cultural integrity of member states. This was a new twist in the multifunctionality argument. Members of this group, in particular Korea, were also notable for their strong support for the commencement of negotiations on the Singapore issues. Also of note was the lack of a presence from the Cairns group in Cancún. This seems to have been the result of several of the key developing country members focusing their efforts on pushing forward the aims of the G22.

Even more notable than the number of coalitions that emerged, however, was the degree to which they combined during the meeting. This was facilitated by the issuing of a second version of the draft text which was, as one WTO official put it, 'liked by nobody'. As Amrita Narlikar and I noted:

[T]he coalitions showed remarkable co-ordination. The ACP, LDC, African Group, Strategic Products Group and G-22 held consultations together. Alliances of sympathy emerged. Hence even though many members of the Africa Group, ACP and LDC were concerned with the issue of their eroding preferences in the face of liberalisation, they supported the position of the G-22. When the Africa Group refused to give in to the Singapore issues on 14 September, it had the moral backing of developing country coalitions across the board. The combination of these coalitions was the so-called G-90.

(Narlikar and Wilkinson, 2004: 457)

Inevitably the meeting collapsed in a hail of acrimony. In the mud-slinging that followed, Cancún USTR Robert Zoellick blamed the agitations, politics of protest, and 'won't do' stances of 'larger developing states' (principally India and Brazil) for the meeting's collapse (Zoellick, 2003); EU Trade Commissioner (and, rather ironically, Supachai's successor as WTO DG) Pascal Lamy once again labelled the WTO a 'medieval' organisation and warned against expectations of a quick resumption of the EU seat at the negotiating table (Lamy, 2003a); and sections of the NGO community celebrated the meeting's significance in the wider battle to resist First World agendas and sink the WTO (put to the tune of 'Can't buy me love' as the meeting closed). Were it not for the conference's ratification of the accession protocols for Cambodia and Nepal and the agreement of a six-paragraph ministerial declaration attesting to 'considerable' progress having been made during the meeting, little of consolation would have been salvaged from Cancún (WTO, 2003a).

More controversially, Conference Chair and Mexican Foreign Minister Luis Ernesto Derbez came in for considerable criticism for his decision to call the meeting to a close only part-way through the final day just at the point wherein movement appeared to be emerging in the entrenched positions of the industrial and developing countries. Derbez's actions were at variance with pre-existing expectations of the passage of ministerials in which vigorous negotiating often begins only in the very late stages and meetings are extended as a result. This was clearly the case in Cancún. The EU, whose position seemed to be set in stone, signalled almost at the close of play that it was prepared to consider 'unbundling' the Singapore issues. This would have left negotiations on the more contentious issues (investment and competition policy) to a later date in return for movement in other areas (largely agriculture) – a position confirmed by Lamy in his final press conference to the meeting (Lamy, 2003a). Moreover, murmurs from the US team suggested that further concessions were also possible, but that to trigger these required a willingness to negotiate from developing states. The absence of any movement on the latter's part made the collapse almost inevitable.

Yet Derbez's decision to call the conference to a close was probably not, as some have suggested, the result of his inexperience of chairing such meetings. At least one commentator has argued that Derbez's decision was, in large measure, part of a negotiating strategy operationalised at the behest of USTR Zoellick to get 'other players to return [to the negotiations] with more chips' (Bhagwati, 2004c: 63). In pursuing this line of argument, Jagdish Bhagwati suggests that Zoellick's frustration with developing countries during the meeting was fuelled by their refusal to respond to pre-conference signals and movements made by the US (such as the agreement to a waiver to the TRIPs agreement for generic drugs and signals that the US would wind down export subsidies). Zoellick's resolve was hardened when, in the final moments of the meeting, a walk-out was staged by representatives from least developed African and Caribbean countries and it became inevitable that the meeting would be abandoned, thereby generating pressure to reconvene afresh (and with more chips) at a later date (Zoellick, 2003).

After Cancún

In the settling of dust, matters seemed little better. Hopes that the DDA would be energised by the convening of another ministerial conference relatively soon after Cancún were dashed when it emerged in late February 2004 that the Hong Kong authorities had been unable to agree a date for a meeting, and given the lead time necessary for preparations (an estimated nine months) the meeting would not take place that year; the most talked-about developing country coalition forged in the run-up to and during the meeting (the G22) remained intact (albeit with some attrition to G20); persistent calls from the WTO DG, UN officials (including, again, Kofi Annan), and trade ministers across the developed and developing world for serious negotiating to recommence initially went unanswered; US frustration at the intransigence that crystallised in Cancún was alleviated slightly by progress made in securing bilateral trade deals (Zoellick, 2004: 3, 7–9); even Lamy's efforts to skate over North–South and EU–US tensions in the wake of the meeting proved unconvincing (Lamy, 2003b). Indeed, the only common ground to emerge was that the DDA would not reach a conclusion before the 1 January 2005 deadline.

Yet these declarations of innocence and blame, of victory and defeat and of a resolve to seek trade gains by other means are all part of the rhythm of trade politics. After the initial period of reflection, and much like Seattle, the post-Cancún process saw renewed energy among the WTO membership and the reappearance of a familiar pattern of political bargaining. Breaking the ice, in early 2004 both the US and EU signalled that they were ready to negotiate the elimination of all forms of agricultural export subsidies (including credits and food aid – US tools to promote exports – as well as more traditional means of subsidising exports) (Clapp, 2004: 1444). By June 2004 DG Supachai was praising delegates for the progress that had been made in the agricultural negotiations (albeit peppered with the obligatory encouragement to keep moving forward). Each of the principal protagonists in the Cancún showdown had submitted papers outlining their preferred ways of moving forward – the G20, G10 and G33 – and the EU again stressed its willingness to phase out export subsidies on the condition that other (largely US) forms of subsidising exports were eliminated and that an 'acceptable' outcome could be reached on market access and domestic support (WTO, 2004a).

Negotiations nevertheless continued in their normal fashion. Three weeks before the self-imposed deadline of the end of July 2004, DG Supachai encouraged the G90 to show greater flexibility in their demands, warning of the consequences of not reaching agreement (WTO, 2004b; see also WTO, 2004d). Others, too, sought to influence the discussions by framing them with familiar worries about the consequences of not reaching agreement as well as by the preceding crisis of the Cancún meeting (see World Bank, 2004: ix). GC Chair Shotaro Oshima put together a draft text aimed at bridging outstanding differences in the final stages of the negotiations (which, in a positive development, indicated in the text where agreement had been reached, albeit that this was only in the two least contentious areas: services and dispute settlement negotiations – see WTO, 2004c). In addition to reaffirming the development-centreness of the round, and encouraging members to agree to the negotiating framework set out in Annex A relating to agriculture (which, among other things, highlighted the case of cotton and proposed an overall tiered tariff-cutting formula), the text, for the first time, placed only one of the four Singapore issues firmly on the negotiating table: trade facilitation. Moreover, it clearly stated that investment, competition policy and government procurement would not form part of the DDA (WTO, 2004c: paragraph f).

The rest of the GC session went according to the form book. Meetings among a core group of leading members dominated proceedings (this time the US, EU, India, Brazil and Australia) and eventually brokered an agreement. Although this group comprised members of key coalitions (Brazil and India for the G20 and Australia for the Cairns group) their caucusing and the degree to which other parties to the July discussions were precluded from negotiations proved a source of considerable irritation. In a statement read to the 28 July 2004 meeting of the GC Swiss Confederation, President Joseph Deiss argued that the five (later known as the Five Interested Parties – FIP) should have 'had the courtesy' to consult with the wider membership; a representative of the G20 said, not without a touch of irony bearing in mind developing country complaints about the green room process, they had no objection to small group meetings as long as information about the sessions was disseminated thereafter; and the G10 complained that 'with so little time before the 30 July deadline, they would be forced to accept a text without the opportunity of participating in its drafting' (WTO, 2004e).

Other familiar GATT/WTO traits prevailed at the meeting. The second revision of the text delivered to delegates on what was supposed to be the eve of the GC's conclusion generated myriad responses ranging in degree of hostility (though unlike in Cancún, most agreed that the text was a step in the right direction). GC Chair Oshima told delegates that much work was needed to complete an agreement, including the possibility of continuing through the night; and he also warned of the consequences of not reaching agreement. And small group caucusing and alliance building dominated the session before its end. The meeting nevertheless proved successful. On 1 August 2004 WTO members finally agreed to a framework agreement in agriculture and non-agricultural market access (NAMA); movement forward in service negotiations; a commitment to continue the consultation process on the extension of the TRIPs agreement; the commencement of negotiations on one of the Singapore issues (trade facilitation); the ejection of the remaining three Singapore issues from the DDA; and an extension in the timeframe of the overall negotiations with a view to their conclusion sometime after the WTO's Hong Kong ministerial meeting (December 2005) (WTO, 2004f).

From July 2004 to Hong Kong

Despite the success in agreeing the July 2004 package and the momentum it had generated for the completion of the DDA, the run-up to the WTO's sixth ministerial meeting (Hong Kong, December 2005) was not without warnings of the potential for the meeting to collapse with varying degrees of significance for the DDA as well as for the WTO as an institution. In his assessment of the meeting's likely outcome, for instance, Fred Bergsten argued that unless expectations for the meeting and the round as a whole were significantly scaled down:

> The Doha Round may . . . become the first major multilateral trade negotiation to fail since the 1930s. The collapse could even take place, or be clearly heralded, at the ministerial meeting in Hong Kong. Such an outcome could mark a historic reversal in the irregular but steady progress toward liberalizing world trade over the past sixty years. Since history clearly shows that trade policy must move forward continuously or risk sliding backward into protectionism and mercantilism . . . the consequences of Doha's failure for international security as well as economic relations around the world could be enormous.
>
> (2005: 15–16)

Bergsten was not alone in worrying about the outcome of the Hong Kong meeting. Former USTR Carla Hills argued that 'there is a significant risk that [the negotiations] could collapse or achieve only a fraction of their potential' (Hills, 2005: 25). Former GATT DG Peter Sutherland reminded negotiators that 'a failure of the Doha round would do much damage' both to economic growth and development as well as to 'the notion of multilateralism' (Sutherland, 2005: 46). Outgoing WTO DG Supachai Panitchpakdi warned that the negotiations were 'in trouble' and that 'very little of the political support . . . shown at successive Ministerial meetings [had] been turned into concrete progress in the negotiating groups' (Supachai, 2005). Business leaders suggested that little time remained to 'save' the DDA and that the 'great hopes for global economic growth and development promised by this trade round are now at serious risk' (*Financial Times*, 6 September 2005). Furthermore, Commonwealth Heads of Government Meeting (CHOGM) November 2005 Valletta Statement on Multilateral Trade expressed deep concern 'about the pace of the negotiations' (CHOGM, 2005, paragraph 6).

These warnings were not, of course, without some foundation. In the run-up to the Hong Kong meeting tensions among members remained much in evidence and progress in the negotiations proved frustratingly slow. Despite an agreement to focus on the technical aspects of the agricultural negotiations and to maintain a transparent process, concerns that the FIP were yet again dominating the shape and direction of the discussions were raised by the G10 and various least developed countries; significant divergences emerged in the way in which members interpreted the content of the July 2004 agreement on agriculture; least developed countries expressed concerns about the potential for preferences already in existence to be eroded by commitments made in the DDA; the G10 and the EU expressed concerns about overly ambitious moves to reduce levels of agricultural domestic support; the agricultural negotiations were repeatedly deadlocked over a formula for converting specific duties into percentage base *ad valorem* equivalents (moving from duties based on the volume to the value of imports); and the deadline of July 2005 for agreeing outline modalities for negotiations in agriculture was missed.

Beyond agriculture, matters were little better. A December 2004 Africa group proposal amending the August 2003 decision on TRIPs and public health seeking to loosen the constraints placed upon members importing generic pharmaceuticals was not well received, with particular opposition coming from Australia, Canada, the EU, Hong Kong, Japan, Korea, New Zealand, Norway, Switzerland, Taiwan, Turkey and the US. By March 2005 – two years after the original deadline – more than 40 members (principally, though not exclusively, developing countries) had failed to table offers in the services negotiations. The NAMA negotiations appeared to be in perpetual deadlock; members clashed on the structure of the discussions, the relative merits of pursing single-sector negotiations, the tariff-cutting formula to be deployed (with the majority of the industrial states favouring the Swiss formula, while most developing countries pushed for 'less than reciprocity'), and the July 2005 deadline for agreement on the basic structure of the NAMA negotiations was missed. Deadlines were consistently missed in the Committee on Trade and Development (CTD) for proposing 'clear recommendations' to the GC on special and differential treatment. Little beyond a tacit acceptance that movement would be forthcoming only in the closing stages of the DDA occurred in negotiations on anti-dumping rules. Members were divided on how to deal with the issue of fisheries subsidies. Little progress was made in the services negotiations; pressure by Australia, the EU and US to establish mandatory minimum market access commitments (so-called benchmarks) to increase the level of ambition in the services negotiations was strongly opposed by the majority of developing countries (with the notable exception of India); an Indian-led developing country push for improvements in industrial member commitments to the 'natural movement of persons' under mode 4 of the GATS yielded little; and progress in all areas was hindered by a widespread reluctance to engage in meaningful negotiations without first knowing at least the outline of a deal in agriculture.

The sloth in the negotiations and the re-emergence of tensions therein were fuelled by a series of dispute settlement decisions (for instance, over sugar, cotton, beef hormones, bananas and gambling) as well as over specific issues (such as concerns over the potential damage to the competitiveness of the textile and clothing industries of Bangladesh, the Dominican Republic, Fiji, Jamaica, Madagascar, Mauritius, Mongolia, Nepal, Sri Lanka, Turkey and Uganda from China and India in the wake of the removal of quotas by January 2005). The run-up to the Hong Kong meeting was, nevertheless, qualitatively different to that which had preceded Seattle and Cancún. The election of a successor to Supachai as WTO DG proved remarkably straightforward (with former EU Trade Commissioner Pascal Lamy being elected to the post).[11] More generally, a willingness to keep moving forward with negotiations despite the persistence of significant differences was in evidence. In TRIPs, in November 2005 members agreed to exempt least developing countries from obligations to apply rules protecting patents, copyrights and other intellectual property until 2012; and a 6 December decision saw members agree to a permanent solution to the issue of TRIPs and public health. In agriculture, a formula for *ad valorem* conversion agreed at the 4 May Paris mini-ministerial was accepted by members as an acceptable way forward. Likewise, a G20 proposal on agricultural market access was agreed at the Dalian mini-ministerial meeting (July 2005) as the basis for further discussions. In addition to market access commitments, on 10 October 2005 the US offered to make significant cuts in its domestic agricultural support régime contingent on EU and Japanese reciprocation. The EU made a counter offer shortly thereafter and submitted a further 'new and improved' proposal on 28 October 2005. Proposals were also forthcoming from the G10, G20 and ACP group. In addition, when it became clear that members were unable to bridge remaining differences in agriculture ahead of the Hong Kong meeting (thereby failing to reach agreement on full negotiating modalities – the initial aim of the ministerial) they agreed to scale back expectations, reflect upon the progress that had been made in the draft declaration, and continue negotiations in the wake of Hong Kong with a view to agreeing full modalities in the early part of 2006.

Consistent with the general post-crisis politics that pervaded the post-Cancún era, the immediate run-up to the Hong Kong ministerial saw a general lowering of expectations beyond just agriculture (see Lamy, 2005) and a shift towards reaching agreement on a package to assist the least developed countries – comprising, in addition to reaching a solution on the TRIPs and public health issue, duty-free and quota-free access into developed countries for all LDCs; amendments to existing special and differential provisions in WTO agreements; and a strong Aid for Trade package designed to enable the least developed countries to take advantage of market opening opportunities. Crucially, this lowering of expectations and the focus on a development package – aims all widely agreed to be 'deliverable' prior to the meeting – proved instrumental in ensuring the ministerial's success.

Hong Kong (December 2005)

Despite the signs that an agreement would be reached, for much of the meeting the international print media reported negotiations to be deadlocked, steeped in acrimony and unlikely to succeed (see, for instance, *Wall Street Journal*, 14 December 2005); NGO commentary focused on problems with the negotiating process and the potential consequences for developing countries/labour/the environment should aspects of the draft text not be revised (or removed); while the local press concentrated on the disruptions caused by protestors outside of the meeting (*The Standard*, 16 December 2005; *Sunday Morning Post*, 18 December 2005), the folly of the Hong Kong authorities for agreeing to host the event and the economic costs arising therefrom (see Vines, 2005).

Hong Kong was, however, a much less politically charged affair than the media commentary suggested. What unfolded was merely trade politics as usual, the result of the manner in which the development of multilateral trade regulation has structured the interaction of participating states. Inevitably, agriculture proved to be the principal fault line among members, with development, NAMA and services also figuring prominently. Despite efforts to emphasise that the drafting and redrafting of texts was a 'bottom-up' (that is, member-led) process, the DG, secretariat and the facilitators again came in for criticism for their role in shaping discussions. The pursuit of negotiating leverage encouraged grand coalition-building as existing groups sought to bolster their strength by combining with others (as was the case with the coming together of the G20, G33 and the G90 to form a self-styled Group of 110 – G110). *Ad hoc* groupings of members emerged on specific issues, most notably the 'friends of ambition' in the NAMA negotiations.[12] In addition, politics and grandstanding between key protagonists were played out during press briefings.

Likewise, the negotiations followed a familiar pattern. Discussions began with intensity only on the third and fourth days and were concluded after the obligatory round-the-clock meetings. An impromptu protest outside an

EU press briefing on 15 December saw the secretariat issue a warning to NGOs about such actions and threatened to ban them from further briefings. Korean farmers – who seem to have developed a comparative advantage in such activities – engaged in a variety of demonstrations designed to disrupt the meeting. Despite much talk of a 'development package' for the least developed countries and nods to their plight among their developing and developed counterparts, several of the smallest, most vulnerable developing countries had to rely on imported 'experts' to make up numbers in their delegations; and a few found themselves relying on contacts in the NGO community for updates on progress in the discussions. In addition, green room meetings continued to form the basis of negotiations – albeit that they were renamed gatherings of the 'chairman's consultative group'.

Beneath the theatre of the meeting, the Hong Kong meeting proved to be a quintessential instance of post-crisis politics. For all the debate over duty-free and quota-free access, the end date for a phase-out of export subsidies, market access in agriculture, which coefficients to deploy in the operationalisation of the Swiss formula as a tariff-cutting mechanism in NAMA,[13] the degree of ambition for the services negotiations, the plight of African cotton producers and the provision of Aid for Trade, the meeting was always likely to succeed. The collapse of the Cancún meeting and the political settlement reached in the July 2004 package ensured that despite a general negotiating sloth, each of the principal protagonists approached the meeting in an optimistic and willing fashion. Moreover, in those moments when the discussions were portrayed as deadlocked, the spectre of crisis was wheeled out to focus attention on the need for a successful conclusion. EU Trade Commissioner Peter Mandelson did precisely this in his 15 December press briefing.

The meeting's unfolding reflected the concerted effort to produce a positive result. Negotiations were conducted, in the first instance, in only three areas reflecting those wherein significant tensions existed and where compromises were necessary to generate an agreement – agriculture, NAMA and development; and the content of the discussions was far from ambitious. It was not until the fourth day of the meeting that the negotiating group on services was convened (though informal discussions on services had been taking place between principal protagonists from the meeting's outset), while a fifth group put on call for the duration of the meeting was not operationalised.

The meeting resulted in the production of a 59-paragraph, 11-page ministerial text with six accompanying annexes (relating to: agriculture, market access for non-agricultural products, services, rules, trade facilitation and special and differential treatment) altered slightly from the pre-meeting version. While the declaration provided for only modest movement in the DDA, it was nevertheless a far cry from the six-paragraph declaration released in Cancún. At its core the declaration saw members agree to: (in agriculture) the broad structure for reductions in domestic support and market access as well as to a date of the end of 2013 for the phase-out of export subsidies; (on cotton) the elimination of all forms of export subsidies 'in 2006', and duty-free and quota-free access for products from least development members by the developed countries; (in NAMA) the adoption of the Swiss formula as the mechanism for cutting tariffs, though agreement on the respective coefficients for developed and developing members was not forthcoming; and (in services) movement forward in establishing the parameters of the negotiations without the pre-ministerial desiderata that countries engage in market access negotiations on a plurilateral basis should they be presented with a request to do so (see WTO, 2005). In addition, the Declaration set out five elements of a development package in the form of amendments to the special and differential treatment enjoyed by least developed members. In this regard, members agreed to:

(i)   give requests for waivers under Article IX of the WTO's Establishing Agreement and the Understanding in Respect of Waivers and Obligations under the GATT 1994 'positive consideration' and where possible give a decision within 60 days;
(ii) provide duty-free and quota-free access to all products originating from LDCs into industrial country markets and the markets of those developing countries in a position to do so (with flexibilities and caveats at the margins); ensure the preferential rules of origin applied to imports from LDCs are 'transparent and simple and contribute to facilitating market access'; and implement a surveillance mechanism to ensure compliance;
(iii) reaffirm that LDCs need only undertake commitments and give concessions consistent with their 'individual development, financial or trade needs, or their administrative and institutional capacities'; and that international financial institutions and donors should not place conditions on LDCs inconsistent with their WTO obligations;
(iv) allow LDCs to deviate from their obligations under the TRIMs for seven years (for existing measures) and five years (for new measures) renewable by the GC until a final phase-out date of 2020;
(v)   provide further technical and financial assistance to enable LDCs to meet their obligations and commitments as well as to better realise the opportunities presented by trade liberalisation (that is, provide Aid for Trade) (WTO, 2005: Annex F).

Members also agreed to establish a task force to provide recommendations to the GC by July 2006 on how Aid for Trade might contribute 'most effectively to the development dimension of the DDA' (WTO, 2005: paragraph 57).

There is little to suggest that the round will now not be concluded, or that outcome of the DDA will be significantly different – in terms of the balance of concessions – from previous rounds. The round's conclusion may well see the final bargain heavily peppered with the language of development and include provisions to assist the poorest at the margins that build upon those agreed in Hong Kong, but it will nevertheless bring greater economic opportunities to the industrial states than their developing counterparts. This will inevitably be the case as the gains for the developed members resulting from further liberalisation in NAMA, services and an extension of the TRIPs agreement, among others, far outweigh the benefits that will be accrued by developing states from the moderate liberalisation of agriculture, adjustments to special and differential treatment, the ability to deploy safeguards on special products and so on. As a result, the conclusion of the DDA will inevitably perpetuate and extend the asymmetries in economic opportunity to which WTO rules and their deployment give rise. The conclusion will not, however, be without the drama that has come to characterise WTO negotiations; nor will crisis cease to play an important role therein. Rather, the persistence of asymmetries in economic opportunity arising from WTO rules and their deployment combined with the continuation of practices and procedures that concentrate decision-making power in the hands of the few will ensure that the threat and prospect of the collapse of further ministerial meetings will remain. And until or unless a fundamental overhaul of the way in multilateral trade regulation takes place, an alternative institution emerges wherein trade objectives can be better realised, a dramatic shift occurs in the global balance of power bringing with it sweeping changes in global institutional structures, or else the ideological consensus underpinning the WTO changes radically, crisis will continue to play a role in the institution's further development.

The argument so far

When set within their proper context – that is, within the development of post-war multilateral trade regulation – what the collapse of the Seattle and Cancún meetings clearly illustrates is that they have neither significantly interrupted the institutional development of the GATT/WTO nor precipitated a significant change in the balance of power in trade politics. Moreover, this contextualisation clearly demonstrates that the collapse of these meetings is a direct consequence of the way in which the development of multilateral trade regulation has structured the interaction of member states. At the root of the political contestation given rise to by the development of multilateral trade regulation lies a struggle over economic opportunity. This is manifest, on the one hand, in the pursuit of remedial provisions to address asymmetries of opportunity in multilateral trade regulation by developing, agricultural and textiles producing countries, and on the other, attempts to preserve competitive advantages by the leading industrial states through the pursuit of congruous market opening opportunities (such as in non-agricultural market access and services), greater protection of intellectual property rights and the liberalisation of leading-edge sectors.

Yet, rather than producing institutional inertia, each crisis has actually served to facilitate the further development of multilateral trade regulation. This is the result of an institutional development that has locked member states into a process of negotiation and selective liberalisation framed by a fear of the perceived consequences of a collapse coupled with a shared perception that the gains of multilateral liberalisation far outweigh those that can be realised bilaterally or regionally. This, in turn, ensures that despite the existence of widely acknowledged asymmetries of opportunity, all members consent to their continued involvement. As Andrew Brown and Robert Stern (2005: 1) put it:

> it is, of course, true that the more powerful exercise greater influence and that the weak are often obliged to compromise. Though, in principle, a country is free to withdraw from GATT/WTO, its loss of rights like MFN treatment or access to the dispute settlement machinery is a deterrent. So it is quite possible for an individual state to emerge worse off from a particular round of negotiations and to find itself with no choice but to accept the worsened status.

It is to the conclusion of this book that we now turn.

6   Conclusion

Each of the preceding chapters has explored in detail one aspect of the creation and evolution of multilateral trade regulation with a view to developing a more complete understanding of the causes, consequences and role of crisis in the WTO. This concluding chapter draws together the various pieces of the argument developed throughout the book. My purpose has been to show that the collapse of WTO meetings has so far been misunderstood; that crisis has a more organic connection to the development of multilateral trade regulation than is seldom recognised; and that contemporary trade politics can only be fully comprehended when set within an appreciation of the way in which the institution's creation and evolution have shaped the interaction of its participants. Throughout I have argued that much of the literature fails to see beyond the drama of a collapsed meeting to the root causes of the heightened political contestation underpinning the breakdown. My contention has been that the literature places too much emphasis on the tensions among the membership over substantive issues, and the practices and procedures deployed in the conduct of trade negotiations as explanations of a meeting's collapse without first appreciating that these are actually consequences of the unique and peculiar way in which multilateral trade regulation as an institution has evolved. Throughout I have argued that the heightened political contestation underpinning the collapse of ministerial meetings is the product of asymmetries of economic opportunity that have arisen from the way in which the institution was created, the manner in which it was deployed, and the way it has developed through time.

I have also argued that in focusing too closely on ministerials as isolated moments in time and not placing them in their appropriate historical and institutional context, the literature has failed to acknowledge that, without exception, the breakdown of a meeting has been followed by a period of reflection and renewed focus – what I refer to as a post-crisis politics – which, in turn, has resulted in the further development of multilateral trade regulation. This has been the case following the collapse of each of the five GATT/WTO ministerials that have broken down since 1982. As a consequence, the collapse of a ministerial meeting needs to be understood as a decisive moment in the evolution of multilateral trade regulation wherein its future shape is being contested but where the outcome of that contestation has yet to be settled. However, and most importantly, rather than producing adjustments that attenuate existing asymmetries of opportunity embedded in the institution's legal framework or given rise to by the manner of its deployment, these moments of reflection and renewed energy have facilitated the perpetuation and, on occasion, the amplification of those asymmetries. They have not resulted in any more than minor adjustments to the GATT/WTO's legal framework or the manner in which it has been operationalised. Indeed, substantive remedial action has only been forthcoming in those instances wherein it has also been in the interests of the institution's principal players. The negotiation of the Agreement on Agriculture during the Uruguay round, for instance, would not have been possible had it not been for a US desire to open up EU markets; likewise, the negotiation of the Agreement on Textiles and Clothing was only possible because the production of textiles and clothing in the industrial states had fallen to a point wherein it had ceased to be of major political significance. Yet it is precisely because little has been done to correct the asymmetries of opportunity in the GATT/WTO's legal framework that heightened political contestation continues to be a feature of trade politics, and the collapse of ministerial meetings remains a possibility.

More generally, the book has shown how the development of multilateral trade regulation has come to shape the behaviour of participating states as well as the outcomes that result from their interaction. Like its post-war counterparts – the IMF and World Bank – the system of multilateral trade regulation over which the WTO now presides was fashioned for a specific purpose. That purpose was to assist in the realisation of US post-war economic opportunities. Multilateral trade regulation was not designed to be a vehicle for trade-led growth for all, though it did offer the European Allies a measure of assistance with post-war reconstruction. It is unsurprising, then, that the institution should reflect the interests of its principal architect. It is also inevitable that the institution would evolve in a manner that would reflect both the purpose for which it was originally designed and the relations of power embedded therein.

Reflecting its initial purpose, the GATT was first deployed to facilitate an increase in the volume and value of trade between its principal contracting parties. This led to a concentration on the liberalisation of industrial, manufactured and capital goods markets. Later, key areas of interest to developing countries, and economic and political sensitivity to the advanced industrial states (largely, though not exclusively, the US and later the EU), were removed as legitimate targets of liberalisation: primarily agriculture, and textiles and clothing. Moreover, as each trade round was concluded a new layer of regulation was laid on top of the existing asymmetry thereby perpetuating and amplifying the inequities of economic opportunity therein. The result was to entrench into the very fabric of multilateral trade liberalisation a contestation. This contestation has been played out between those contracting parties better able to take advantage of the economic opportunities presented by the GATT/WTO's peculiar design and operationalisation (largely the leading industrial states) and those not (particularly agricultural and textile producing countries). In turn, this has fuelled tensions between those seeking to take the trade agenda forward to further benefit from multilateral trade regulation (again, largely the leading industrial states) and those seeking to attenuate existing asymmetries of opportunity (much of the rest). In this way, the development of multilateral trade regulation has structured the interaction of participating states such that tensions over aspects of the trade agenda are inevitable by-products. The result has been to imbue ministerial meetings with a propensity to collapse.

What is interesting about the development of multilateral trade regulation is that since it was created it has not departed to any significant degree in form or function from its original design: that is, a critical juncture has not emerged signalling a clear departure from existing practice. It is, in this way, distinct from institutions such as the ILO that have, to ensure their continued relevance, undergone periodic processes of reinvention (see Hughes, 2002; Haworth *et al.*, 2005). What has occurred instead has been a steady consolidation of multilateral trade regulation's form through the growing codification and entrenchment of the rules, practices and procedures developed for its original purpose and their steady extension into other areas of economic activity (services, intellectual property, investment measures and so on). Indeed, at those moments wherein reform was on the agenda the contracting parties/members eschewed a fundamental overhaul in favour of minor fettling at the margins: the operationalisation of Article XXV (Joint Action by the Contracting Parties) of the GATT in the wake of the ITO's failure; the consolidation of existing procedures and ways of operating in the face of the demise of the OTC; the addition of Part IV in an effort to satisfy growing criticism of the General Agreement's incongruity with the economic needs of developing states; the pursuit of detailed legalisms during the Tokyo agenda as means of creating greater certainty in trade rules but without attenuating the asymmetries therein; the deepening, widening and further codification of existing trade rules (though not their substantive alteration), and creation of the WTO during the Uruguay round; and the pursuit of a 'development agenda' during the DDA based on traditional negotiating trade-offs and bargains. These minor concessions have had the effect of momentarily satisfying recalcitrant states. They have not, however, substantively refashioned or significantly overhauled multilateral trade regulations.

One reason for the GATT/WTO's incremental development is that the institution has been relatively successful in fulfilling its original purpose and, as a result (and in spite of some domestic political rhetoric to the contrary, particularly in the US), it has enjoyed the continued support of its dominant members. Moreover, as post-war liberalisation has steadily removed barriers to trade among the industrial states, leaving only those that are 'the hardest to tackle' (Bergsten, 2005: 16), the GATT and now the WTO has become an important machinery in which industrial states are able to, at best protect, and at least forestall, those areas of declining competitiveness – such as agriculture, textiles and clothing, certain manufactures and so on. In this way, multilateral trade regulation has remained an important tool of foreign economic policy for the leading industrial states.

A second reason for the incremental development of multilateral trade regulation is that the configuration of power in which it was forged has not altered significantly to bring about the institution's overhaul. While it is the case that the end of the Cold War saw the Soviet Union fall by the wayside, the USSR was not a participant in the GATT, nor was it an institution designed to serve Soviet economic interests. Moreover, while the EU has come to rival, in the economic realm at least, the US, and Japan and the East Asian NICs have also become key players, they have not challenged American supremacy to such an extent that existing institutions are either abandoned or fundamentally overhauled. What has occurred instead has been the use of an existing institutional architecture by those powers that have come to be significant. This is because the economic development of these states has evolved in such a way that their interests are now also (broadly) served by the way in which the GATT/WTO is deployed as a machinery for liberalisation (albeit with notable areas of conflict such as agriculture). This use of an existing institutional architecture has, in turn, had the effect of reinforcing the existing balance of power.

Moreover, while the GATT and the WTO were not constructed in such a way that their institutional architectures formally reflected the prevailing configuration of power – with, for example, the creation of an executive committee as had been envisaged under the ITO, OTC and suggested during the Uruguay round – their legal frameworks, the manner which they were deployed as a means of liberalising trade (of which the principal-supplier rule played a crucial role), their decision-making procedures (including green room diplomacy), and the creation of *de facto* ruling bodies (such as the CG18 and the quad) clearly reflected that power structure. And while it may be the case that key developing countries such as India and Brazil (but also South Africa and to a lesser extent China – at least for the moment) have come to play a role in core decision-making fora, as is the case with the reforms that have been made to the international financial architecture (and in particular the creation of the Group of 20 Finance Ministers – G20 Finance), most of their counterparts nevertheless remain on the periphery.

A third reason for the incremental development of multilateral trade regulation (as well as for the heightened political contestation and the propensity for ministerial meetings to collapse that have become features therein) has been the lack of an alternative fora in which trade objectives might be realised. Challenges to the authority of the GATT/WTO as the primary machinery for trade liberalisation have emerged. The most significant alternative vision was provided by UNCTAD, though both the ITO and OTC also offered competing (albeit only slightly differing) versions of multilateral trade regulation. However, they have all, without exception, been unsuccessful. Both the ITO and OTC failed to come to fruition, while the decision to give UNCTAD a formal and permanent presence, but not powers to go beyond the issuing of recommendations, neutered the institution. Moreover, bilateral and regional initiatives have proved to be only a limited means by which trade objectives can be realised; they are relatively more costly and time-consuming than multilateral negotiations and promise fewer results, though they nevertheless have value as strategically and economically important tools of foreign policy. The result has been to make the WTO administered system of multilateral trade liberalisation the *only* game in town. In so doing, it has ensured that the WTO is a site of contestation between competing forces. And until a competing machinery emerges around which a consensus is built, or else a fundamental rupture in the WTO's evolutionary trajectory occurs (either causing the institution to be radically overhauled or bringing about its collapse – neither of which seems likely given the consensus that currently exists on trade-led growth as the model of economic development and the WTO's position as the only forum in which that objective is pursued on a multilateral basis), multilateral trade regulation will remain the site of contestation.

The lack of a reform process in multilateral trade regulation has also heightened political contestation in another way. Although it was the case that a large proportion of the GATT's contracting parties were only party to the General Agreement in name and were not involved in trade negotiations until the Uruguay round (and even then in only a peripheral fashion) the pursuit of trade deals as single undertakings has seen the institution struggle to take account of the myriad trade interests that are now encompassed by its membership. In a purely numerical sense, it is much easier to reach agreement among 23 parties (as during the original GATT negotiations) sharing broadly similar trade objectives than it is among 149 members of vastly differing economic complexions. When married to a trade institution that is merely a development of an original machinery for negotiating among a limited subset of states, it is unsurprising that almost every facet of trade negotiations is contested. Put differently, and to paraphrase Feis's observation of the ITO Havana negotiations, it is only to be expected that almost everyone is trying to fashion the negotiations in the service of their special necessities, ideas, wishes or prejudices (see Feis, 1948: 51).

Exacerbating tensions among members further are the decision-making procedures that have evolved through time and become established features of the institution's operation. We need think no further than the persistence of green room diplomacy as the preferred means of nurturing agreement, the deployment of confessions to reveal delegations' bottom lines, the appointment of friends of the Chair, the absence of agreed procedures for the conduct and organisation of negotiations, and the role of various 'forum-plus' tactics such as strong-arming delegates, linkage to non-trade (particularly security) concerns and the like as instantly recognisable facets of this.

Yet it is not only these practices and procedures that contribute to the heightening of political contestation; it is the organisational culture that has emerged in tandem with the development of multilateral trade regulation. Not only are institutional factors implicated in the collapse of ministerials; a culture of expectation has evolved surrounding the acknowledgement that meetings do collapse and that this is part of the normal rhythm of trade politics (as seasoned trade practitioners and secretariat officials alike testify). Likewise, an expectation has emerged that negotiating only begins with vigour in the closing stages of negotiations (whether during rounds or ministerials); and the collapse of some projects has come to be accepted precisely because the trade bicycle keeps moving forward and an outcome will eventually be produced. Indeed, as the large majority of GATT/WTO negotiations have clearly demonstrated, the real deadline is the date at which US presidential authority expires (particularly when there is no realistic hope that authority will be extended). The Kennedy and Uruguay rounds provide good examples to support this claim.

While it remains the case that demonstrations during ministerials have not in themselves been the causal factors of a meeting's collapse, the growth of civil society interest in multilateral trade regulation has nevertheless raised awareness and, on occasion, contributed to the heightening of political tensions over particular issues. This is evident on at least four levels: first, through the contribution of demonstrations during, and public interest in, the WTO ministerial meetings; second, through the growing use of particular NGOs as sources of expertise (particularly by developing countries seeking to advance their understanding of, and position in, trade negotiations); third, through the contribution of civil society organisations to debate in the run-up to, during and following a ministerial meeting; and fourth, through the growing number of NGO representatives attending WTO ministerials as members of official state delegations.

What we can also see in exploring the emergence and subsequent development of multilateral trade regulation, then, is a series of developments that structure the relations of participating states in such a way that they give rise to heightened political contestation. This, in turn, lends ministerial meetings a propensity to collapse. The crises brought about by the collapse of a meeting – as well as the threat thereof – has helped take multilateral trade regulation forward (and the asymmetry of economic opportunity embedded therein) at moments wherein significant blockages have existed. That is, crisis has opened up opportunities for further development. In this way crisis has played a dynamic role in the development of multilateral trade regulation rather than the institution-threatening, balance-of-power adjusting or inertia-generating function assumed in much of the literature. In those moments when a crisis has prevailed, the fear of what might happen should the trade bicycle be allowed to stall has served to concentrate minds. This concentration of minds has been played out not only as a worry that an unchecked surge in protectionist sentiment might usher in the kind of nationalist insularity that characterised the inter-war period, but also as a realisation by all of the trading powers (large and small) that the route to trade-led growth lies not in the conclusion of myriad bilateral and regional agreement but rather though a multilateral agreement.

In sum, the root causes of the collapse of WTO ministerial meetings lie in the particular manner in which the institution of multilateral trade regulation was created and has evolved through time. Moreover, in those moments wherein political contestation appears intractable, the collapse of a ministerial meeting has preceded the emergence of a post-crisis politics more conducive to movement forward. Until or unless a dramatic shift in the global balance of power occurs (in which a vastly different institutional architecture is put into place), an alternative ideological consensus develops, a viable competing institutional framework emerges, and/or a fundamental overhaul of the WTO takes place, the collapse of ministerial meetings and the onset of a post-crisis politics thereafter will continue to be significant features of multilateral trade regulation.

Notes

1 The WTO, crisis and the governance of global trade

1 By which I mean that body of rules and attendant practices and procedures designed to facilitate an increase in the volume and value of trade first put into place under the General Agreement on Tariffs and Trade (GATT) and significantly extended but nevertheless continued under the WTO.

2 Green room meetings take their name from the colour of the decoration of the conference room in the GATT/WTO Secretariat where they were originally held (see Odell, 2005: 433–434).

3 In July 2001 then WTO DG Mike Moore appointed Bhagwati and 11 others to a newly established 'advisory' panel. The panel's aim was to examine 'how the WTO should respond to the needs of member governments and their citizens at a time when an increasingly integrated global economy has brought about profound economic and political change'. In addition to Bhagwati, the panel comprised Robert Baldwin, Peter Eigen, Victor Halberstadt, Koichi Hamada, Patrick Messerlin, Konrad Von Moltke, Sylvia Ostry, Ademola Oyejide, Manmohan Singh, LeRoy Trotman and Ernesto Zedillo. For a collection of papers by most of the panel see Moore, 2004. See also www.wto.org/english/news_e/pres01_e/pr236_e.htm

4 Persons appointed to assist in the facilitating negotiations – also known as 'facilitators'.

2 Forging multilateral trade regulation: the post-war settlement and the rise of GATT

1 The Preparatory Committee consisted of Australia, Belgium, Brazil, Canada, Chile, China, Cuba, Czechoslovakia, France, India, Lebanon, Luxembourg, the Netherlands, New Zealand, Norway, South Africa, the Soviet Union, the United Kingdom, and the United States. Syria also took part in the Geneva discussions as a member of a customs union with Lebanon. The Soviet Union declined to take part in the negotiations, and Belgium, Luxembourg and the Netherlands were represented jointly as a customs union (ITO Report, 1947a: 362).

2 Three of the states chose not to sign the Charter: Argentina, Poland (both of which had previously announced their intention to abstain) and Turkey (whose delegation stated that its instructions had been delayed). Turkey signed the Charter on 26 June 1948 (see ITO Report, 1948b: 365; 1949: 160).

3 The ITO Charter was to come into effect 60 days after just over half (27) of the signatories had ratified the document. Failing that, the Charter would come into effect if 20 states had ratified it by 24 March 1949. If by 30 September

1949 these requirements still had not been met, under the guidance of the UN Secretary-General, those states that had ratified the Charter were to be consulted to determine the conditions under which they would be willing to bring the Charter into effect. The result was to continually extend the timeframe in which signatories were able to ratify the Charter and, by so doing, elongating the institution's demise.

3 Establishing asymmetry: liberalising trade under the GATT

1 The low tariff countries included Austria, the Netherlands, Belgium, Luxembourg, Canada, Denmark, France, Germany, Italy, Norway and Sweden.
2 The 21 were Argentina, Brazil, Burma, Cambodia, Ceylon, Chile, Cuba, Ghana, Haiti, India, Indonesia, Israel, Federation of Malaya, Federation of Nigeria, Pakistan, Peru, Tanganyika, Tunisia, United Arab Republic, Uruguay and Yugoslavia.
3 The 14 contracting parties were Australia, Austria, Belgium, Brazil, Cuba, France, Haiti, India, Luxembourg, the Netherlands, New Zealand, the Federation of Rhodesia and Nyasaland, the Union of South Africa and the United Kingdom (which, incidentally, was most vociferous of all).
4 The title of 'Executive Secretary' as head of the GATT secretariat was changed by a decision of 23 March 1965 to 'Director General' (GATT, 1965: 19).

4 Fashioning the WTO: formalising multilateral trade regulation

1 The CG18 was a group of industrial and developing countries elected annually by the contracting parties designed to discuss key issues and to debate the future direction of the trade agenda. The US, Canada, EEC, Australia, New Zealand, Switzerland and one Nordic country and Brazil, Egypt, India, an ASEAN state and Hungary were more or less permanent members. The group's lack of formal status reflected and served to consolidate the informality that characterised the GATT despite the Tokyo codification process.
2 The Cairns group was formed in the opening stages of the Uruguay round. The group sought to lobby for the inclusion of agriculture under GATT rules. The group took its name from the city in Northeastern Queensland, Australia where it first met. It comprised: Argentina, Australia, Brazil, Canada, Chile, Colombia, Fiji, Hungary, Indonesia, Malaysia, New Zealand, Philippines, Thailand and Uruguay.
3 The Group of Rio consisted of Argentina, Bolivia, Brazil, Colombia, Chile, Ecuador, Mexico, Paraguay, Peru, Uruguay and Venezuela.

5 Perpetuating asymmetry: the collapse of ministerial meetings and the Doba Development Agenda

1 *Amicus curiae* submissions are those filed by persons or bodies that are not party to a case or dispute.
2 Bangladesh, Bhutan, India, Maldives, Nepal, Pakistan, Sri Lanka.
3 Bangladesh (speaking on behalf of the LDC group), Bolivia, Brunei Darussalam, Cuba, Dominican Republic, Guyana, Haiti, Honduras, India, Indonesia, Jamaica, Kenya, Kuwait, Malawi, Malaysia, Nigeria, Pakistan, Paraguay, Philippines, Qatar, Fiji, Sierra Leone, St Kitts and Nevis, Tanzania (speaking on behalf of SADC), Thailand, Trinidad and Tobago, Uganda, Zambia.
4 The negotiations were chaired by George Yeo (Singapore – Agriculture), Pierre Pettigrew (Canada – Implementation and Rules), Mopho Malie (Lestho – Market

Access), Lockwood Smith (New Zealand – Singapore Agenda and other issues), Juan Gabriel Valdes (Chile) and Anup Kumar (Fiji – Systemic Issues), and Anabel González (Costa Rica – Labour Standards).

5   The LMG was formed in the run-up to the Singapore ministerial meeting (i) in response to developed country pressure to begin negotiations on new issues; and (ii) to press for implementation issues to be addressed prior to a new round commencing. Originally comprising Cuba, Egypt, India, Indonesia, Malaysia, Pakistan, Tanzania and Uganda, its membership was expanded to include the Dominican Republic, Honduras, Sri Lanka and Zimbabwe. Jamaica became a permanent observer with Kenya also attending meetings. (See Narlikar and Odell, 2003: 7–8).

6   The streams were chaired by Luis Ernesto Derbez (Mexico – Intellectual Property Rights and Public Health/Access to Medicines); Pascal Couchepin (Switzerland – Implementation); George Yeo (Singapore – Agriculture); Heraldo Munoz Valenzuela (Canada – Environment); Peirre Pettigrew (Canada – Singapore Issues); Alec Erwin (South Africa – Rule-making); and Tebelelo Seretse (Botswana – other issues). The conference was chaired by Qatari Minister of Finance, Economy and Trade Yussef Hussain Kamal.

7   The five negotiating groups, with their respective chairs, were: Agriculture (George Yeo Yong-Bon – Singapore); Non-agricultural Market Access (Henry Tang Ying-Yen – Hong Kong); Development (Mukhisa Kituyi – Kenya); Singapore Issues (Pierre Pettigrew – Canada); Miscellaneous (Clement Rohee – Guyana).

8   The G20 comprised Argentina, Brazil, Bolivia, China, Chile, Colombia, Costa Rica, Cuba, Ecuador, El Salvador, Guatemala, India, Mexico, Pakistan, Paraguay, Philippines, Peru, Thailand, South Africa, and Venezuela. The Strategic and Safeguard alliance originally consisted of Barbados, Botswana, Cuba, Dominican Republic, Ecuador, Honduras, Indonesia, Jamaica, Kenya, Mongolia, Nicaragua, Nigeria, Pakistan, Panama, Peru, Philippines, Tanzania, Trinidad and Tobago, Turkey, Uganda, Venezuela, Zambia and Zimbabwe.

9   In reality the G90 comprised 64 member states: Angola, Antigua and Barbuda, Bangladesh, Barbados, Belize, Benin, Botswana, Burkina Faso, Burundi, Cambodia, Cameroon, Central African Republic, Chad, Congo, Côte d'Ivoire, Cuba, Democratic Republic of the Congo, Djibouti, Dominica, Dominican Republic, Egypt, Fiji, Gabon, The Gambia, Ghana, Grenada, Guinea, Guinea Bissau, Guyana, Haiti, Jamaica, Kenya, Lesotho, Madagascar, Malawi, Maldives, Mali, Mauritania, Mauritius, Morocco, Mozambique, Myanmar, Namibia, Nepal, Niger, Nigeria, Papua New Guinea, Rwanda, Saint Kitts and Nevis, Saint Lucia, Saint Vincent and the Grenadines, Senegal, Sierra Leone, Solomon Islands, South Africa, Suriname, Swaziland, Tanzania, Togo, Trinidad and Tobago, Tunisia, Uganda, Zambia and Zimbabwe.

10   Bulgaria, Chinese Taipei, Korea, Iceland, Israel, Japan, Liechtenstein, Mauritius, Norway and Switzerland.

11   Three other candidates stood for the post. In the order in which they dropped out of the election after not gaining sufficient support (from first to stand down to last), they were: Luiz Felipe de Seixas Corrêa (Brazilian Ambassador to the WTO); Jaya Krishna Cuttaree (Mauritian Minister for Foreign Affairs and Trade); and Carlos Pérez del Castillo (former Uruguayan Ambassador to the WTO).

12   Comprising Australia, Canada, Chile, Costa Rica, the EU, Japan, Hong Kong, Korea, New Zealand, Norway, Singapore, Switzerland and the US.

13   Two coefficients were discussed: a lower coefficient to provide for deeper cuts by industrial members; and a coefficient enabling developing countries to pursue shallower tariff reductions.

Bibliography

Aggarwal, Vinod K. 1983), 'The unraveling of the Multi-Fiber Arrangement, 1981: an examination of international regime change', *International Organization*, 37: 4 (Autumn).

Annan, Kofi (2001), 'Laying the foundations of a fair and free world trade system', in Gary P. Sampson (ed.), *The Role of the World Trade Organization in Global Governance* (Tokyo: United Nations University Press).

Anonymous ('A Canadian Economist') (1944), 'Economic reconstruction in Europe', *International Affairs*, 20: 4 (October).

Arai, Hisamitsu (2000), 'Some reflections on the Seattle Ministerial: toward the relaunching of a new round', in Jeffrey J. Schott (ed.), *The WTO after Seattle* (Washington DC: Institute for International Economics).

Ariff, M. (1989), 'TRIMs: a North–South divide or a non-issue?', *The World Economy*, 12: 3.

Balassa, Bela (1980), 'The Tokyo round and the developing countries', *Journal of World Trade Law*, 14: 2.

Bello, Walden (2002), 'Learning from Doha: a civil society perspective from the south', *Global Governance*, 8: 3.

Bergsten, C. Fred (2005), 'Rescuing the Doha round', *Foreign Affairs*, special edition (December).

Bhagwati, Jagdish (1999), 'An unjustified sense of victory', *Financial Times* (21 December).

Bhagwati, Jagdish (2001), 'After Seattle: free trade and the WTO', *International Affairs*, 77: 1 (January).

Bhagwati, Jagdish (2002), *Free Trade Today* (Princeton, NJ: Princeton University Press).

Bhagwati, Jagdish (2004a), *In Defense of Globalization* (Oxford: Oxford University Press).

Bhagwati, Jagdish (2004b), 'Trading for development: how to assist poor countries', in Mike Moore (ed.), *Doha and Beyond: The Future of the Multilateral Trading System* (Cambridge: Cambridge University Press).

Bhagwati, Jagdish (2004c), Don't cry for Cancun', *Foreign Affairs*, 83: 1 (January/February).

Bhagwati, Jagdish and Patrick, Hugh T. (eds) (1990), *Aggressive Unilateralism: American's 301 Trade Policy and the World Trading System* (Ann Abor: University of Michigan Press).

Blackhurst, Richard (1998), 'The capacity of the WTO to fulfil its mandate', in Anne O. Krueger (ed.), *The WTO as an International Organization* (Chicago, IL: Chicago University Press).

Blair, Tony (1998), Statement to the WTO Geneva Ministerial Meeting, 19 May.

Brewer, Thomas L. and Young, Stephen (1999), 'WTO disputes and developing countries', *Journal of World Trade*, 33: 5 (October).

Brittan, Leon (1996), 'Statement to the WTO Singapore Ministerial Conference', WT/MIN(96)/ST2, 9 December.

Bronkers, Marco C. E. J. (1994), 'The impact of TRIPs: intellectual property protection in developing countries', *Common Market Law Review*, 31.

Bronkers, Marco C. E. J. (2001), 'More power to the WTO?', *Journal of International Economic Law*, 4: 1.

Brown, Andrew G. and Stern, Robert M. (2005), 'Achieving fairness in the Doha Development Round', paper presented to the conference on 'Perspectives on the WTO Doha Development Agenda Multilateral Trade Negotiations', International Policy Center, Gerald R. Ford School of Public Policy, Department of Economics, Law School, University of Michigan, 21 October.

Brown, William Adams Jr. (1950), *The United States and the Restoration of World Trade* (Washington, DC: Brookings Institution).

Bulmer, Simon and Burch, Martin (1998), 'Organizing for Europe: Whitehall, the British state and European Union', *Public Administration*, 76: 4 (Winter).

Cairns group (1993), Communiqué, 13th Cairns Group Ministerial Meeting, Geneva, Switzerland, 18 October.

Cardoso, Fernando Henrique (1998), Statement by the President of Brazil to the WTO Geneva Ministerial Meeting, 19 May.

Castillo, Carlos Pérez del and Panitchpakdi, Supachai (2003), letter to Cancún Conference Chair Derbez, 31 August.

Chadha, Rajesh, Hoekman, Bernard, Martin, Will, Oyejide, Ademola, Pangestu, Mari, Tussie, Diana and Zarrouk, Jamel (2000), 'Developing countries and the next round of WTO negotiations', *The World Economy*, 23: 4 (April).

Charnovitz, Steve (1987), 'The influence of international labour standards on the world trading regime: a historical overview', *International Labour Review*, 126: 5.

Charnovitz, Steve (2001), 'The environmental significance of the Doha Declaration', *Bridges Monthly Review*, 5: 9 (November/December).

CHOGM (2005), Valletta Statement on Multilateral Trade, Malta, 26 November.

Clapp, Jennifer (2004), 'WTO agricultural trade battles and food aid', *Third World Quarterly*, 25: 8.

Clinton, Bill (1998), Statement to the WTO Geneva Ministerial Meeting, 18 May.

Clinton, Bill (1999), 'Transcript of interview with President Clinton', *Seattle Post-Intelligencer* (1 December).

Cohn, Theodore H. (2005), *Global Political Economy* (London: Pearson and Longman, 3rd edn).

Coleman, Zach (2005), 'The man in the hot seat', *The Standard (Hong Kong)*, 10 September.

Cox, Robert W. (1996), *Approaches to World Order* (Cambridge: Cambridge University Press).

Crick, W. F. (1951), 'International financial relations: some concealed problems', *International Affairs*, 27: 3 (July).

Curzon, Gerard (1965), *Multilateral Commercial Diplomacy: The General Agreement on Tariffs and Trade and its Impact on National Commercial Policies and Techniques* (London: Michael Joseph).

Curzon, Gerard (1969), 'The General Agreement on Tariffs and Trade: pressures and strategies for task expansion', in Robert W. Cox (ed.), *International Organisation: World Politics* (London: Macmillan).

Curzon, Gerard and Curzon, Victoria (1974), 'GATT: Trader's Club', in Robert W. Cox and Harold K. Jacobson (eds), *The Anatomy of Influence: Decision Making in International Organization* (London: Yale University Press, 1974, 2nd edn).

Curzon, Gerard and Curzon, Victoria (1976), 'The management of trade relations in the GATT', in Andrew Schonfield (ed.), *International Economic Relations of the Western World 1959–1971, Volume 1* (London: Oxford University Press).

Curzon, Gerard and Curzon, Victoria (1989), 'Non-discrimination and the rise of "material" reciprocity', *The World Economy*, 12: 4 (December).

Dam, Kenneth W. (1970), *The GATT: Law and International Economic Organization* (Chicago, IL: University of Chicago Press).

Das, Bhagirath Lal (1998), *The WTO Agreements: Deficiencies, Imbalances and Required Changes* (London: Zed Books).

Diebold Jr., William (1952), 'The end of the ITO', *Essays in International Finance*, 16, International Finance Section, Department of Economics, Princeton University, NJ.

Drahos, Peter (2003), 'When the weak bargain with the strong: negotiations in the World Trade Organization', *International Negotiation*, 8: 1.

Esserman, Susan and Howse, Robert (2003), 'The WTO on trial', *Foreign Affairs*, 82: 1 (January/February).

Esty, Daniel C. (2002), 'The World Trade Organization's legitimacy crisis', *World Trade Review*, 1: 1.

Evans, John W. (1968), 'The General Agreement on Tariffs and Trade', *International Organization*, 22: 1 (1968).

Evans, John W. (1971), *The Kennedy Round in American Trade Policy: the twilight of the GATT?* (Cambridge, MA: Harvard University Press).

Fawcett, J. E. S. (1951), The Havana Charter, *The Year Book of World Affairs*, 5.

Feis, Herbert (1948), 'The Geneva Proposal for an International Trade Charter', *International Organization*, 2: 1 (February).

Finger, J. Michael (1991), 'That old GATT magic no more casts its spell (how the Uruguay round failed)', *Journal of World Trade*, 25: 1 (February).

Finlayson, Jock A. and Zacher, Mark W. (1981), 'The GATT and the regulation of trade barriers: regime dynamics and functions', *International Organization*, 35: 4 (Autumn).

G20 (2005), 'New Delhi Declaration', New Delhi, India, 19 March.

G20 Finance (2005), Communiqué, Meeting of Finance Ministers and Central Bank Governors, Xianghe, Hebei, China, 15–16 October.

Gardner, Richard N. (1956), *Sterling–Dollar Diplomacy: Anglo–American collaboration in the reconstruction of multilateral trade* (Oxford: Clarendon Press).

Gardner, Richard N. (1964), 'GATT and the United Nations Conference on Trade and Development' *International Organization*, 18: 4 (Autumn).

Gardner, Richard N. (1969), *Sterling–Dollar Diplomacy: The Origins and Prospects of our International Economic Order* (London: McGraw-Hill, 2nd edn).

GATT (1947), *General Agreement on Tariffs and Trade* (Geneva: GATT).

GATT (1952a), *Basic Instruments and Selected Documents Volume I: Text of the Agreement and other Instruments and Procedures* (Geneva: GATT).

GATT (1952b), *Basic Instruments and Selected Documents Volume II: Decisions, Declarations, Resolutions, Rulings and Reports* (Geneva: GATT).

GATT (1953a), *International Trade, 1952* (Geneva: GATT).

GATT (1953b), *Basic Instruments and Selected Documents First Supplement* (Geneva: GATT).

GATT (1954), *Basic Instruments and Selected Documents Second Supplement* (Geneva: GATT).

GATT (1955a), *International Trade, 1954* (Geneva: GATT).

GATT (1955b), *Basic Instruments and Selected Documents Third Supplement: Decision, Resolutions, Reports, etc. of the Ninth Session* (Geneva: GATT).

GATT (1955c), *Basic Instruments and Selected Documents First Supplement* (Geneva: GATT, revised).

GATT (1956), *Basic Instruments and Selected Documents Fourth Supplement: Decisions, Reports, etc. of the Tenth Session* (Geneva: GATT).

GATT (1957), *Basic Instruments and Selected Documents Fifth Supplement: Decisions, Reports, etc. of the Eleventh Session* (Geneva: GATT).

GATT (1958a), *Trends in International Trade: A Report by a Panel of Experts* (Geneva: GATT).

GATT (1958b), *Basic Instruments and Selected Documents Sixth Supplement: Decisions, Reports, etc. of the Twelfth Session* (Geneva: GATT).

GATT (1959), *Basic Instruments and Selected Documents Seventh Supplement: Decisions, Reports, etc. of the Thirteenth Session* (Geneva: GATT).

GATT (1960), *Basic Instruments and Selected Documents Eighth Supplement: Decisions, Reports, etc. of the Fourteenth and Fifteenth Sessions* (Geneva: GATT).

GATT (1961), *Basic Instruments and Selected Documents Ninth Supplement: Decisions, Reports, etc. of the Sixteenth and Seventeenth Sessions* (Geneva: GATT).

GATT (1962), *Basic Instruments and Selected Documents Tenth Supplement: Decisions, Reports, etc. of the Eighteenth and Nineteenth Sessions* (Geneva: GATT).

GATT (1963), *Basic Instruments and Selected Documents Eleventh Supplement: Decisions, Reports, etc. of the Twentieth Session* (Geneva: GATT).

GATT (1964), *Basic Instruments and Selected Documents Twelfth Supplement: Decisions, Reports, etc. of the Twenty-first Session* (Geneva: GATT).

GATT (1965), *Basic Instruments and Selected Documents Thirteenth Supplement: Decisions, Reports, etc. of the Second Special Session and the Twenty-second Session* (Geneva: GATT).

GATT (1966), *A Study on Cotton Textiles* (Geneva: GATT).

GATT (1968), *Basic Instruments and Selected Documents Fifteenth Supplement: Protocols, Decisions, Reports 1966–1967 and the Twenty-fourth Session* (Geneva: GATT).

GATT (1974), *Basic Instruments and Selected Documents Twentieth Supplement: Decision, Report 1972–1973 and the Twenty-ninth Session* (Geneva: GATT).

GATT (1984), *Textiles and Clothing in the World Economy: Background Study Prepared by the GATT Secretariat to Assist Work Undertaken by the Contracting Parties in Pursuance of the Decision on Textiles and Clothing taken at the November 1982 Ministerial Meeting* (Geneva: GATT).

GATT (1986), Punta Del Este Declaration [launching the Uruguay round], 20 September.

GATT (1994), *The Results of the Uruguay Round of Multilateral Trade Negotiations: The Legal Texts* (Geneva: GATT).

GATT Report (1957a), *International Organization*, 11: 1 (winter).

Golt, Sidney (1978), *The GATT Negotiations 1973–79: The Closing Stage* (London: British–North American Committee).

Goodwin, G. L. (1956), 'GATT and the Organisation for Trade Co-operation', *The Year Book of World Affairs*, 10.

Goodwin, G. L. (1965), 'The United Nations Conference on Trade and Development: beginning of a new era?', *The Year Book of World Affairs*, 19.

Gorter, Wytze (1954), 'GATT after six years: an appraisal', *International Organization*, 8: 1 (February).

Graz, Jean-Christophe (1999), 'The political economy of international trade: the relevance of the ITO project', *Journal of International Relations and Development*, 2: 3.

Graz, Jean-Christophe (2004), 'Transnational mercantilism and the emergent global trading order', *Review of International Political Economy*, 11: 3 (August).

Guinness, A. R. (1944), 'International trade and the making of peace', *International Affairs*, 20: 4.

Hale, Angela (ed.) (1999), *Trade Myths and Gender Reality: Trade Liberalisation and Women's Lives* (Uppsala: Fyris-Tryck AB).

Hall, Peter and Taylor, Rosemary (1998), 'The potential of historical institutionalism: a response to Hay and Wincott', *Political Studies*, 46: 5 (December).

Haque, Inaamul and Wajid, Majid Ali (2005), 'WTO's July package and developing countries: preferring pragmatism to ideology', unpublished paper.

Harbinson, Stuart (2002), 'Lessons from the launching of the Doha round negotiations', paper prepared for the Trade Policy Roundtable, Cordell Hull Institute, Washington, 18 April.

Hart, Michael (1995), 'The GATT Uruguay round, 1986–1993', in Fen Olser Hampson (ed.), *Multilateral Negotiations: Lessons from Arms Control, Trade and the Environment* (Baltimore, MD: Johns Hopkins University Press).

Haworth, Nigel and Hughes, Steve (1997), 'Trade and international labour standards: issues and debates over a social clause', *Journal of Industrial Relations*, 39: 2 (June).

Haworth, Nigel, Hughes, Steve and Wilkinson, Rorden (2005), 'The international labour standards regime: a case study in global regulation', *Environment and Planning A*, 37: 11 (November).

Hay, Colin and Wincott, Daniel (1998), 'Structure, agency and historical institutionalism', *Political Studies*, 46: 5 (December).

Healy, Stephen, Peace, Richard and Stockbridge, Michael (1998), *The Implications of the Uruguay Round Agreement on Agriculture for Developing Countries* (Rome, FAO).

Hills, Carla A (2005), 'The stakes of Doha', *Foreign Affairs*, special edition (December).

Hoda, Anwarul (2001), *Tariff Negotiations and Renegotiations under the GATT and WTO: Procedures and Practices* (Cambridge: Cambridge University Press).

Hoekman, Bernard (1993), 'New issues in the Uruguay round and beyond', *Economic Journal*, 103: 421 (November).

Hoekman, Bernard and Kostecki, Michel (1995), *The Political Economy of the World Trading System* (Oxford: Oxford University Press).

Hogan, Michael J. (1987), *The Marshall Plan: America, Britain and the Reconstruction of Western Europe, 1947–1952* (Cambridge: Cambridge University Press).

Hudec, Robert E. (1990), *The GATT Legal System and World Trade Diplomacy* (Salem, MA: Butterworth Legal Publishers, 2nd edn).

Hudec, Robert E. (1998), 'The new WTO dispute settlement procedure: an overview of the first three years', *Minnesota Journal of Global Trade*, 8: 1.

Hughes, Steve (2002), 'Coming in from the cold: Labour, the ILO and the international labour standards regime', in Rorden Wilkinson and Steve Hughes (eds), *Global Governance: Critical Perspectives* (London: Routledge).

Hughes, Steve and Wilkinson, Rorden (1998), 'International labour standards and world trade: no role for the World Trade Organisation?', *New Political Economy*, 3: 3 (November).

Hughes, Steve and Wilkinson, Rorden (2001), 'The global compact: promoting corporate responsibility?', *Environmental Politics*, 10: 1 (Spring).

Ibrahim, Tigani E. (1978), 'Developing countries and the Tokyo round', *Journal of World Trade Law*, 12: 1.

Ikenberry, G. John (1992), 'A world economy restored: expert consensus and the Anglo-American postwar settlement', *International Organization*, 46: 1 (Winter).

ITO Report (1947a), *International Organization*, 1: 2 (June).

ITO Report (1947b), *International Organization*, 1: 3 (September).

ITO Report (1948a), *International Organization*, 2: 1 (February).

ITO Report (1948b), *International Organization*, 2: 2 (June).

ITO Report (1949), *International Organization*, 3: 1 (February).

ITO Report (1950a), *International Organization*, 4: 2 (May).

ITO Report (1950b), *International Organization*, 4: 3 (August).

ITO Report (1951a), *International Organization*, 5: 1 (February).

ITO Report (1951b), *International Organization*, 5: 2 (May).

ITO Report (1951c), *International Organization*, 5: 3 (August).

ITO Report (1952a), *International Organization*, 6: 1 (February).

ITO Report (1952b), *International Organization*, 6: 4 (November).

ITO Report (1953), *International Organization*, 7: 4 (November).

ITO Report (1955a), *International Organization*, 9: 1 (February).

ITO Report (1955b), *International Organization*, 9: 2 (May).

ITO Report (1955c), *International Organization*, 9: 4 (November).

ITO Report (1956a), *International Organization*, 10: 3 (August).

Jackson, John H. (1987), 'Multilateral and bilateral negotiating approaches for the conduct of US trade policies', in Robert M. Stern (ed.), *US Trade Policies in an Changing World Economy* (Cambridge, MA: MIT Press).

Jackson, John H. (1990a), *Restructuring the GATT System* (London: Pinter).

Jackson, John H. (1990b), 'Reflections on restructuring the GATT', in Jeffrey J. Scott (ed.), *Completing the Uruguay Round* (Washington, DC: Institute for International Economics).

Jackson, John H. (1993), 'A new constitution for world trade? Reforming the GATT system', in Robert M. Stern (ed.), *The Multilateral Trading System* (Michigan, OH: Michigan University Press).

Jackson, John H. (1997), 'The great 1994 sovereignty debate: United States acceptance and implementation of the Uruguay round results', *Columbia Journal of
Transnational Law*, 36: 157.

Jackson, John H. (1998), 'Designing and implementing effective dispute settlement
procedures: WTO dispute settlement, appraisal and prospects', in Anne O. Krueger
(ed.), *The WTO as an International Organization* (Chicago, IL: University of
Chicago Press).

Jackson, John H. (2000), *The Jurisprudence of GATT and the WTO: Insights on
Treaty Law and Economic Relations* (Cambridge: Cambridge University Press).

Jackson, John H. and Sykes, Alan O. (1997), 'Introduction and overview', in John
H. Jackson and Alan O. Sykes (eds), *Implementing the Uruguay Round* (Oxford:
Clarendon Press).

Jawara, Fatoumata and Kwa, Aileen (2003), *Behind the Scenes at the WTO: The
Real World of International Trade Negotiations* (London: Zed Books).

Johnson, Harry G. (1968), 'US economic policy toward the developing countries',
Economic Development and Cultural Change, 16: 3 (April).

Josling, Tim (1990), 'The GATT: its historical role and importance to agricultural
policy and trade', in Hans J. Michelmann *et al.* (eds), *The Political Economy of
Agricultural Trade and Policy* (Boulder, CO: Westview Press).

Kapoor, Ilan (2004), 'Deliberative democracy and the WTO', *Review of International
Political Economy*, 1: 3 (August).

Keohane, Robert O. (1989), *International Institutions and State Power* (Boulder,
CO: Westview Press).

Keohane, Robert O. (2002), *Power and Governance in a Partially Globalized World*
(London: Routledge).

Knorr, Klaus (1948), 'The Bretton Woods institutions in transition', *International
Organization*, 2: 1 (February).

Kock, Karin (1969), *International Trade Policy and the GATT, 1947–1967*
(Stockholm: Almqvist and Wiksell).

Krueger, Anne O. (ed.) (1998), *The WTO as an International Organization* (Chicago,
IL: Chicago University Press).

Kwa, Aileen (2003), *Power Politics in the WTO* (Bangkok: Focus on the Global
South, 2nd edn).

Lall, K. B (1965), address to the 7th World Conference of the Society for International
Development, Washington, DC (March). Reprinted in WCSID, *International
Development* (New York: WCSID).

Lamy, Pascal (2003a), Final press conference to the Cancún Ministerial Meeting,
14 September.

Lamy, Pascal (2003b), 'Trade crisis', speech to the European Institute, Washington,
4 November.

Lamy, Pascal (2005), Report to WTO General Council, 10 November.

Lang, Ian (1996), Statement to the WTO Singapore Ministerial Meeting, WT/
MIN(96)/ST/9, 9 December.

Lee, Donna (1998), 'Middle powers in the global economy: British influence during
the opening phase of the Kennedy Trade Round negotiations, 1962–4', *Review of
International Studies*, 24: 4 (October).

Lee, Donna (2001), 'Endgame at the Kennedy round: a case study of multilateral
economic diplomacy', *Diplomacy and Statecraft*, 12: 3 (September).

Lee, Donna (2004), 'Understanding the WTO dispute settlement process', in Brian Hocking and Steven McGuire (eds), *Trade Politics* (London: Routledge, 2nd edn).

Lee, Eddy, (1997), 'Globalisation and labour standards: a review of issues', *International Labour Review*, 136: 2 (Summer).

LeQuesne, Caroline (1996), *Reforming World Trade: The Social and Environmental Priorities* (Oxford: Oxfam).

Lowndes, Vivien (1996), 'Varieties of new institutionalism: a critical appraisal', *Public Administration*, 74: 2 (Summer).

Luke, David F. (1996), 'The impact of the Uruguay round on trade preferences', *Journal of World Trade*, 30: 3 (June).

Marceau, Gabrielle and Pedersen, Peter N. (1999), 'Is the WTO open and transparent? A discussion of the relationship of the WTO with non-governmental organisations and civil society's claims for more transparency and public participation', *Journal of World Trade*, 33: 1.

March, James G. and Olsen, Johan P. (1996), 'Institutional perspectives on political institutions', *Governance*, 9: 3 (July).

McGrew, Tony (1999), 'The World Trade Organization: technocracy or banana republic?', in Annie Taylor and Caroline Thomas (eds), *Global Trade and Global Social Issues* (London: Routledge).

McMichael, Philip (2000), 'Sleepless since Seattle: what is the WTO about?', *Review of International Political Economy*, 7: 3 (Autumn).

Melendez-Ortiz, Ricardo (2004), 'The multilateral trade system at the end of history?', remarks made at the 'WTO After Cancun: What Development Prospects' Conference, Danish Institute for International Studies, Copenhagen, 1 March.

Mkapa, Benjamin William (2004), 'Cancun's false promise: a view from the South', *Foreign Affairs*, 83: 3 (May/June).

Moore, Mike (1999a), 'Labour is a "false debate" . . .', *WTO Press Release*, No. 152 (25 November).

Moore, Mike (1999b), 'The WTO is not a world government . . .', *WTO Press Release*, No. 155 (29 November).

Moore, Mike (2003), *A World Without Walls: Freedom, Development, Free Trade and Global Governance* (Cambridge: Cambridge University Press).

Moore, Mike (ed.) (2004), *Doha and Beyond: The Future of the Multilateral Trading System* (Cambridge: Cambridge University Press).

Moore, Mike and Harbinson, Stuart (2001), Letter to WTO Conference Chair Yousef Hussain Kamal, 5 November.

Mori, Katsuhiko (2004), 'The Cancun breakdown and the WTO's Doha development agenda in global governance', *International Politics*, 41: 3 (September).

Murphy, Craig N. (1994), *International Organization and Industrial Change: Global Governance since 1850* (Cambridge: Polity Press)

Murphy, Craig N. (2005), *Global Institutions, Marginalization and Development* (London: Routledge).

Narlikar, Amrita (2002), 'The politics of participation: decision-making processes and developing countries in the WTO', *The Round Table: The Commonwealth Journal of International Affairs*, Vol. 364 (April).

Narlikar, Amrita (2003), *International Trade and Developing Countries: Bargaining Coalitions in the GATT and WTO* (London: Routledge).

Narlikar, Amrita (2004a), 'The ministerial process and power dynamics in the world trade organization: understanding failure from Seattle to Cancun', *New Political Economy*, 9: 3 (September).

Narlikar, Amrita (2004b), 'The World Trade Organization: a case for G20 action on institutional reform', paper presented at the 'Breaking the Deadlock in Agricultural Trade Reform and Development Conference', University of Oxford, 8–9 June.

Narlikar, Amrita and Odell, John S. (2003), 'The strict distributive strategy for a bargaining coalition: the like minded group in the World Trade Organization', unpublished paper prepared for the Conference on 'Developing Countries and the Trade Negotiation Process', UNCTAD, 6–7 November.

Narlikar, Amrita and Tussie, Diana (2004), 'The G20 at the Cancun ministerial meeting: developing countries and their evolving coalitions in the WTO', *World Economy*, 27: 7 (July).

Narlikar, Amrita and Wilkinson, Rorden (2004), 'Collapse at the WTO: A Cancún post-mortem', *Third World Quarterly*, 25: 3 (April).

North, Douglass C. (1990), *Institutions, Institutional Change and Economic Performance* (Cambridge: Cambridge University Press).

Nyhan, Paul (1999), 'Clinton's proposals praised by labor groups', *Seattle Post-Intelligencer* (2 December).

O'Brien, Patrick and Pigman, Geoffrey Allen (1992), 'Free trade, British hegemony and the international economic order in the nineteenth century', *Review of International Studies*, 18: 2 (April).

Odell, John S. (2001), 'A few tricks of the negotiating table, but can they produce a rabbit by November?', *World Trade Agenda* (2 July).

Odell, John S. (2002), 'The Seattle impasses and its implications for the WTO', in Daniel Kennedy and James Southwick (eds), *The Political Economy of International Trade Law: Essays in Honor of Robert Hudec* (Cambridge: Cambridge University Press).

Odell, John S. (2004), 'Chairing a WTO negotiation', paper prepared for the Conference on Developing Countries in the Doha Round: WTO Decision Making Procedures and WTO Negotiations on Trade in Agricultural Goods and Services, Robert Schuman Centre for Advanced Studies, Florence, 2–3 July (revised 15 September).

Odell, John S. (2005), 'Chairing a WTO negotiation', *Journal of International Economic Law*, 8: 2.

Odell, John S. and Eichengreen, Barry (1998), 'The United States, the ITO, and the WTO: exit options, agent slack, and presidential leadership', in Anne O. Krueger (ed.), *The WTO as an International Organization* (Chicago, IL: Chicago University Press).

Office of the Press Secretary (1993), Transcript of a Press Conference by the President and Prime Minister Keating of Australia in the East Room, 14 September.

Ostry, Sylvia (1997), *The Post-Cold War Trading System* (London: University of Chicago Press).

Panagariya, Arvind (2005), 'Liberalizing agriculture', *Foreign Affairs*, Special Issue (December).

Patterson, Gardner (1966), *Discrimination in International Trade: The Policy Issues 1945–1965* (Princeton, NJ: Princeton University Press).

Patterson, Lee Ann (1997), 'Agricultural policy reform in the European Community: a three-level game analysis', *International Organization*, 51: 1 (winter).

Paulson, Michael (1999), 'Clinton says he will support trade sanctions for worker abuse', *Seattle Post-Intelligencer* (1 December).

Payne, Anthony J. (2005), *The Global Politics of Unequal Development* (Basingstoke: Palgrave).

Penrose, E. F. (1953), *Economic Planning for Peace* (Princeton, NJ: Princeton University Press).

Petersmann, Ernst-Ulrich (1997), *The GATT/WTO Dispute Settlement System: International Law, International Organizations and Dispute Settlement* (London: Kluwer Law).

Pigman, Geoffrey Allen (1998), 'The sovereignty discourse and the US debate on joining the World Trade Organisation', *Global Society*, 12: 1.

Preeg, Ernest H. (1970), *Traders and Diplomats: An Analysis of the Kennedy Round of Negotiations under the General Agreement on Tariffs and Trade* (Washington, DC: Brookings Institution).

Raghavan, Chakravarthi (1982), 'GATT sheds its fig leaf', *SUNS – South–North Development Monitor*, 30 November.

Raghavan, Chakravarthi (1991), 'G77 assail "single undertaking" and MTO efforts in round', *SUNS – South–North Development Monitor*, 18 March.

Raghavan, Chakravarthi (1996a), 'Consensus by absence at SMC preparations', *SUNS – South–North Development Monitor*, 31 October.

Raghavan, Chakravarthi (1996b), 'Open differences, and some confrontation, at SMC', *SUNS – South–North Development Monitor*, 10 December.

Raghavan, Chakravarthi (2000), 'After Seattle, world trade system faces uncertain future', *Review of International Political Economy*, 7: 3 (autumn).

Reif, Linda C. (1995), 'History of the Uruguay round', in Joseph F. Dennin (general ed.), *Law and Practice of the World Trade Organization – Booklet A* (New York: Oceana Publications).

Rhodes, Carolyn (1995), *Reciprocity, US Trade Policy, and the GATT Regime* (Ithaca, NY: Cornell University Press).

Ricupero, Rubens (2001), 'Rebuilding confidence in the multilateral trading system: closing the "legitimacy gap"', in Gary P. Sampson (ed.), *The Role of the World Trade Organization in Global Governance* (Tokyo: United Nations University Press).

Robertson, Charles L. (1969), 'The creation of UNCTAD', in Robert W. Cox (ed.), *International Organisation: World Politics* (London: Macmillan).

Ruggie, John Gerard (1982) 'International regimes, transactions and change: embedded liberalism in the postwar economic order', *International Organization*, 36: 2.

Ruggie, John Gerard (1993a), 'Multilateralism: the anatomy of an institution', in John Gerard Ruggie (ed.), *Multilateralism Matters: The Theory and Praxis of an Institutional Form* (New York: Columbia University Press).

Ruggie, John Gerard (ed.) (1993b), *Multilateralism Matters: The Theory and Praxis of an Institutional Form* (New York: Columbia University Press).

Ruggiero, Renato (1998), Opening Address to the WTO Geneva Ministerial Meeting, 18 May.

Sampson, Gary P. (2000), 'The World Trade Organization after Seattle', *World Economy*, 23: 9.

Sampson, Gary P. (2001), 'Overview', in Gary P. Sampson (ed.), *The Role of the World Trade Organization in Global Governance* (Tokyo: United Nations University Press).

Santer, Jacques (1998), Statement to the WTO Geneva Ministerial Meeting, 19 May.

Sauvé, Pierre (2000), 'Developing countries and the GATS 2000 round', *Journal of World Trade*, 34: 2 (April).

Scammell, W. M. (1952), 'International economic co-operation and the problem of full employment', *The Year Book of World Affairs*, 6.

Schechter, Michael G. (2005), *United Nations Global Conferences* (London: Routledge).

Schott, Jeffrey J. (2000), 'The WTO after Seattle', in Jeffrey J. Schott (ed.), *The WTO after Seattle* (Washington: Institute for International Economics).

Schott, Jeffrey J. and Watal, Jayashree (2000), 'Decision making in the WTO', in Jeffrey J. Schott (ed.), *The WTO after Seattle* (Washington, DC: Institute for International Economics).

Sell, Susan K. (2000), 'Big business and the new trade agreements: the future of the WTO', in Richard Stubbs and Geoffrey R. D. Underhill (eds), *Political Economy and the Changing Global Order* (Oxford: Oxford University Press, 2nd edn).

Sell, Susan K. (2002), 'The agreement on trade related aspects of intellectual property rights and the access to medicines campaign', *Wisconsin International Law Journal*, 20: 3 (summer).

Simpson, Seamus and Wilkinson, Rorden (2002), 'Regulatory change and telecommunications governance', *Convergence: The Journal of Research into New Media Technologies*, 8: 2 (summer).

Smith, James (2004), 'Inequality in international trade? Developing countries and institutional change in WTO dispute settlement', *Review of International Political Economy*, 11: 3 (August).

Srinivasan, T. N. (1998), *Developing Countries and the Multilateral Trading System* (Boulder, CO: Westview Press).

Steinmo, Sven, Thelen, Kathleen and Longstreth, Frank (eds) (1992), *Structuring Politics: Historical Institutionalism in Comparative Analysis* (Cambridge: Cambridge University Press).

Stern, Robert M. (1987a), (ed.), *US Trade Policies in a Changing World Economy* (Cambridge, MA: MIT Press).

Stern, Robert M. (1987b), 'Introduction', in Robert M. Stern (ed.), *US Trade Policies in a Changing World Economy* (Cambridge, MA: MIT Press).

Stigliani, Nicholas A. (2000), 'Labor diplomacy: a revitalised aspect of US foreign policy in the era of globalization', *International Studies Perspectives*, 1: 2 (August).

Stiglitz, Joseph E. and Charlton, Andrew (2004), 'The development round of trade negotiations in the aftermath of Cancun: a report prepared for the Commonwealth Secretariat' (New York: Initiative for Policy Dialogue, Columbia University, 1 July).

Strange, Susan (1997), *Casino Capitalism* (Manchester: Manchester University Press).

Supachai, Panitchpakdi (2003), Speech to the Global Unions Conference on 'Making globalisation work for the poor: respect for development, worker rights and sustainability at the fifth WTO ministerial conference', Cancún, 9 September.

Supachai, Panitchpakdi (2005), Statement to informal meeting at the level of Heads of Delegation, Geneva, 8 July.

Sutherland, Peter (2005), 'Correcting misperceptions', *Foreign Affairs*, special edition (December).

Sutherland, Peter, Sewell, John and Weiner, David (2001), 'Challenges facing the WTO and policies to address global governance' in Gary P. Sampson (ed.), *The*

Role of the World Trade Organization in Global Governance (Tokyo: United Nations University Press).

Thelen, Kathleen (1999), 'Historical institutionalism in comparative politics', *Annual Review of Political Science*, 2 (June).

Thelen, Kathleen and Steinmo, Sven (1992), 'Historical institutionalism in comparative politics', in Sven Steinmo, Kathleen Thelen and Frank Longstreth (eds), *Structuring Politics: Historical Institutionalism in Comparative Analysis* (Cambridge: Cambridge University Press).

Toynbee, Arnold J. (1947), 'The international economic outlook', *International Affairs*, 23: 4 (October).

UNCTAD V (1979), *Multilateral Trade Negotiations: Evaluation and Further Recommendations Arising Therefrom* (Manila: UNCTAD), 7 May.

UNDP (1997), *Human Development Report 1997* (New York: Oxford University Press).

Ungphakorn, Peter Mytri (1994), 'When the European Community's ambassador kissed the Malaysian Trade Minister', *TDRI* [Thailand Development Research Institute] *Quarterly Review*, 9: 4 (December).

United Nations Conference on Trade and Employment (1948), *Final Act and Related Documents*, 21 November 1947 to 24 March 1948, Havana, Cuba.

US State Department (1997), 'Eizenstat announces US/EU understanding on Cuba, (EU suspends challenge to Helms-Burton in WTO), April 11.

Viner, Jacob [1931] (1951), 'The most-favored-nation clause in American commercial treaties', reprinted in Jacob Viner, *International Economics* (London: George Allen & Unwin).

Viner, Jacob (1947), 'Conflicts of principle in drafting a trade charter', *Foreign Affairs*, 25: 4 (July).

Vines, Stephen (2005), 'WTO host of trouble', *The Standard* (Hong Kong), 16 December.

Wade, Robert Hunter (2003), 'What strategies are viable for developing countries today? The World Trade Organization and the shrinking of "development space"', *Review of International Political Economy*, 10: 4 (November).

Wade, Robert Hunter (2004), 'The Ringmaster of Doha', *New Left Review*, 25 (January–February).

Wallach, Lori and Woodall, Patrick (2004), *Whose Trade Organization?* (New York: The New Press).

Wells, Sidney (1969), 'Developing countries, GATT and UNCTAD', *International Affairs*, 45: 1.

Whalley, John (1990), 'Non-discriminatory discrimination: special and differential treatment under the GATT for developing countries', *The Economic Journal*, 100: 403 (December).

Wilcox, Clair (1949a), *A Charter for World Trade* (London: Macmillan).

Wilcox, Clair (1949b), 'The promise of the World Trade Charter', *Foreign Affairs*, 27: 3 (April).

Wilkinson, Rorden (1999a), 'Labour and trade-related regulation: beyond the trade – labour standards debate?', *British Journal of Politics and International Relations*, 1: 2 (June).

Wilkinson, Rorden (1999b), 'Footloose and fancy free?: The multilateral agreement on investment', *Environmental Politics*, 8: 4 (Winter).

Wilkinson, Rorden (2000), *Multilateralism and the World Trade Organisation: The Architecture and Extension of International Trade Regulation* (London: Routledge)

Wilkinson, Rorden (2001), 'The WTO in crisis: exploring the dimensions of institutional inertia', *Journal of World Trade*, 35: 3 (June).

Wilkinson, Rorden (2002a), 'Peripheralising labour: The ILO, WTO and the completion of the Bretton Woods project', in Jeffery Harrod and Robert O'Brien (eds), *Globalized Unions? Theory and Strategies of Organized Labour in the Global Political Economy* (London: Routledge).

Wilkinson, Rorden (2002b), 'The contours of courtship: the WTO and civil society', in Rorden Wilkinson and Steve Hughes (eds), *Global Governance: Critical Perspectives* (London: Routledge).

Wilkinson, Rorden (2002c), 'The World Trade Organisation', *New Political Economy*, 7: 1 (March).

Wilkinson, Rorden (2002d), 'A tale of four ministerials: the WTO and the rise and demise of the trade–labour standards debate', *IPEG Papers in Global Political Economy*, No. 3 (April).

Wilkinson, Rorden (2003), 'ACUNS in Cancún', *ACUNS Informational Memorandum*, No. 57 (autumn).

Wilkinson, Rorden (2004), 'Crisis in Cancún', *Global Governance*, 10: 2 (March).

Wilkinson, Rorden (2005), 'Managing global civil society: the WTO's engagement with NGOs', in Randall Germain and Michael Kenny (eds), *The Idea of Global Civil Society: Ethics and Politics in a Globalising Era* (London: Routledge).

Wilkinson, Rorden and Hughes, Steve (2000), 'Labor standards and global governance: examining the dimensions of institutional engagement', *Global Governance*, 6: 2 (April–June).

Wilkinson, Rorden, Haworth, Nigel and Hughes, Steve (2001), 'Recasting labor diplomacy', *International Studies Perspectives*, 2: 2 (May).

Winham, Gilbert R. (1986), *International Trade and the Tokyo Round* (Princeton, NJ: Princeton University Press).

Winters, L. Alan (1990), 'The road to Uruguay', *The Economic Journal*, 100: 403 (December).

Wolf, Martin (2001), 'What the world needs from the multilateral trading system', in Gary P. Sampson (ed.), *The Role of the World Trade Organization in Global Governance* (Tokyo: United Nations University Press).

Wolfe, Robert (2004), 'Crossing the river by feeling the stones: where the WTO is going after Seattle, Doha and Cancun', *Review of International Political Economy*, 11: 3 (August).

World Bank (2004), *Global Economic Prospects: Realizing the Development Promise of the Doha Agenda* (Washington, DC: World Bank).

World Commission on the Social Dimensions of Globalization (2004), *A Fair Globalization: Creating Opportunities for All* (Geneva: ILO).

WTO (1995a), *The World Trade Organisation: Trading into the Future* (Geneva: WTO).

WTO (1995b), 'WTO Director-General hails financial services accord', *Press Release*, No. 18 (26 July).

WTO (1996) Singapore Ministerial Declaration, adopted 13 December.

WTO (1997a), 'Ruggiero congratulates governments on landmark telecommunications agreement', *Press Release*, No. 67 (17 February).

WTO (1997b), 'Successful conclusion of the WTO's financial services negotiations', *Press Release*, No. 86 (15 December).

WTO (1998), Geneva Ministerial Declaration, adopted 20 May.

WTO (1999), 'WTO DG Moore announces selection of four deputies', *Press Release*, No. 144 (3 November).

WTO (2001a), Doha Ministerial Declaration, WT/MIN(01)/DEC/1, 20 November.

WTO (2001b), Decision on Implementation-related issues and concerns, WT/MIN (01)/17, 20 November.

WTO (2001c), Declaration on the TRIPs agreement and public health, WT/MIN(01)/DEC/2, 20 November.

WTO (2001d), *The WTO . . . and why it matters: a guide for officials, legislators, civil society and all those interested in international trade and global governance* (Geneva: WTO).

WTO (2001e), 'Moore says draft texts form solid basis for ministerial negotiations', *Press Release*, No. 250 (28 October).

WTO (2003a), 'Final ministerial statement of the Cancún Ministerial Conference', adopted 14 September, WT/MIN (03)/20.

WTO (2003b), 'Decision removes final patent obstacle to cheap drug imports', *Press Release* No. 350 (30 August).

WTO (2003c), Comments on the EC communication on the modalities for the Singapore issues – Communication from Bangladesh, Cuba, Egypt, India, Indonesia, Kenya, Malaysia, Nigeria, Pakistan, Venezuela, Zambia and Zimbabwe (WT/GC/W/491), 8 July.

WTO (2004a), 'Supachai commends negotiators, urges more progress', *Press Release*, No. 379 (4 June).

WTO (2004b), 'Supachai urges G-90 ministers, all ministers to show flexibility', *Press Release*, No. 382 (12 July).

WTO (2004c), 'Doha work programme: Draft General Council Decision of July 2004', JOB(04)/96, 16 July.

WTO (2004d), 'Supachai calls on WTO governments to reach agreement', *Press Release*, No. 383 (19 July).

WTO (2004e), 'Supachai welcomes from the five as a key first step', *News Item*, 29 July.

WTO (2004f), 'Doha work programme: decision adopted by the General Council on 1 August 2004', WT/L/579, 2 August.

WTO (2005), Hong Kong Ministerial Declaration adopted 18 December, WT/MIN(05)/W/3/Rev.2.

Yeo Cheow Tong (1996), Concluding remarks by the Chair of the Ministerial Conference, WTO Singapore Ministerial Meeting (13 December).

Zoellick, Robert B. (2003), 'America will not wait for the won't do countries', *Financial Times*, 22 September.

Zoellick, Robert B. (2004), Statement to the Committee on Ways and Means, US House of Representatives, 11 March.

Index

Tables in *Italic*